THE NEW FREEZER COOKBOOK

THE
NEW FREEZER
COOKBOOK

HELGE RUBINSTEIN
and
SHEILA BUSH

Line drawings by Madeleine David

AURUM PRESS

First published 1995 by Aurum Press Limited,
25 Bedford Avenue, London WC1B 3AT

A catalogue record for this book is available from the
British Library.

ISBN 1 85410 337 7

Book design by Jessica Caws
Printed and bound in Great Britain by Hartnolls Ltd, Bodmin

Contents

Introduction

This book is designed to help cooks make the most of their freezers, by using fresh raw materials when they are at their best, cheapest and most plentiful in the garden, shops and markets. We have found that owning a freezer has enabled us to produce a wider range of delicious and fresher food with far less time spent shopping or cooking, and has also cut down household costs.

The book is divided into four main sections, each devoted to one of the seasons, listing the foods available, with brief freezing instructions where appropriate and a number of seasonal recipes. Obviously, since nature herself is bountiful in fits and starts, some sections are fat and full, and others slender. Also, since almost every kind of food is becoming available all the year round, our choice of season may sometimes seem arbitrary; but we have picked in every case the season when the food in question is at its best and most abundant.

We all have our own ways of using the freezer: some people buy meat in bulk, for drawing on during the year; others pick and store vegetables and fruit in season, or make double quantities of dishes and freeze one for later use. In the 22 years since the publication of our *Penguin Freezer Cookbook*, the popularity of home freezers has grown enormously, not least because of the great variety of ready-prepared dishes available nowadays. Excellent though these are, they cannot compete with the dishes that you cook yourself, or make it any the less attractive to store freshly picked fruit and vegetables.

A freezer should be an ally and not a tyrant: use it in whatever way best suits your particular needs and way of life. We hope that this book will help you to do so, and to *enjoy* your freezer.

Basic Guidelines

THE FREEZER AS STORE CUPBOARD

Bread
Breadcrumbs (fresh)
Bouquets garnis (see pp. 29–30)
Butter
Cheese, in the piece or grated. Hard cheese becomes crumbly if it is frozen for
    too long. Cottage, curd and low-fat soft cheeses do not freeze well.
Chicken breasts
Cream, double or whipping. Stir or whip well before serving. Single cream does
    not freeze satisfactorily.
Egg whites
Commercially frozen fish
Meringues
Milk (in cartons)
Pastry
Cooked rice. Freeze in small quantities for stuffing poultry, pimentos, tomatoes,
    etc., and adding to soups or stews.
Stock
Tomato sauce
Flavoured yoghurt

The following do not freeze successfully:
Mayonnaise
Eggs in the shell
Hard-boiled eggs
Salad vegetables
Plain yoghurt

SAFETY RULES

- All food should be frozen while it is still absolutely fresh. Never leave it lying about in the kitchen.

- Cooked food should be frozen immediately it is cold.

- If food needs to be thawed when it is taken out of the freezer, put in a cool, clean place. The refrigerator is best, especially for meat and fish.

- Poultry must always be thawed completely before cooking.

- Meat should normally be allowed to thaw before cooking. We have noted in the individual recipes where this is not necessary.

- Dishes made from fish or meat that has been frozen raw can be frozen once the dish has been cooked.

- From the point of view of safety, fruit and vegetables can be refrozen in cooked dishes. However, in general this is best avoided, since the texture and flavour suffer.

PACKAGING

Packaging for the freezer is important. Unless plastic bags or other containers are absolutely airtight, dry patches, known as freezer burn, and ice crystals will appear, spoiling the taste and texture of the food. Airtight packaging is especially important in the case of food with a strong smell, such as tomato sauce, for the smell will spread to other foods. Glass containers can be used, but 1 in (2.5 cm) headroom must be left between the food and the cover, to allow for expansion. If the food is to be thawed in a microwave, foil or other metal containers must not be used.

It is not recommended to wrap fatty foods in cling film.

STORAGE TIMES

There are no hard and fast rules as to how long food may be stored in the freezer. In our experience most food keeps well for six months or longer, with the exception of ices and mousses, which are best eaten as fresh as possible.

Some basic raw materials, such as good-quality meat, keep perfectly well for a year or more. But there is nothing to be said for long-term storage for its own sake – however well pheasant or hare may keep, it is not going to seem very appetizing in July. And if you don't eat up your summer vegetables and fruit before the winter is out, you will miss half the joy of the new season's garden produce.

FISH

Fish is only worth freezing raw if it practically jumps out of the sea into the freezer. Since very few people can get it as fresh as this, we have confined ourselves mainly to recipes for salmon and a few other fish that do freeze well, and to dishes using commercially frozen fish.

MEAT AND POULTRY

Although most kinds of meat and poultry are not really seasonal, there are months of the year when certain dishes are specially welcome, or when the vegetables with which they are cooked are more readily available. Beef casseroles and stews, for example, are more likely to be eaten in the winter, and light chicken dishes in the summer. It is with this in mind that we have distributed the meat and poultry dishes within the four seasons.

Lamb is the exception, for the new season's English, Welsh or Scottish lambs come into the shops in spring; and while they are a delicacy to be eaten and enjoyed straight away, they also retain their flavour well when frozen.

It is hardly worth saying that free-range chickens will always have a better flavour and texture than battery-reared birds. Here again, if you are able to obtain such chickens, it is worth having a supply in the freezer.

Chicken carcasses, raw or cooked, can be frozen for making stock and used straight from the freezer.

VEGETABLES

Most vegetables freeze well. In general, they should be either blanched or cooked before they are frozen: methods of freezing are given for each vegetable in the season when it is at its best. It is worth experimenting with the different methods, and also with various ways of cooking vegetables when they come out of the freezer, to find out what suits you.

The following points may be helpful:

- Vegetables should be picked when they are young and tender, and frozen as soon as possible after picking.

- Blanch in small quantities, so that the water is off the boil for the shortest possible time.

- When you plunge the vegetables into cold water after blanching, add ice-cubes to help them to cool quickly.

- Freeze in small quantities. Two or three small bags of vegetables will cook or heat through more rapidly and evenly than one big lump.

- If you freeze vegetables for later use in recipes, write the weight on the label.

- When you take vegetables out of the freezer, they should always be cooked or heated while they are still frozen. (Sweet corn is the exception.) If they have been blanched, remember that the blanching will have partially cooked them, so they will not need more than about half the usual cooking time.

- Vegetables that are cooked before freezing should in general be frozen with their cooking liquid – this assumes that you cook them simply in a little butter and water. The liquid can be used during the reheating, and very little more, if any, should be needed.

- Vegetables with a high water content, such as marrows, will only freeze satis-factorily if they are cooked first.

- Salad vegetables, such as watercress, lettuce and cucumber, will be no good for eating raw after freezing. They can, however, be frozen cooked.

- We do not recommend freezing new potatoes, as the texture and flavour suffer.

FRUIT

Most fruit freezes excellently, and if you have a garden, or access to fresh supplies of soft and stoned fruit, they are among the most rewarding of all foods to freeze. The following points are worth remembering:

• Only ripe, good-quality fruit should be used, but fruit which is slightly overripe or otherwise not quite perfect can be made into a purée before freezing.

• Fruit should be frozen as quickly as possible after picking.

• If syrup is used, it must be quite cold before it is poured over the fruit.

• If the fruit is likely to be used in recipes afterwards, it is helpful to write on the label of each packet the weight of the fruit and the amount of sugar used.

• Bananas and avocado pears do not freeze well; grapes are only worth freezing in the form of juice.

Whether you freeze fruit sweetened or unsweetened is a matter of preference. Some people prefer to freeze soft fruit without sugar, because it keeps its shape better. On the other hand, if sugar is added the fruit keeps longer, has a better flavour, and forms a delicious natural juice as it thaws. The addition of sugar is not so important for tough-skinned fruit such as gooseberries, which do not form a juice. Stoned fruit is excellent frozen in syrup.

Fruit should be thawed slowly to conserve the delicacy, colour and freshness of taste. Never leave longer than necessary after thawing. Soft fruit, in particular, tends to collapse and lose its shape and flavour if it is left too long after it has been taken out of the freezer. A 1-lb (450-g) bag of fruit frozen with sugar will take two to four hours to thaw at room temperature, rather longer if it has been frozen in syrup, and at least double this time in a refrigerator. But no hard and fast rules can be laid down about times, which vary considerably according to the temperature, quantity and type of fruit, and so on.

Mousses, soufflés and ices deteriorate in texture and flavour if they are kept in the freezer for long, but they are excellent if freshly made from frozen fruit.

ICE-CREAMS, WATER-ICES AND SORBETS

A constant supply of homemade ices – which are invariably better and usually cheaper than the bought variety – is one of the especial joys of owning a freezer.

All ices are at their best when freshly made. Sorbets, in particular, should be eaten within a week and fruit ice-creams within a fortnight. So during the soft-fruit season make only the ices you will eat immediately, and freeze as much fruit purée as you can. You can then make fresh-tasting ices throughout the winter months, as the sweetened fruit purées keep remarkably well in the freezer.

USING THIS BOOK

Since one of the most valuable ways of using a freezer is to work on the principle of 'make two – eat one – freeze one', we have wherever relevant given instructions both for immediate eating and for freezing. The quantities for most of the recipes can be multiplied almost indefinitely, the only limitations being the size of your saucepans, oven, freezer and pocket. We have as a general rule given quantities for six people. There are a few exceptions, and in such cases this is stated in the individual recipes. But this can only be a rough guide. As that great cook Alice B. Toklas said tetchily when asked how many people a particular recipe would serve, 'How should I know how many it serves? It depends on their appetites, what else they have for dinner – whether they like it or not ... Such questions! Typically home economics ... so finicky.'

In a number of recipes some of the ingredients appear below the main list and in bold type; this means that they should be added just before serving, and so, if the dish is for the freezer, they should only be added after freezing.

Spring

CRAB • LAMB • VEAL • ASPARAGUS • BROAD BEANS
BROCCOLI • HERBS • SPINACH • WATERCRESS
RHUBARB • ELDERFLOWER

Crab

CRAB BISQUE

1 large whole cooked crab   *1 oz (25 g) flour*
2 onions   *2 egg yolks*
2 carrots   *¹/₂ pt (300 ml) single cream*
2 tbsp gin (optional)   *salt and pepper*
1 lemon
parsley, fennel, bayleaf   **a dash of Pernod (optional)**
1 oz (25 g) butter

Wash the crab thoroughly, crack it open and take out all the meat, discarding the inedible lungs or 'dead man's fingers'.

Put the shells in a large saucepan, add the roughly chopped onions and carrots, place on a high flame for a few moments and pour on the gin, leaving it to evaporate for one minute over the flame. The gin may be omitted, but it makes a perceptible difference to the luxurious taste of the soup. Add enough cold water to cover the shells (about 4 pt/2.4 litres), bring to the boil, skim, add the peel and juice of the lemon and the herbs and simmer for about one hour. Strain.

Flake the meat from the claws and set aside. Blend the brown meat with a little of the stock and stir into the soup. Bring slowly to the boil.

Make a beurre manié by working the flour into the butter and drop into the soup, stirring while it dissolves and the soup thickens. Whisk the egg yolks briefly with the cream and add to the soup, continuing to stir over a low heat. Do not allow the soup to boil once the eggs have been added. Add the reserved meat and heat through. Season and serve, with a dash of Pernod in each bowl if you like.

To freeze: cool and freeze in waxed or plastic containers.

To serve after freezing: tip the frozen soup into a saucepan and reheat very gently. On no account allow to boil, as this will curdle the eggs.

CRAB QUICHE

6 oz (175 g) crabmeat, fresh	1 tsp French mustard
or frozen	1 oz (25 g) grated Cheddar
10 oz (275 g) shortcrust pastry	or Gruyère cheese (optional)
(see p. 000)	1/2 pt (300 ml) single cream
2 whole eggs and 4 egg yolks	salt and pepper

If you are using frozen crabmeat do not freeze this dish.

Line one 10-in (25-cm) or two 7-in (18-cm) buttered flan tins with the pastry and bake blind for 10 minutes in a moderate oven (350°F/175°C/gas 4).

Beat the whole eggs and the yolks lightly until they are well amalgamated. Add the mustard and the cheese and season. Slowly beat in the cream, stir in the crabmeat and pour into the pastry cases. Return to the oven for 35 to 40 minutes.

To serve immediately: cook for a further five minutes.

To freeze: cool and freeze.

To serve after freezing: place the frozen quiche in a hot oven (425°F/220°C/gas 7). After 20 minutes lower the temperature to 350°F/175°C/gas 4, and leave for a further 30 to 40 minutes until it has heated right through. Place a piece of baking parchment or foil over the top if necessary, to prevent excessive browning.

~

CRABMEAT IN SAUCE

Served on croûtons this dish makes a delicious first course. Frozen crabmeat can be used straight from the freezer, but do not then freeze the dish.

8 oz (225 g) crabmeat, fresh	1 tbsp sherry or brandy
or frozen	1/2 tsp French mustard
1 oz (25 g) butter	2 tbsp cream
1 oz (25 g) flour	squeeze of lemon juice
1/2 pt (300 ml) milk	salt and pepper

Flake fresh crabmeat. Make a sauce with the butter, flour and milk, and cook until it is thick and smooth. Add the crabmeat, the sherry or brandy, the mustard, cream and a squeeze of lemon juice, and season to taste.

To serve immediately: heat gently without allowing the mixture to boil, and serve as above.

To freeze: cool and freeze.

To serve after freezing: tip the frozen mass into a saucepan and reheat gently, stirring frequently. You may need to add another tablespoon of cream if the mixture seems a little dry. Serve as above.

Lamb

If you are able to buy a whole or half lamb direct from a farm which will joint it for you, it is well worth buying one for storing in the freezer. The following recipes suggest ways of using the various joints.

NAVARIN OF LAMB PRINTANIER

1 leg or shoulder of lamb, fresh or frozen
1 oz (25 g) butter
1 tbsp oil
1 lb (450 g) button onions, fresh or frozen blanched
1 oz (25 g) flour
1 pt (600 ml) stock
1 clove garlic
a sprig of rosemary

1 lb (450 g) baby carrots, fresh or frozen blanched
1 lb (450 g) baby turnips, fresh or frozen blanched
1 lb (450 g) small new potatoes
8 oz (225 g) fresh broad beans or peas (podded weight), or frozen blanched
salt and pepper

Frozen lamb should be allowed to thaw at least partially before cooking. Frozen vegetables do not need to be thawed before they are added.

Heat the butter and oil in a heavy pan or flameproof casserole. Sauté the onions until they are a light-golden brown. Take them out and sear the meat on all sides. Remove the meat, sprinkle the flour into the pan and cook gently for a few minutes, stirring all the time. Add the stock gradually and continue stirring until the sauce is smooth. Put back the meat and add the crushed clove of garlic, salt, pepper and rosemary. Cover and leave to simmer for one hour.

Add the root vegetables and simmer for another 40 minutes.

Add the beans or peas. If they are frozen, stir them in well. When they are cooked test for seasoning. Carve the meat into thick slices before serving.

BLANQUETTE OF LAMB

This dish is particularly good served with rice or noodles.

1 shoulder of lamb, fresh or frozen
1 onion stuck with 2 or 3 cloves
bouquet garni
8 oz (225 g) button onions, fresh, or frozen blanched or in white sauce (see p. 74)
8 oz (225 g) button mushrooms, fresh, or frozen sautéed
2 oz (50 g) butter
2 oz (50 g) flour
1/4 pt (150 ml) double or whipping cream
a squeeze of lemon juice
salt and pepper

Frozen meat is best used straight from the freezer, so that the juices will go into the stock. Frozen onions and frozen sautéed mushrooms can also be used straight from the freezer.

Place the shoulder of lamb in a large pan, cover with cold water and bring very slowly to the boil. Make sure that the water does not reach boiling point before the meat has completely thawed. Skim the stock, add the onion stuffed with cloves, the bouquet garni and the seasoning, and simmer, covered, for 1–1½ hours, according to the size of the shoulder. When the meat is just done (if you prick it with a fork the liquid that comes out should be colourless), lift out and allow to cool.

Carve into slices or cubes, discarding any fat. Skim the fat off the broth and remove the onion.

Add fresh or frozen blanched onions and cook in the broth for 10 to 15 minutes, when they should be tender but not mushy. Sauté fresh mushrooms briefly in a little of the butter.

Make a beurre manié with the remaining butter and the flour. Slowly dissolve this in the broth and cook gently, stirring all the time, until the sauce begins to thicken. If you are using onions frozen in white sauce, add now. Add the sautéed mushrooms. Stir in the cream. Add the meat and the squeeze of lemon juice, and season.

To serve immediately: heat through gently and serve.

To freeze: cool and freeze.

To serve after freezing: tip the frozen blanquette into a saucepan and heat through very gently – do not allow to boil. Serve as above.

BOILED LAMB IN CAPER SAUCE

1 leg or shoulder of lamb, fresh	*2 oz (50 g) butter*
or frozen	*2 oz (50 g) flour*
1 onion	*1 tbsp capers (or more)*
1 carrot	*2 tbsp cream*
bouquet garni	*salt and pepper*

Frozen lamb is best used straight from the freezer for this recipe, so that the juices will go into the stock.

Place the leg or shoulder in a large pan, cover with cold water and bring very slowly to the boil, making sure that the water does not reach boiling point until the meat has completely thawed. Skim, add the roughly chopped onion and carrot, the bouquet garni and seasoning, and simmer very slowly until the meat is just done (anything between one and two hours, depending on the size of the joint). Remove the meat, transfer to a serving dish and keep warm while making the sauce. Strain the broth and set aside.

Melt the butter in a pan, add the flour and cook very gently for two minutes, stirring all the time. Gradually add ³/₄ pt (450 ml) of the lamb broth, stir until smooth, add the capers and the cream and test for seasoning. If you like a slightly sharp taste, you can also add a little of the caper vinegar.

To serve immediately: carve the meat at table and hand the sauce separately.

To freeze: allow the meat to cool and carve into thick slices. Freeze with the sauce.

To serve after freezing: tip the frozen mass into a pan and heat very slowly. Allow at least 40 minutes for this. You may wish to add some more capers and caper vinegar at this stage, as the capers seem to lose some of their sharpness in freezing.

NOTE Pour the remaining broth into a clean pan, add the lamb bone and a tablespoon of dried oregano, and boil briskly until it is reduced by half. Strain, cool and freeze for later use as stock. Or serve as broth, adding salt, pepper, oregano and lemon juice.

LEG OR SHOULDER OF LAMB COOKED IN DESSERT WINE WITH GARLIC

The long, slow cooking of this dish brings out the sweet flavour of the lamb, and even garlic haters will enjoy it, as the garlic melts and merely deepens the flavour of the sauce. The dish is best when cooked with dessert wine, such as a Monbazillac, but any good white wine, provided it is not too dry, will do, and you can always add a dash of Madeira or sweet sherry if the sauce tastes a little tart.

1 leg or shoulder of lamb, fresh *2 tbsp brandy*
 or frozen *1 bottle sweet white wine*
1 onion, stuck with 4 cloves *2 whole heads of garlic*
1 carrot *(or more)*
bouquet garni *salt and pepper*
2 tbsp oil

Frozen lamb must be allowed to thaw completely before cooking.

Bring to the boil a pan of water large enough to hold the lamb, add the onion, carrot and bouquet garni, and boil rapidly for 15 minutes. Add the lamb and boil gently for another 15 minutes. Remove the meat from the pan and wipe dry. (The cooking water can be boiled with the bone later, for use as stock.)

Heat the oil in a flameproof casserole and brown the lamb on all sides. Pour off any excess fat. Add the brandy and set alight. When the flames have died down, add the white wine and the garlic cloves, peeled. Bring to the boil, season, cover closely, lower the heat, and simmer very slowly over a low flame, or in a low oven (300°F/150°C/gas 2), for five to six hours. The meat will be nut brown and ready to fall off the bone, and the garlic will have melted into the sauce.

To serve immediately: carve the meat into chunks and serve, with the sauce, with mashed or gratin potatoes.

To freeze: take the meat off the bone, cool and freeze with the sauce.

To serve after freezing: heat through gently from frozen and serve as above.

NOTE This dish can also be made with chops. In this case, the cooking time will only be three hours.

NECK OF LAMB BOULANGÈRE

This makes an inexpensive but very satisfying family supper.

neck of lamb chops (1 or 2	*¹/₂ pt (300 ml) stock or water*
chops per person), fresh or	*for every 2 lb (900 g)*
frozen	*potatoes*
1 baking potato per person	*parsley*
1 clove garlic	*salt and pepper*

The meat can be used straight from the freezer, but will be more tender if it has been allowed to thaw at least partially.

Peel the potatoes, cut them into ¹/₄-in (¹/₂-cm) slices and lay on the bottom of a large roasting tin. Sprinkle with salt and pepper. Rub both sides of each chop with a cut clove of garlic and with salt and pepper and place on top of the potatoes. Add the stock or water. Cook in a medium oven (375°F/190°C/gas 5) for 1–1¹/₂ hours, or until the meat and potatoes are cooked. Sprinkle with plenty of finely chopped parsley before serving.

~

ITALIAN LAMB STEW

2–3 lb (900 g–1¹/₂ kg) neck	*1 small tin tomato purée*
of lamb chops, fresh or frozen	*1 tsp each of oregano, thyme*
1 oz (25 g) butter	*and rosemary*
1 tbsp oil	*salt and pepper and 1 lump*
1 lb (450 g) onions	*of sugar*
1 clove garlic	
¹/₂ pt (300 ml) red wine	**parsley**

Frozen chops should be allowed to thaw at least partially – about three hours should be enough.

Melt the butter and oil in a flameproof casserole. Slice the onions and brown gently with the garlic for a few minutes, then add the lamb chops and brown on both sides. Pour on the red wine and allow to boil fiercely for a few minutes until it has reduced by almost half. Add the tomato purée, herbs, sugar, seasoning and some water if necessary, enough for the meat to be just covered by liquid. Cover the casserole and leave to simmer for about two hours, until the meat is tender.

To serve immediately: remove excess fat. Sprinkle with plenty of parsley and serve.

To freeze: lift out the chops and remove the meat carefully from the bones. Chill the sauce, and when it is cold remove the fat. Combine the meat with the sauce and freeze.

To serve after freezing: tip the frozen stew into a pan and heat through very slowly. Sprinkle with parsley before serving.

~

DEVILLED BEST END OF NECK

An agreeable variation on plain roast best end of neck. Allow about two chops per person.

2 large best ends of neck, whole, fresh or frozen	parsley, tarragon, marjoram
1 large clove garlic	4 oz (100 g) fresh white breadcrumbs
4 tbsp French mustard	Worcestershire sauce
1 large onion	black peppercorns, very coarsely crushed
small piece of finely pared lemon peel	1 oz (25 g) butter

Frozen meat should be allowed to thaw before cooking.

Rub the meat well with the cut clove of garlic, and spread the mustard liberally on both sides. Chop the onion, lemon peel and herbs finely, mix with the breadcrumbs, spread over the outside of the meat and pat on firmly. Sprinkle on a little Worcestershire sauce and plenty of coarsely crushed peppercorns, dot with butter and cook in a hot oven (450°F/230°C/gas 8) for 45 minutes to one hour.

NOTE You can cook a saddle of lamb in the same way, but the roasting time will be longer.

ROAST BREAST OF LAMB

Although breast is perhaps the least-prized cut, the meat is tender and tasty.

> *2 breasts of lamb, fresh or*   *chopped herbs (thyme, oregano*
>   *frozen*   *or rosemary)*
> *1 clove garlic (optional)*   *salt and pepper*
> *French mustard*

Frozen meat should be allowed to thaw thoroughly before roasting.

Score the skin, rub with a cut clove of garlic and spread thickly with French mustard, salt (coarse sea salt if possible), coarsely ground black pepper and herbs. Roast in a medium oven (375°F/190°C/gas 5) for one hour.

~

STUFFED ROAST BREAST OF LAMB

> *2 boned breasts of lamb, fresh*   *4 oz (125 g) fresh breadcrumbs*
>   *or frozen*   *1 egg*
> *1 onion*   *1 clove garlic (optional)*
> *1 tbsp chopped parsley*   *1 tbsp French mustard*
> *1 tbsp chopped marjoram*   *knob of butter*
> *grated peel of 1 lemon*   *salt and pepper*

Frozen meat should be allowed to thaw thoroughly.

Mix the finely chopped onion, the parsley, marjoram and lemon peel with the breadcrumbs, season, and bind with the egg.

Lay out the breasts of lamb on a flat board and rub both sides with the cut clove of garlic, a little mustard and some salt and pepper, and spoon the stuffing evenly over each one. Roll them up, tie with string or thread, dot with a little butter and roast for about one hour in a hot oven (425°F/220°C/gas 7).

This dish is also good served cold, provided the meat is not too fatty.

Veal

BLANQUETTE OF VEAL

2–3 lb (1–1½ kg) shoulder or
  breast of veal, preferably on
  the bone
½ lemon
1 onion
1 carrot
bouquet garni
3 oz (75 g) butter

3 oz (75 g) flour
8 oz (225 g) button onions,
  fresh or frozen in white sauce
8 oz (225 g) button
  mushrooms
2 egg yolks
½ pt (300 ml) single cream
salt and pepper

Frozen onions can be used straight from the freezer.

Take the meat off the bone, cut into bite-sized cubes and put in a large bowl. Cover with cold water, add a slice of lemon and leave overnight to blanch the meat. Drain, put the meat in a large pan together with the bone, cover with cold water and bring slowly to the boil. Drain, rinse the pan, cover the meat and bone with fresh cold water and again bring to the boil. Add another slice of lemon, the roughly quartered onion and carrot, the bouquet garni and the seasoning, and leave to simmer for about 1½ hours, until the meat is tender. Strain, set aside the cooking liquid, and take any further meat off the bone.

Melt the butter in a clean pan, add the flour and cook, stirring, for three minutes. Slowly add up to 2 pt (1 litre) of the cooking liquid (if there is more, freeze it separately and use for veal stock on other occasions), together with the onions and mushrooms, and simmer slowly until the sauce begins to thicken.

Beat the cream into the egg yolks and add to the sauce. Stir over a very low heat, and be careful not to allow to boil. Check for seasoning and add a squeeze of lemon juice. Return the meat to the sauce.

To serve immediately: heat all through together, without allowing to boil, and serve with rice.

To freeze: cool and freeze.

To serve after freezing: tip the frozen blanquette into a pan and heat through gently. Allow at least 45 minutes for this, as it must be done very slowly and on no account be allowed to boil. Serve with rice.

VEAL GOULASH

Goulash can be served with rice, noodles or potatoes, but in Austria and Hungary it is traditionally served with little dumplings called Nockerln (see p. 25). If possible, buy the veal on the bone, as you can then make wonderful jellied veal stock from the bones.

2 lb (1 kg) shoulder or breast of veal	bayleaf, pinch of oregano and thyme
4 oz (100 g) paprika speck or streaky bacon	1 green pimento, fresh or frozen (optional)
2 onions	8 oz (225 g) mushrooms, fresh or frozen
1 clove garlic	1/4 pt (150 ml) sour cream
approx. 1 tsp paprika	salt and pepper
2 tbsp flour	
1/2 pt (300 ml) stock	

Frozen pimento and mushrooms can be used straight from the freezer.

Cut the meat and the speck or bacon into small cubes, and fry gently in a flameproof casserole. Add the sliced onions and garlic and sauté until golden brown. Sprinkle on the paprika. It is difficult to give an exact quantity for this, as paprika varies so much in strength: the fresher it is, the hotter it will be. Add the flour and cook gently for another two minutes, stirring well. Add the stock, herbs and seasoning, and continue to stir while it comes to the boil. Cover and simmer very slowly, or place in a low oven (300°F/150°C/gas 2) for about 1½ hours, until the meat is tender. Half an hour before the end of the cooking time add the chopped green pimento and the chopped or sliced mushrooms. Just before serving, stir in the sour cream and test for seasoning. The dish is now ready to serve.

To freeze: cool and freeze.

To serve after freezing: return the frozen goulash to a flameproof casserole and warm over a low heat, allowing 45 minutes to one hour. You may need to add a little more stock.

NOCKERLN (DUMPLINGS)

8 oz (225 g) flour   *¹/₂ pt (300 ml) milk*
2 oz (50 g) dried breadcrumbs   *1 oz (25 g) butter*
1 egg

Mix the flour and breadcrumbs, beat in the egg and make a stiff batter with the milk. Beat well.

Heat a large panful of salted water, and when it is boiling drop in teaspoonfuls of batter one by one, about 8 to 10 at a time, depending on the size of your pan. Leave to boil for about 10 minutes, by which time the dumplings should have risen to the surface. Take out of the water with a slotted spoon. Repeat until all the batter has been used up. Rinse the dumplings briefly under a cold tap, and heat in a frying pan in a little butter.

These dumplings make an excellent simple supper dish. After you have boiled and rinsed them, roll them in breadcrumbs, fry in butter until golden brown and serve with scrambled eggs or tomato sauce. Puréed tomatoes (see p. 129) go well with this dish.

Asparagus

The season for asparagus is short and it is a luxury food whether you buy it or grow it. So enjoy it fresh while you can and don't bother to freeze it unless you have a glut. However, for anyone who does have some to spare, here are two recipes which do freeze well and can be made in conjunction with one another.

ASPARAGUS TART

2 lb (1 kg) asparagus	¹/₄ pt (150 ml) single cream
10 oz (275 g) shortcrust pastry	1 oz (25 g) grated cheese
(see p. 218)	salt and pepper
6 eggs	

Line one 10-in (25-cm) or two 7-in (18-cm) buttered flan tins with the shortcrust pastry. Bake blind in a hot oven (400°F/200°C/gas 6) for 10 to 15 minutes.

Trim the asparagus, discarding any tough stalks, and cook until just tender. If you haven't an asparagus pan, keep the tips out of the water as far as possible, so that they are steamed rather than boiled.

Lift carefully out of the pan and drain well. Arrange the asparagus tips with the tender parts of the stalks in the pastry cases. Reserve the cooking water and any stalks that are left over for making soup (see following recipe). Beat the eggs lightly with the cream, add the cheese, season, and pour over the asparagus. Bake in a medium oven (375°F/190°C/gas 5) for 40 minutes.

To serve immediately: cook for a further five minutes, until the top is golden brown.

To freeze: cool and freeze.

To serve after freezing: place the frozen tart in a hot oven (425°F/220°C/gas 7) for 20 minutes. Turn the oven down to 350°F/175°C/gas 4 and cook for another 30 to 40 minutes, according to the size of the tart, until it has heated right through. Place a piece of buttered paper over the top if necessary to prevent excessive browning.

ASPARAGUS SOUP

1 lb (450 g) asparagus	*1¹/₂ oz (40 g) butter*
1¹/₂ pt (900 ml) light stock or	*1¹/₂ oz (40 g) flour*
water or *use asparagus stalks*	*3 egg yolks*
and stock from previous	*¹/₄ pt (150 ml) single cream*
recipe	*salt and pepper*
1 tsp sugar	

Trim the asparagus and cook in the stock or water, adding the sugar to take away any bitterness. If you haven't an asparagus pan, keep the tips out of the water as far as possible, so that they are steamed rather than boiled. Reserve the tips. Alternatively, use the stalks and stock left over from the recipe for asparagus tart.

Melt the butter in a pan, add the flour and cook gently for five minutes, stirring all the time. Gradually add about a pint (600 ml) of the cooking liquid and stir until smooth. Blend the stalks with the remaining liquid. Sieve and add to the soup.

Combine the yolks with the cream and add to the soup. Add any asparagus tips and reheat gently, but do not allow the soup to boil. Season and serve.

To freeze: cool and freeze.

To serve after freezing: tip the frozen soup into a saucepan and reheat very gently. On no account allow it to boil, as this would curdle the eggs.

Broad Beans

Broad beans, tender and straight out of the garden, are particularly good for freezing.

To freeze blanched: shell the beans and blanch them for two minutes. Drain, cool as quickly as possible, and freeze.

To serve after freezing: tip the frozen beans into a saucepan containing about 1 in (2 cm) of boiling water and cook gently until they are soft, breaking up the mass carefully with a fork once or twice. Be careful not to overcook the beans, which can easily happen if they are very young. Drain and serve with plenty of butter, or stir in a little cream (about 2 tbsp to 8 oz/225 g of beans) and some chopped parsley. Another way of serving broad beans is to make some béchamel sauce, stirring in lots of finely chopped parsley so that the sauce is quite green, and pour this over the beans.

LAMB WITH BROAD BEANS AND LEMON SAUCE

1 shoulder or leg of lamb,
fresh or frozen
2 lb (900 g) fresh broad beans
or 1 lb (450 g) frozen
1 clove garlic

1/4 pt (150 ml) stock or water
2 egg yolks
1/4 pt (150 ml) single cream
juice of 1 lemon
salt and pepper

Frozen lamb should be allowed to thaw before roasting. Frozen beans can be used straight from the freezer, but do not then freeze the dish.

Rub the meat all over with the cut surface of the garlic, and with salt and pepper. Put in a roasting tin, placing the remains of the garlic underneath. Roast in a medium oven (375°F/190°C/gas 5) for about one hour, depending on the size of the joint. The meat should be pink but not raw at the centre, a little less cooked than you would ultimately like to eat it, as it will be reheated in the sauce. Take it out of the oven and pour off the fat. Remove the garlic.

Meanwhile gently boil the broad beans until they are just tender. Drain, but do not throw away the water.

Carve the meat into thick slices, being careful to preserve all the juice, and set aside. Place the roasting pan with the skimmed meat juice on a very low heat, and add the stock or water and the egg yolks lightly beaten into the cream. Stir constantly over a low heat until the sauce thickens, but do not allow to boil. Gradually add the lemon juice and as much of the bean water as the sauce will take without becoming too thin. Check for seasoning.

To serve immediately: return the meat to the pan and allow to heat through, still being very careful not to allow the sauce to boil. Add the beans and serve.

To freeze: cool and freeze.

To serve after freezing: allow to thaw for at least five or six hours and reheat. Add a little more stock if necessary, and serve. This dish must not be heated straight from the freezer as the long period of heating would overcook the beans and make them tough and dry.

Broccoli, Sprouting Broccoli and Curly Kale

These are all very good vegetables to freeze, since they retain excellent colour, flavour and texture.

To freeze blanched: break the heads into florets of roughly equal size or cut the shoots to about the same length. Wash thoroughly. Blanch for two minutes. Drain, cool and freeze.

To serve after freezing: melt a little butter in a heavy pan. Add the frozen vegetables and heat very gently, stirring with a fork from time to time to break up the mass. Season lightly. The vegetables will be cooked in a few minutes.

These vegetables can also be cooked in a little salted water, but they keep their flavour and shape better if only butter is used, or at most a couple of tablespoons of water.

Herbs

Perennial herbs are at their best and freshest in spring, so that is the time to freeze them. It is well worth freezing any herbs you use in large quantities or in a great many dishes. Mint, parsley, chives, basil and tarragon, for instance, are a boon to have in the freezer, and bouquets garnis are worth their weight in gold.

Herbs have an extremely strong odour, and will contaminate other foods unless they are stored in airtight containers. This applies particularly to mint; even the smallest quantity, insufficiently wrapped, can make the whole freezer smell. So store them in screw-topped jars.

The taste and strength of herbs frozen raw are sometimes unpredictable, but when they are used in dishes which are cooked before freezing they do not seem to change at all.

Freeze the herbs in either of the following ways:

1 Prepare a really large number of bouquets garnis with two or three sprigs of

parsley, a sprig each of marjoram and thyme and a bay leaf. Tie them in small bunches and pack loosely in an airtight jar.

2 Parsley, mint, tarragon and any other herbs that you will use separately and in larger quantities can be packed into individual airtight jars. Use straight from the freezer, crumbling out as much as you need.

~

MEAT AND POULTRY WITH HERBS

Meat and poultry are excellent with herbs, which give a deliciously subtle flavour. If you are roasting a joint of beef, take off the string and fat in which the butcher has rolled it, and cover the meat lavishly with salt, pepper and several tablespoonfuls of chopped fresh or frozen herbs – parsley, rosemary, marjoram, thyme, and anything else you may have. Replace the fat and the string, and roast in the ordinary way.

A leg or shoulder of lamb can be scored very deeply – almost to the bone – in half-a-dozen places, and sprigs of rosemary tucked into the cuts. Pour over 3 or 4 tbsp of olive oil and roast. The rosemary, as well as giving the meat a pleasantly piquant taste, becomes crisp in the cooking, and some or all of it can be served up with the meat.

For roasting poultry, put some of the herbs inside the bird and cover it with the rest.

If you are pot-roasting a joint, you can insert chopped herbs, mixed with a little butter, into the cuts. Put some olive oil or dripping into a flameproof casserole, and brown the meat well all over. Add about ½ pt (300 ml) of red or white wine and cook gently (about 1½–2 hours for a medium joint) until the meat is tender. Skim the fat off the juice remaining in the casserole and either serve the rest of the liquid as it is or use it for making gravy.

For an economical but excellent meal, try roast breast of lamb stuffed with herbs (see p. 22).

CHICKEN WITH TARRAGON

*1 roasting chicken (about
    4 lb/2 kg), fresh or frozen
about 6 sprigs of tarragon
2 tbsp butter
2 tbsp olive oil
1 onion*

*1 carrot
approx. 1/2–3/4 pt (300–450 ml)
    stock
1 tbsp flour
2 tbsp sherry (optional)
salt and pepper*

Frozen chicken must be allowed to thaw before roasting.

Put half the tarragon inside the chicken, together with half the butter and a little salt and pepper. Melt the oil and the rest of the butter in a flameproof casserole, and use some of this to brush over the chicken. Gently cook the sliced onion and carrot and the remaining sprigs of tarragon for a few minutes, keeping aside a few tarragon leaves for the gravy. Add the chicken to the casserole and brown thoroughly all over. Season, baste the chicken well with the butter and oil in the casserole, and cook in the middle of a medium oven (350°F/175°C/gas 4) for 1–1½ hours. Baste once or twice.

When the chicken is tender, take out of the casserole and joint. For immediate eating keep warm while you make the sauce.

Strain the liquid in which the chicken was cooked and remove the fat. Put 1 tbsp of this fat back into the casserole, add the flour and mix well, scraping up any coagulated juices. Make the cooking liquid up to 1 pt (600 ml) with stock and add gradually, stirring until the sauce is smooth and has thickened. Add the sherry and the reserved tarragon leaves (chopped) and test for seasoning.

To serve immediately: arrange the chicken on a dish and hand the sauce separately.

To freeze: cool and freeze the chicken in the sauce.

To serve after freezing: allow to thaw overnight in the refrigerator or for at least five to six hours at room temperature. Put into a flameproof casserole, and warm through in a moderate oven or over a very low heat for 45 minutes to one hour.

CHICKEN BREASTS WITH HERB SAUCE

*4–6 boned chicken breasts, fresh
or frozen
3 tbsp finely chopped herbs,
fresh or frozen: thyme, basil,
tarragon, marjoram and
parsley*

*4 oz (100 g) butter
¹/₄ pt (150 ml) double or
whipping cream
¹/₄ pt (150 ml) chicken stock
salt and pepper*

Allow frozen chicken breasts to thaw before using.

Chop the herbs very finely and mix well, being careful to include only a small quantity of basil and tarragon, which are the strongest in flavour. Mix with the butter into a smooth paste. Season. Place the chicken breasts in a buttered baking tray skin side up, and spread the herbed butter to cover each evenly.

Bake in a medium oven (375°F/190°C/gas 5) for 30 minutes, basting from time to time. Take out of the oven, pour the cream over the breasts, and return for a further 10 minutes. Remove from the oven and transfer the breasts to a warmed serving dish.

Add the stock to the pan, reduce rapidly by half, stirring briskly with a fork. Season, pour the thickened sauce over the chicken and serve.

~

CORIANDER CHICKEN BREASTS

*4–6 chicken breasts, skinned,
fresh or frozen
¹/₂ pt (300 ml) yoghurt
2 tbsp olive oil
juice of ¹/₂ lemon
2 tsp Dijon mustard
2 tsp Worcestershire sauce
2 tsp coriander seeds, crushed*

*2 cloves garlic, finely chopped
¹/₂ oz (12 g) root ginger,
finely chopped
salt and pepper*

*2 tbsp finely chopped fresh
coriander or parsley leaves*

Frozen chicken breasts must be allowed to thaw before marinating.

Mix together all the ingredients except the chicken breasts in an ovenproof dish, and marinate the breasts for several hours, or overnight in the refrigerator. Bake in a moderately hot oven (375°F/190°C/gas 5) for 25 to 30 minutes, or until cooked.

To serve immediately: sprinkle with the finely chopped coriander or parsley and serve hot with rice. Alternatively, serve at room temperature with a rice salad.

To freeze: cool and freeze.

To serve after freezing: leave to thaw overnight in the refrigerator, or for at least five to six hours. Serve as above.

~

HERB BUTTER

4 oz (125 g) butter
1 tbsp chives
2 tsp parsley
1/2 tsp marjoram
2 crushed cloves garlic
  (optional)

1/2 tsp finely grated lemon
  peel (optional)
salt and pepper

Soften the butter, and mix well with the finely chopped herbs, garlic, and lemon peel. Season, wrap well and freeze.

To make herb bread: cut a medium-sized French loaf into 1–1½ in (2–4 cm) slices almost down to the bottom crust, and spread the herb butter generously on one side of each of the slices. Wrap the loaf in foil and put in a hot oven (400°F/200°C/gas 6) for about 15 minutes. Take out of the foil and separate the slices before serving.

PESTO GENOVESE

This famous sauce is used with many kinds of pasta, and also to flavour minestrone. For perfection, only the young leaves should be used; but since the plants are sometimes difficult to grow in cooler climates you may need to use some of the more mature leaves as well.

3 oz (75 g) basil leaves, weighed after stripping from the stalks	*2 oz (50 g) pine kernels*
	salt
2–3 medium cloves garlic	*2 oz (50 g) Parmesan cheese*
approx. ½ pt (300 ml) olive oil	

Crush the garlic on a wooden board with a little salt – the flat blade of a knife is useful for this. The amount of garlic is a matter of taste, so it is better to start with only two cloves, knowing that you can if you want add more.

To serve immediately: blend all the ingredients until the sauce is quite smooth. It should be the colour of fresh garden peas, with tiny bits of darker basil floating in it. Stir in the freshly grated cheese and season with a little salt but no pepper.

To freeze: blend all the ingredients except the cheese. Freeze in airtight containers, as the smell is extremely penetrating.

To serve after freezing: grate the cheese finely and stir into the pesto when it has thawed.

~

PARSLEY SOUP

This soup is equally good served hot or cold.

large bunch of fresh parsley (approx. 4 oz/ 100 g)	*2 pt (1 litre) stock*
	salt and pepper
2 onions	
2 potatoes	*cream for serving (optional)*
2 oz (50 g) butter	

Cut the tops off the parsley stalks and set aside. Sweat the chopped onions and potatoes in the butter for five minutes, then add the stock and the parsley stalks and cook for 10 minutes or until the potato is soft. Remove the stalks and blend the soup and the parsley tops. Season.

To serve immediately:

To serve hot – reheat and serve with a swirl of cream in each bowl.

To serve cold – chill before serving.

To freeze: cool and freeze.

To serve after freezing:

To serve hot – tip the frozen soup into a pan, reheat gently and proceed as above.

To serve cold – allow to thaw at room temperature or in the refrigerator.

~

FISH PIE

Fish and parsley sauce go well together, and this easy recipe brings out the flavour of both. Any white fish, or salmon, or a combination of the two, can be used for this recipe. The pie is excellent made with frozen fish, but should not then be frozen.

2 lb (900 g) fish fillets	*butter and hot milk for mashing*
3 lb (1¹/₂ kg) potatoes	*the potatoes*
1¹/₄ pt (750 ml) milk	*4 oz (100 g) prawns*
2 oz (50 g) butter	*(optional)*
2 oz (50 g) flour	*salt and freshly ground pepper*
4–6 tbsp chopped parsley	*1 oz (25 g) butter*
(or more)	

There is no need to thaw frozen fish.

Boil the potatoes. Gently simmer the fish in the milk for 10 to 15 minutes. When it is cooked, drain, reserving the milk, remove the skin and flake the flesh. Alternatively, place the fish in a pan, add the milk, bring slowly to the boil, and as soon as it has boiled remove from the heat, cover the pan and leave. The fish will be cooked by the time it is cool enough to handle.

Make a sauce with the butter, the flour and the reserved milk. Season and stir in the chopped parsley – the more the better.

When the potatoes are cooked, drain and return to the pan. Add plenty of butter and hot milk, beating well until light and fluffy. Season generously with pepper (one of the secrets of good mashed potatoes).

Stir the fish into the sauce, add the prawns if you are using them, and transfer to an ovenproof dish. Spoon the mashed potatoes evenly over the fish.

To serve immediately: dot with 1 oz (25 g) butter and heat through in a moderate oven (350°F/175°C/gas 4) for about 30 minutes, until hot and bubbling. Put under a hot grill for a few minutes before serving so that the top is golden brown and slightly crusty.

To freeze: cool and freeze.

To serve after freezing: allow to thaw for at least four hours and heat through as above.

MINT ICE-CREAM

The delicate green colour and unexpected taste of this ice-cream and of the mint sorbet that follows make them refreshing desserts. Pick the mint when it is young and tender.

> *1 handful of mint leaves*   *juice of one lemon*
> *stripped off the stems*   *¹/₄ pt (150 ml) whipping cream*
> *4 oz (100 g) sugar*   *or crème fraîche*
> *¹/₄ pt (150 ml) water*

Bring the water and sugar to the boil, stirring until all the sugar has dissolved. Boil for three minutes and allow to cool.

Wash the mint leaves and place in a blender, pour over the syrup and blend thoroughly. Strain through a nylon sieve, pressing as much of the mint through as possible. Add the strained lemon juice, pour into an ice-tray and freeze for about one hour, until 'soft frozen'. Blend again, and fold into the lightly whipped cream. Pour into a serving dish and freeze.

To serve: remove from the freezer one hour before serving and leave in the refrigerator.

~

MINT SORBET

> *1 handful of mint leaves,*   *4 oz (100 g) sugar*
> *stripped off the stems*   *juice of 1 lemon*
> *¹/₄ pt (150 ml) water*   *2 egg whites*

Frozen egg whites must be allowed to thaw to room temperature.

Make in the same way as mint ice-cream, substituting the stiffly beaten egg whites for the whipped cream.

To serve: remove from the freezer 10 to 15 minutes before serving.

Spinach

Spinach is one of the best stand-byes to keep in the freezer. It can be used at very little notice in most of the recipes which follow.

Blanching it is a long job, for only a little can be processed at a time. It is much simpler, and just as good, to cook it before freezing.

To freeze cooked: strip off any long or tough stalks, wash the leaves thoroughly, and put in a large, heavy pan without any added water. Cook until tender. The time taken will depend on how young and fresh the spinach is: if it is really young, and straight out of the garden, it shouldn't take more than five to six minutes, but a little longer may be necessary if it is older and not so fresh.

When it is cooked, strain and plunge into cold water for a couple of minutes. Drain, and squeeze out the moisture very thoroughly. Freeze in small quantities, left whole or chopped.

To serve after freezing: put the frozen spinach in a heavy pan. Season and add a knob of butter, a grating of nutmeg and, if you like, a little milk or cream. Heat very gently, stirring from time to time. Test for seasoning and serve.

SPINACH SOUP

1 lb (450 g) fresh spinach or	*salt and pepper*
6 oz (175 g) frozen (cooked)	
1 oz (25 g) butter	*1 pt (600 ml) milk*
½ oz (12 g) flour	*cream for serving*
1 pt (600 ml) stock	

Cook the fresh spinach as described above. If you are using frozen spinach, there is no need to wait for it to thaw.

Make a roux with the butter and flour and add the stock, stirring all the time. When it boils, add the spinach and simmer for a few minutes after it has thawed. Season and mix in a blender.

To serve immediately: add the milk and cook for a further 10 minutes. Test for seasoning, pour into bowls and add a swirl of cream to each serving.

To freeze: cool and freeze. You can add the milk before freezing, but the soup will take up more room in the freezer.

To serve after freezing: add the milk to the frozen soup and heat gently, stirring from time to time. Test for seasoning, pour into bowls and serve as above.

SOLE FLORENTINE

This dish can be made with almost any white fish, fresh or frozen, but if you are using frozen fish do not freeze the dish. These quantities will serve four people.

> *1½ lb (675 g) fish fillets*
> *1½ lb (675 g) fresh spinach*
> *or 12 oz (350 g) frozen*
> *(cooked)*
> *4 oz (100 g) butter*

> *2 oz (50 g) flour*
> *1 pt (600 ml) milk*
> *4 oz (100 g) grated cheese*
> *salt, pepper, nutmeg*

Frozen fish should be allowed to thaw partially. If you are using fresh spinach, cook as described on p. 37. If you are using frozen spinach there is no need to wait for it to thaw.

Melt 1 oz (25 g) of the butter in a pan and stir in the cooked spinach. If you are using frozen spinach a little more butter will be necessary. Season. Place the spinach in a baking dish and lay the fish fillets on top.

Make a sauce with 2 oz (50 g) butter, the flour and the milk. Stir in most of the grated cheese and season with salt, pepper and grated nutmeg. Pour over the fish, sprinkle with the remaining cheese and dot with a few knobs of butter. Bake in a medium oven (375°F/190°C/gas 5) for 20 minutes (or for 30 minutes if partly frozen fish is used) until the top is golden brown.

To freeze: cool and freeze.

To serve after freezing: place in a hot oven (450°F/230°C/gas 8) for 20 minutes. Turn the oven down to 350°/175°C/gas 4, and cook for a further 30 to 40 minutes.

FLORENTINE EGGS

A good, quickly made supper dish.

12 oz (350 g) frozen spinach	*2 tbsp flour*
6 eggs	*1 pt (600 ml) milk*
4 oz (100 g) butter	*2 oz (50 g) grated cheese*
approx. 2 tbsp cream	*salt, pepper, nutmeg*

Put the frozen spinach into a pan with half the butter and the cream and warm gently. Make a sauce with the remaining butter, the flour and the milk, season, and when the sauce has thickened pour about half into another pan and keep warm. Add the spinach to the sauce remaining in the pan and stir well. Test for seasoning, and turn into a shallow ovenproof dish. Keep warm.

Poach the eggs, which should be slightly underdone when you take them out of the water. Arrange them on top of the spinach, and pour over the remaining sauce, to which about half the cheese and a couple of gratings of nutmeg have been added. Sprinkle the remaining cheese on top, and brown quickly under the grill.

If you make this dish with fresh spinach, you will need 1¹/₂–2 lb (675–900 g).

SPINACH GNOCCHI

These little dumplings make a delicious starter, or they can be served as a main dish.

6 oz (175 g) frozen spinach
4 oz (100 g) ricotta or cottage
cheese
2 oz (50 g) butter
1½ oz (40 g) self-raising flour
1 egg

1 oz (25 g) Cheddar cheese,
grated
salt, pepper, nutmeg
grated Parmesan cheese for
serving

Thaw the spinach and chop finely. Mix well with the ricotta or cottage cheese (if you are using the latter, pass it through a sieve first). Put into a small pan with half the butter and stir over a low heat for about five minutes. Remove from the heat and add the flour, Cheddar cheese and beaten egg. Season with salt, pepper and plenty of freshly grated nutmeg.

Leave in the refrigerator for at least four or five hours, or in the freezer for about 45 minutes: this will make the mixture firm and easy to handle. When you are ready to cook the gnocchi, flour your hands, and with a teaspoon scoop out a little of the mixture. Roll very lightly into a small sausage shape – no more than 1½ in (4 cm) long and ¾ in (2 cm) in diameter – dust with flour, and lay on a floured board until all the gnocchi are ready.

Bring a large pan of water to the boil, and gently drop in the gnocchi one by one, not letting the water go off the boil. Simmer with the pan uncovered. As soon as the gnocchi come to the surface (four or five minutes), take out with a slotted spoon and put in a warmed vegetable dish.

Meanwhile, melt the rest of the butter in a small pan until it is bubbly and pale nut-brown. Pour over the gnocchi and serve at once, handing round plenty of grated Parmesan cheese.

This quantity will make about 40 gnocchi.

SPINACH SOUFFLÉ

This soufflé is enough as a starter for three to four people.

3 oz (75 g) frozen spinach	*3 eggs and 1 extra white*
1 oz (25 g) butter	*3 oz (75 g) grated cheese*
4–5 tbsp cream	*salt and pepper*

Tip the frozen spinach into a pan with about half the butter and half the cream and warm through gently until it has thawed. Blend. Beat the yolks with the remaining cream, add the spinach and season. Finally fold in the stiffly beaten whites. Pour into a 2-pt (1-litre) buttered soufflé dish and dot with the rest of the butter. Cook in the centre of a moderate oven (350°F/175°C/gas 4) for about 35 minutes. Serve immediately.

If fresh spinach is used, about 8 oz (225 g) will be needed.

~

SPINACH WITH RICE

This is a simple but delicious and unusual supper dish.

12 oz (350 g) frozen spinach	*1/4 pt (150 ml) cream*
12 oz (350 g) risotto rice	*5–6 oz (150–175 g)*
3 oz (75 g) butter	*grated cheese*
2 1/2 tbsp flour	*salt, pepper, nutmeg*
1 1/4 pt (750 ml) milk	

Frozen spinach can be used straight from the freezer.

Put the rice on to cook and meanwhile make a sauce in a large pan with the butter, flour and milk. Add the spinach and simmer gently for 10 to 15 minutes, chopping the spinach roughly as it thaws. Add the cream, the grated cheese, the seasoning and two or three grates of nutmeg.

When the rice is ready drain it well and add to the mixture. Stir well over a low heat until it is very hot and serve immediately.

If you make this dish with fresh spinach, you will need about 1 1/2 lb (675 g).

SPINACH PANCAKES

This is an excellent dish to keep as a stand-by for unexpected visitors, as the pancakes can be put straight from the freezer into a hot oven, and freezing even seems to improve their taste and texture.

BATTER
1/2 pt (300 ml) milk
1/2 pt (300 ml) water or beer
8 oz (225 g) flour
4 eggs
salt and pepper

SAUCE
1 1/2 oz (40 g) butter
1 1/2 oz (40 g) flour
1 pt (600 ml) milk
salt and pepper

FILLING
1–1 1/2 lb (450–675 g) fresh
spinach or 8 oz (225 g)
frozen
3–4 tbsp cream
2–3 oz (50–75 g) butter
2 oz (50 g) mushrooms, fresh
or frozen sautéed
2 oz (50 g) grated cheese

2 oz (50 g) grated cheese

Frozen spinach and mushrooms can be used straight from the freezer when making this dish.

Make the batter with the milk, water or beer, flour and eggs, and season well. Allow to stand for at least an hour.

Meanwhile prepare the filling. If you are using fresh spinach, cook as described on p. 37 and chop finely. Put in a pan with half the cream and 1 oz (25 g) butter (for frozen spinach you may need a little more of both). Warm through gently. Chop fresh mushrooms and sauté for a few minutes in the rest of the butter. Mix the mushrooms, fresh or frozen, with the spinach, cheese and remaining cream.

Make a sauce with the butter, flour and milk. Stir this into the spinach mixture, test for seasoning and keep warm if the pancakes are to be eaten immediately.

Give the batter another beat before you start to make the pancakes. These should be quite small – if you use a frying pan which is 5 in (12 cm) in diameter, this quantity will make about 30. Spread a small quantity of the spinach filling on each pancake and roll up.

To serve immediately: arrange the pancakes in a shallow ovenproof dish, sprinkle the grated cheese on top, and warm through in a moderate oven (350°F/175°C/gas 4) for about 20 minutes.

To freeze: allow to cool. Wrap in the quantities you would normally need for a meal and freeze. Two pancakes make a fairly substantial starter.

To serve after freezing: place the pancakes straight from the freezer in a shallow ovenproof dish, sprinkle with grated cheese and put in the upper part of a hot oven (450°F/230°C/gas 8) for about 30 minutes.

~

SPINACH STALKS AND SWISS CHARD

One of the most useful varieties of spinach to grow is Swiss chard – the type with big leaves and thick white stalks – because both stalks and leaves can be used.

To freeze the stalks blanched: when you have stripped off the leaves take the best and largest of the stalks, trim so that they are roughly the same length, and blanch for two minutes. Drain, cool and freeze.

To serve after freezing: cook until soft in a little butter.

NOTE Blanched chard stalks can also be used instead of pasta when making meat or vegetable lasagne.

Watercress

WATERCRESS SOUP

4 bunches watercress
2 oz (50 g) butter
4 onions
4 medium potatoes
2 pt (1 litre) stock or water

salt and pepper

1 pt (600 ml) milk
a little cream for serving

Wash the watercress well, and pick off any thick or hairy stalks.

Melt the butter in a large pan, add the roughly chopped onions and potatoes and sweat gently for about five minutes. Pour on the stock or water, add half the watercress, season, and simmer for about 20 minutes, or until the potatoes are cooked. Blend until smooth. Then either blend again briefly with the remaining watercress, or chop the cress roughly and add, so that you have a pale-green soup with large flecks of dark-green, fresh-tasting cress.

To serve immediately: return to the stove and add the milk, check for seasoning, and heat through. Pour into bowls and add a swirl of cream to each helping.

To freeze: allow to cool and freeze.

To serve after freezing: tip the frozen soup into a pan, add the milk and heat through gently. Serve as above.

Rhubarb

Rhubarb keeps its flavour and colour perfectly when it is frozen without sugar.

To freeze: wash the stalks or wipe them with a damp cloth, cut into convenient lengths and freeze.

To serve after freezing: put the frozen rhubarb in a stainless steel or enamel saucepan, with 1 tbsp of water to prevent it from sticking, and sugar in the proportion of 4–6 oz (100–175 g) to 1 lb (450 g) rhubarb. Leave over the gentlest possible heat until the rhubarb is cooked. This can also be done in a double saucepan or a covered casserole in a moderate oven.

RHUBARB CRUMBLE

1 lb (450 g) rhubarb, fresh or
frozen
4 oz (100 g) brown sugar
grated rind of 1 orange
(optional)

6 oz (175 g) flour
4 oz (100 g) white sugar
2 oz (50 g) butter

Frozen rhubarb can be used straight from the freezer, but do not then freeze the dish.

Place the rhubarb, cut into small pieces, in an ovenproof dish. Sprinkle on the brown sugar and the grated orange rind and leave for about an hour to draw out the juice and for frozen rhubarb to thaw.

Mix the flour with the white sugar and rub in the butter. Spread this mixture over the top of the rhubarb and pat down firmly.

To serve immediately: place in a medium oven (375°F/190°C/gas 5) and cook for about one hour, until the crumble is golden brown.

To freeze: make sure the crumble is very firmly patted down before freezing.

To serve after freezing: place the frozen crumble in a hot oven (425°F/220°C/gas 7) for half an hour, then turn the oven down to 375°F/190°C/gas 5, and cook for a further hour.

NOTE Crumble made with fresh rhubarb can be cooked and then frozen, but it should be taken out of the oven before it browns. After freezing it will need only about half an hour in the oven once the temperature has been lowered.

RHUBARB AND GINGER ICE-CREAM

If you use castor sugar the ice-cream will be a delicate pink. Soft brown sugar will give a richer flavour, but the colour will be less appealing.

1 lb (450 g) rhubarb, fresh or   *4 pieces preserved ginger*
    frozen   *3–4 tbsp preserved ginger syrup*
8 oz (225 g) soft brown or   *¹/₂ pt (300 ml) double or*
    castor sugar   *whipping cream*

Frozen rhubarb can be used straight from the freezer.

Place the rhubarb, cut into pieces, in a bowl, sprinkle on the sugar and leave for two to three hours to draw out the juice.

Put the rhubarb with its juice into a heavy saucepan and stew gently over a low heat, stirring from time to time until you have a smooth purée. It should not be necessary to add any water, and the rhubarb, especially if it is fresh and young, should just melt. However, if it is at all stringy, pass through a sieve. Leave to cool.

Finely chop the preserved ginger and add to the rhubarb together with the ginger syrup. Lightly whip the cream and fold in. Taste, and add more ginger if you wish, remembering that freezing will slightly diminish the sharpness. Freeze.

To serve: remove from the freezer and leave in the refrigerator for about half an hour before serving.

~

RHUBARB MOULD

This is blander than most rhubarb dishes, and is popular with children.

2 lb (900 g) frozen rhubarb   *2 oz (50 g) cornflour*
approx. 1 lb (450 g) sugar

Place the frozen rhubarb in a bowl, sprinkle on the sugar and leave for two to three hours to draw out the juice.

Tip the rhubarb into a pan, add enough water to cover, bring to the boil and simmer, covered, until the rhubarb is very tender. Mix the cornflour to a smooth paste with 2 tbsp water. Stir into the rhubarb and boil for five minutes, stirring all the time, until the mixture thickens and loses any cloudiness. Test for sweetness. Rinse out a bowl or mould with cold water. Pour in the rhubarb mixture and chill. Turn out when set, sprinkle a little sugar on top, and serve with cream.

RHUBARB COBBLER

1–1½ lb (450–675 g) frozen   *3 oz (75 g) butter*
   rhubarb   *1 egg*
6–8 oz (175–225 g) sugar   *a little milk*
6 oz (175 g) self-raising flour

Place the frozen rhubarb in an ovenproof dish
with all but 1 oz (25 g) of the sugar, and leave for
two to three hours. Rub the flour into the butter
and add the remaining sugar, the beaten egg and a
very little milk – enough to make a stiff, cake-like
mixture. Spread this on top of the rhubarb. Bake
in a moderate oven (350°F/175°C/gas 4) for
about 45 minutes, until the top is golden brown and crusty.

NOTE This pudding can be made equally well with apples. Plums or blackberries can also be used instead of rhubarb, either on their own or combined
with apple.

~

FOAMY RHUBARB TART

1 lb (450 g) frozen rhubarb   *2 eggs*
6 oz (175 g) sweetened   *2 tbsp double cream, crème*
   shortcrust pastry (see p. 218)   *fraîche or sour cream*
6 oz (175 g) sugar   *grated rind of 1 lemon*

Place the frozen rhubarb in a bowl with 4 oz (100 g) of the sugar and leave for
two to three hours to draw out the juice.

Line a buttered 8-in (20-cm) flan tin with the shortcrust pastry and bake blind
for 10 minutes in a hot oven (425°F/220°C/gas 7). Strain the rhubarb, reserving
the juice, and spread on the pastry case. Sprinkle on the rest of the sugar and
bake for 30–40 minutes in a medium oven (375°F/190°C/gas 5) until the
rhubarb is tender.

Beat the egg yolks lightly and add the rhubarb juice, the grated lemon rind
and the cream. Fold in the stiffly beaten egg whites, pour over the tart, and
return to the oven until it has set (about 25 minutes).

Serve hot or cold.

Elderflower

The season for making these two recipes is very short. The elderflower heads must be picked when they are fully out but before they have begun to turn brown, and they are best gathered when the sun is on them, as this brings out the full fragrance. Shake lightly to remove any bugs and discard thick stalks.

ELDERFLOWER LEMONADE

at least 2 dozen elderflower   4–6 lemons
  heads   2 pt (1 litre) water
2 lb (1 kg) sugar

Put the sugar in a large, shallow bowl. Add the thinly pared lemon rind and place the elderflower heads on top. Pour on the boiling water. Stir once or twice to dissolve the sugar and leave to steep for several hours.

Strain the syrup and add the lemon juice.

To serve immediately: dilute with three or four parts of water (sparkling water makes this a particularly refreshing drink).

To freeze: pour into small tubs or ice-cube trays and freeze. As the syrup will not freeze completely it is best to cover the trays with film.

To serve after freezing: put three or four cubes into each glass or a tubful into a jug, and top up with water.

~

ELDERFLOWER SORBET

This is particularly good served with gooseberry tart (see p. 86).

1 pt (600 ml) elderflower   1 egg white (optional)
  syrup

The frozen egg white must be allowed to thaw to room temperature.

Freeze the syrup (see previous recipe). When frozen blend until white and fluffy. Fold in the stiffly beaten egg white, pour into a chilled serving dish and return to the freezer.

Serve straight from the freezer, as this sorbet melts very fast.

Summer

SALMON • FRENCH BEANS • RUNNER BEANS • BEETROOT • CARROTS • CAULIFLOWER
COURGETTES • CUCUMBER • LETTUCE • MARROW • ONIONS • PEAS • TURNIPS
APRICOTS • CHERRIES • CURRANTS • GOOSEBERRIES • MELONS
PEACHES AND NECTARINES • PINEAPPLE • PLUMS
RASPBERRIES • STRAWBERRIES

Salmon

No fish freezes more successfully than salmon, or is better worth preserving in this way, providing it is very fresh. But do not keep it in the freezer for more than two months. Salmon is equally successful frozen raw or cooked, but raw whole fish must be gutted and cleaned before freezing. Freeze whole or cut into convenient portions.

KOULIBIAC

This Russian dish is excellent for making a little salmon go a long way. The quantities given are for six people, but they can be multiplied indefinitely. A really big koulibiac makes a splendid centrepiece for a buffet party.

Koulibiac made with fresh salmon may be frozen cooked or uncooked: the two methods are equally successful. But if you are freezing it omit the eggs.

1 lb (450 g) cooked salmon, fresh or frozen
1 large onion
3 oz (75 g) butter
8 oz (225 g) mushrooms, fresh or frozen sautéed
8 oz (225 g) cooked long grain rice (approx. 3 oz/75 g raw)
8 oz (225 g) puff pastry
2 hard-boiled eggs
a little milk or egg yolk

salt, pepper and a little lemon juice

SAUCE
1/2 pt (300 ml) single cream
1/2 pt (300 ml) fish or other light stock
1 tbsp chopped herbs, ideally a combination of parsley, chives and fennel
a little finely grated lemon peel
salt and pepper

Frozen salmon should be allowed to thaw for two to three hours so that you can flake it, but if you are using it, do not freeze the koulibiac. Frozen sautéed mushrooms can be used straight from the freezer.

Sauté the finely chopped onion in 1 oz (25 g) of the butter, and when it is transparent add the roughly chopped fresh or the frozen sautéed mushrooms, and cook for a further five minutes. Mix with the boiled rice and season liberally with salt, pepper and lemon juice.

Roll out the pastry thinly into a rectangle. (If you are making a larger koulibiac, see below.) Place on a buttered baking tray lined with baking parchment. Spread half the rice mixture down the centre of the rectangle, flake the salmon over this and cover with the sliced hard-boiled eggs. Spread the rest of the rice on top, and dot with the remaining butter. Fold up the sides of the pastry towards the top and pinch the sides and ends together, sealing them with a little water if necessary.

If you are making a large koulibiac, you will probably find it easier to roll out the pastry into two equal rectangles. Spread the rice and fish mixture over the whole of one rectangle, leaving a 1-in (2-cm) margin all round, then place the second rectangle over the top and seal all edges as before. For this larger koulibiac, increase the cooking times given below.

To make the sauce: boil the cream for a few minutes to reduce and thicken. Add the stock, the herbs and the lemon peel. Season.

To serve immediately: brush the top of the koulibiac with milk or egg yolk and place in a hot oven (425°F/220°C/gas 7) for half an hour. Turn the oven down to 350°F/175°C/gas 4 and continue to cook for a further 20 minutes, or until the pastry is golden brown. Serve hot with the cream sauce.

To freeze uncooked: freeze the uncooked koulibiac for 24 hours on the baking tray, wrap and freeze. Freeze the sauce separately.

To freeze cooked: cook the koulibiac as for immediate eating, cool, and freeze as above. Freeze the sauce separately.

To serve after freezing:

Frozen uncooked – put the frozen koulibiac into a hot oven (425°F/220°C/gas 7) for half an hour, then turn the oven down to 350°F/175°C/gas 4. Continue to cook for a further 45 to 50 minutes, or until the pastry is golden brown.

Frozen cooked – put the frozen koulibiac in a hot oven (425°F, 220°C, gas 7) for half an hour, then turn the oven down to 350°F/175°C/ gas 4, and leave for another 20 minutes. Place a piece of buttered paper or foil over the top for the last 20 minutes if necessary to prevent the top from getting too browned.

Sauce: heat gently from frozen and serve separately.

SALMON SOUFFLÉ

8 oz (225 g) cooked salmon,	2 oz (50 g) butter
fresh or frozen	2 oz (50 g) flour
2 oz (50 g) finely grated	1/2 pt (300 ml) milk
cheese – Parmesan, Gruyère	4 eggs
or Cheddar	salt and pepper

Allow frozen salmon to thaw for two to three hours, or until it will flake.

Butter a 2-pt (1-litre) soufflé dish and sprinkle a little of the grated cheese round the sides.

Make a sauce with the butter, flour and milk. Remove from the heat and add the egg yolks one by one, beating them in well. Stir in the salmon and the rest of the cheese and season to taste. Whip the egg whites stiffly, fold into the mixture, and pour into the prepared soufflé dish. Cook in the centre of a moderate oven (375°F/190°C/gas 5) for 35 to 40 minutes, by which time the top should have risen and be golden brown, and the inside should still be creamy. Serve at once.

> NOTE To make a more substantial dish, use more salmon and line the bottom of the dish with the extra fish, flaked.

~

SALMON MOUSSE

This is a good way to use up a small amount of cooked salmon, but if you are using frozen cooked salmon do not freeze the mousse. These quantities will make an ample starter for six, but they can be multiplied indefinitely.

8 oz (225 g) cooked salmon,	1/8 pt (80 ml) white wine
fresh or frozen	1/2 pt (300 ml) fish or other
3 shallots or a dozen spring	light stock
onions	1/2 pt (300 ml) double or
1/2 oz (12 g) butter	whipping cream
1/4 oz (6 g) gelatine	salt and pepper

If you are using frozen cooked salmon, allow it to thaw for three or four hours.

Chop the shallots or onions and sweat very gently in the butter until they are soft but not coloured. Dissolve the gelatine in the white wine and heat until it has completely dissolved. Add to the onions and blend with the salmon. Season and leave to cool. Whip the cream very lightly so that it doubles in bulk without becoming stiff and fold into the salmon mixture when it has cooled. Pour into a ring or fish mould or a soufflé dish.

To serve immediately: chill in the refrigerator for about two hours or until the mousse has set. Turn out of the mould or serve in the soufflé dish.

To freeze: freeze when the mousse is quite cold.

To serve after freezing: allow to thaw at room temperature for six or seven hours, turn out and serve.

NOTE To make this dish more luxurious, line the mould with slices of smoked salmon.

~

SALMON TART

1 lb (450 g) cooked salmon,	¹/₂ oz (12 g) butter
fresh or frozen	5 eggs
10 oz (275 g) shortcrust pastry	¹/₂ pt (300 ml) single cream
(see p. 218)	salt and pepper
1 large onion	

Allow frozen salmon to thaw for two to three hours so that you can flake it, but if you are using frozen fish do not freeze the tart.

Line one 10-in (25-cm) or two 7-in (18-cm) buttered flan tins with the pastry.

Sauté the chopped onion in the butter. Flake the salmon into the flan cases, spread the sautéed onion on top, beat the eggs with the cream, season, and pour this mixture into the flan cases. Cook in a moderate oven (375°F/190°C/gas 5) for 30 to 40 minutes.

To serve immediately: cook for a further five minutes until the top is a rich golden colour. Serve hot or cold.

To freeze: cool and freeze.

To serve after freezing: place the frozen tart in a hot oven (425°F/220°C/gas 7) for 20 minutes, then turn the oven down to 350°F/175°C/gas 5, and leave for another 20 to 30 minutes, according to the size of the tart, until it has heated right through. Place a piece of buttered paper or foil over the top, if necesssary, to prevent excessive browning.

If you want to serve the tart cold, place in a hot oven for 30 minutes only.

French Beans

French beans are best frozen blanched, but they do not retain their superlative taste as well as many other vegetables. So it pays to give them rather special treatment afterwards.

To freeze blanched: trim the ends off the beans. Blanch for two minutes, drain, cool and freeze.

To serve after freezing: any of the three following methods of cooking helps to preserve the taste and colour of the beans.

1 Cook the frozen beans in a little boiling salted water until they are tender, which shouldn't take more than about five minutes if they are really fresh and young. Drain, put a good knob of butter in the pan and gently reheat the beans for a few minutes, shaking the pan so that they become coated with the butter.

2 Put some olive oil into a pan – about 3 tbsp for 1 lb (450 g) of beans – add a little pepper and salt and sauté the frozen beans until they are tender. This will take 10 to 15 minutes.

3 Cook the beans in water as for method 1, drain them, and while they are still hot mix them with French dressing and a little finely chopped onion or shallot. Chill before serving.

MINESTRONE

Minestrone is one of those comfortable soups which can be made in all sorts of ways. The quantities of vegetables given are approximate – vary both amounts and varieties according to your taste and what you have available. The haricot beans must be left to soak overnight. For freezing, omit the cabbage until the minestrone comes to be eaten. These quantities will serve 8 to 10 people.

8 oz (225 g) French or runner beans, fresh or frozen blanched

8 oz (225 g) haricot beans
2 onions
3 carrots
1 potato
4 celery stalks
2 leeks
4 rashers bacon (optional)
2 tbsp olive oil

8 oz (225 g) tomatoes
1–2 tbsp concentrated tomato purée
approx. 3 pt (1½ litres) water
salt and pepper
1 tsp sugar

approx. 8 oz (225 g) shredded cabbage
pasta (optional)
grated Parmesan

If any of the vegetables are frozen, add them to the soup as soon as they have thawed enough to slice.

Chop the onions, carrots, potato, celery and leeks fairly finely, and cut the bacon into dice. Cook briskly in the olive oil in a big pan for 5 to 10 minutes. Add the drained haricot beans, the tomatoes skinned and roughly chopped, the green beans cut into small pieces and the tomato purée. Pour on the boiling water, add salt and pepper and sugar, and simmer gently for about 1½ hours, or until the haricot beans are quite soft.

To serve immediately: add the shredded cabbage and cook for another half an hour. The haricot beans give the minestrone body, but if you like pasta, break some spaghetti into small pieces and add about 10 minutes before the end of the cooking time. Test for seasoning and serve with grated Parmesan.

To freeze: cool and freeze.

To serve after freezing: tip the frozen soup into a pan and bring gently to the boil. Continue as for serving immediately.

~

SALADE NIÇOISE

1 lb (450 g) French beans,	*1 tin tuna fish*
fresh or frozen	*3 hard–boiled eggs (quartered)*
6–8 tbsp French dressing	*approx. 10 anchovy fillets*
1 lb (450 g) tomatoes	*approx. 4 oz (100 g) black*
1 cos lettuce	*olives*

Cook the beans in a little salted water until tender. Drain, mix with 2–3 tbsp French dressing and chill. Cut the tomatoes into quarters. Wash the lettuce leaves, dry well, and toss in a little French dressing. Line a large bowl with lettuce leaves and arrange the remaining ingredients in the centre. Pour 2 or 3 more tbsp of French dressing over the salad before serving.

Runner Beans

Of all the vegetables in the garden, the useful and prolific runner bean is probably frozen in greater quantities than any other. It is best frozen blanched. Freeze only young, fresh beans.

To freeze blanched: cut the ends off the beans, and if necessary pare off the sides. Cut into slices and blanch for two minutes. Drain, cool and freeze.

  To serve after freezing: put the frozen beans into salted boiling water and heat through, gently breaking up the frozen mass with a fork. They will take about five minutes to cook after they have come to the boil.

Beetroot

Beetroot are worth freezing if they are young and tender.

To freeze cooked: wash the beetroot and cook in salted boiling water until soft – this will take 30 to 50 minutes according to size. Cool, and rub off the skins. Freeze.

  To serve after freezing: allow to thaw and use in salad, or heat in a little water and serve hot with béchamel sauce.

BORTSCH

1 lb (450 g) raw beetroot	*1 spoonful of sour cream or*
3 pt (2 litres) light stock or	* yoghurt for each serving*
* water*	
large bouquet garni	*pickled cucumbers* ⎫
a good squeeze of lemon juice	*parsley* *finely*
salt and pepper	*hard-boiled egg* ⎭ *chopped*

Peel the beetroot and cook all but a small amount in the stock or water with the bouquet garni until tender and until the stock has taken on a deep-red colour.

Lift out the beetroot and set aside to use later as a vegetable or in salad. Test the soup for seasoning and add the lemon juice. Shred the reserved raw beetroot and add to the soup.

To serve immediately: serve hot or chilled, with a teaspoon of sour cream or yoghurt in each bowl. Sprinkle with a little of the garnish.

To freeze: cool and freeze.

To serve after freezing:

To serve hot – tip the frozen soup into a pan and heat gently. Serve as above.

To serve cold – allow to thaw and serve as above.

Carrots

Carrots are worth freezing if they are very young and tender and have a good flavour. They freeze well either blanched or cooked. Blanching is useful if they are to be added to stews and casseroles, while cooking is much better if they are to be eaten as a vegetable in their own right.

Wash the carrots and scrape or scrub them. Leave whole if they are small, or else cut lengthwise or in rings.

To freeze blanched: blanch for three minutes. Drain, cool and freeze.

To freeze cooked: for each 1 lb (450 g) carrots you will need a knob of butter, 1 tbsp of water, 1 tsp or more of sugar and a little salt. Simmer all the ingredients together for about 10 minutes. It is important not to cook the carrots too much, as they will go on cooking after they have been taken off the heat. Turn into a large basin with the cooking liquid, allow to cool, and freeze the carrots with their liquid.

To serve after freezing blanched: if the carrots are to be used in stews or casseroles, they can be added straight from the freezer. If they are to be served as a vegetable, tip them, still frozen, into a heavy pan with a knob of butter, 2 or 3 tbsp of water to keep them from catching, a little salt, and a sprinkling of sugar. Cook very gently for about 30 minutes, or until they are soft, separating them carefully with a fork as they thaw. Test for seasoning and serve.

To serve after freezing cooked: tip the frozen carrots into a pan and heat through gently, separating them with a fork as they thaw. Add more butter if necessary. Test for seasoning and serve.

CARROT AND ORANGE SOUP

2 lb (900 g) carrots, fresh or   *2 pt (1 litre) stock or*
   frozen blanched   *water*
2 medium onions   *salt and pepper*
1 oz (25 g) butter

1 orange   ***chopped parsley***

Frozen carrots can be used straight from the freezer.

Chop the onions and fresh carrots roughly. Cook the vegetables gently in the butter for a few minutes. Add the grated orange peel and the stock or water and simmer for 15 to 20 minutes, until the vegetables are soft. Blend. Stir in the juice from the orange, but be careful not to add too much, or you may lose the delicate carrot flavour. Season.

To serve immediately: reheat and serve with chopped parsley.
To freeze: cool and freeze.
To serve after freezing: gently warm the frozen soup and serve as above.

NOTE Lemon can be substituted for the orange, and is just as delicious.

~

CARROT AND CORIANDER SOUP

1 lb (450 g) carrots, fresh or   *³/₄ pt (750 g) water*
   frozen blanched   *a squeeze of lemon juice*
2 tbsp oil   *sugar*
1 oz (25 g) butter   *salt and pepper*
1 onion
1 potato   ***2 tbsp chopped coriander***
1 pt (600 ml) light stock   ***leaves***

Frozen carrots can be used straight from the freezer.

Heat the oil and butter in a pan and gently cook the chopped onion, carrots and potato for five minutes. Add the stock and water and cook for about 25 minutes until the carrots are soft. Blend and season, adding a little lemon juice and sugar to taste.

To serve immediately: add the chopped coriander leaves and serve piping hot.
To freeze: cool and freeze.
To serve after freezing: heat the frozen soup gently, adding the chopped coriander leaves and adjusting the seasoning if necessary.

~

KIDNEY AND SAUSAGE CASSEROLE WITH CARROTS AND PEAS

This appetizing dish is a useful way of stretching a small amount of meat.

6 lambs' kidneys, fresh or frozen	1¹/₂ tbsp flour
8 oz (225 g) chipolata sausages, fresh or frozen	³/₄ pt (450 ml) stock
	2 tbsp red wine or sherry
1 lb (450 g) small young carrots, fresh or frozen blanched	2 tsp concentrated tomato purée
	2 bay leaves
	salt and pepper
2 oz (50 g) butter or 2 tbsp olive oil	
8 oz (225 g) button onions, fresh or frozen blanched	1¹/₂ lb (675 g) fresh peas or 12 oz (350 g) frozen blanched
8 oz (225 g) mushrooms, fresh or frozen sautéed	

Frozen kidneys and sausages should be allowed to thaw, but carrots, onions, peas and mushrooms can be used straight from the freezer.

Skin the kidneys, cut in half and take out the core. Sauté with the sausages in the butter or oil in a flameproof casserole until they are lightly browned. The sausages, in particular, should be well coloured. Add the onions and the sliced fresh or frozen sautéed mushrooms, reduce the heat and cook slowly for five minutes or until they are soft. Stir in the flour and continue to cook gently, stirring, until it is browned. Add the stock, red wine or sherry, tomato purée, bay leaves and carrots. Season, cover the casserole with a well-fitting lid, and put in a medium oven (350°F/175°C/gas 5) for one hour.

To serve immediately: add the peas and cook for half an hour longer. If you are using frozen peas, stir in well. When they are cooked test for seasoning and serve.
To freeze: cool and freeze.
To serve after freezing: tip the frozen casserole into a pan and heat gently for about 30 minutes, until it has thawed. Add the peas and continue to cook for another 30 minutes. Test for seasoning and serve.

GLAZED CARROTS

2 lb (900 g) carrots, fresh or frozen blanched	2 tbsp sugar
	salt
approx. ½ pt (300 ml) stock	
4 oz (100 g) butter	*chopped parsley for serving*

Frozen carrots can be used straight from the freezer, but do not then freeze th
dish.

Leave fresh carrots whole if they are quite small; otherwise cut into rings or slices

Put the carrots in a pan with the other ingredients and simmer for about 4(
minutes, until they are soft and the cooking liquid has evaporated. Frozen carrot
won't take quite so long.

It is impossible to be exact about the quantity of stock that will be required. I
there is too much it won't evaporate and the carrots won't glaze, while if there i
too little they won't become soft. So keep an eye on them for the last quarter o
an hour or so, and if necessary either add a little more stock or take the lid of
the pan and turn up the heat to allow the liquid to evaporate more rapidly.

To serve immediately: test for seasoning and serve sprinkled with chopped parsley.

To freeze: take off the heat while there is still a little liquid in the pan. Cool
and freeze with the liquid.

To serve after freezing: tip the frozen carrots into a pan and heat through
separating them carefully with a fork. Serve as above.

~

CARROTS WITH MUSHROOMS

2 lb (900 g) carrots, fresh or frozen blanched	8 oz (225 g) mushrooms, fresh or frozen sautéed
2 tbsp oil	salt and pepper
2 onions	

Frozen carrots and mushrooms can be used straight from the freezer, but do no
then freeze the dish.

Leave fresh carrots whole if they are quite small; otherwise cut into rings. Mel
the oil in a large pan, sauté the finely chopped onions for a few minutes and add
the carrots. Season, cover and cook over a low heat for 30 minutes. Add th
sliced fresh or sautéed frozen mushrooms and continue to simmer, covered, unti
the carrots are cooked. Frozen blanched carrots will not take as long as fres
ones. Check the seasoning and serve.

To freeze: cool and freeze.

To serve after freezing: tip the frozen vegetables into a pan and heat gently, separating carefully with a fork from time to time.

~

CARROT CAKE

This moist, wholesome loaf, which can be sliced and buttered like bread or iced and eaten as a cake, keeps particularly well in the freezer.

1 lb (450 g) carrots	*2 tsp ground cinnamon*
finely grated rind and juice of	*pinch of ground allspice*
1 lemon or orange	*4 oz (100 g) hazelnuts, walnuts*
6 oz (175 g) butter	*or pecans (optional)*
12 oz (350 g) soft brown sugar	
or honey	ICING (OPTIONAL)
4 eggs	*4 oz (100 g) butter*
1 tsp vanilla essence	*4 oz (100 g) cream cheese*
8 oz (225 g) plain flour	*2 tbsp honey or icing sugar*
8 oz (225 g) wholemeal flour	*a little grated lemon or*
1 tsp salt	*orange rind*
2 tsp baking powder	

Butter two 1-lb (450-g) loaf tins and line with baking paper.

Grate the carrots and sprinkle on the lemon or orange juice. Cream the butter with the sugar or honey until light and fluffy, beat in the eggs one by one and add the vanilla essence and the lemon or orange rind.

Sift the flours, salt, baking powder and spices together at least twice, until light and well blended.

Add the dry ingredients alternately with the carrots to the creamed mixture and fold in lightly but thoroughly. Fold in the roughly chopped nuts.

Pour into the prepared tins and bake in a medium oven (350°F/175°C/gas 4) for one hour, or until a skewer inserted into the centre comes out clean. Remove from the oven and leave to cool in the tins for 15 minutes, then turn on to a wire rack and leave to cool completely.

To serve immediately: beat the icing ingredients together until very light and fluffy, then spread thickly over the tops of the cakes.

To freeze: wrap and freeze.

To serve after freezing: unwrap and leave to thaw at room temperature for three to four hours. Ice as above.

Cauliflower

To freeze blanched: break the head into roughly equal florets, wash, and blanch for two minutes. Drain, cool and freeze.

To serve after freezing: tip the frozen cauliflower into a little boiling water and cook gently until soft. Serve with melted butter or dried breadcrumbs fried in butter and sprinkled thickly over the cauliflower. Or cover with a cheese sauce, sprinkle some grated cheese on top, and brown under the grill.

Courgettes

Courgettes can be frozen unblanched, but if they are likely to be in the freezer for more than a month or so it is better to blanch them.

To freeze blanched: trim each end and wipe with a damp cloth. Blanch for two minutes. Freeze.

To serve after freezing: allow the courgettes to thaw just enough to cut into $1/2$-in (1-cm) slices. Sauté in olive oil or butter, or a mixture of the two, sprinkled with salt and pepper and two or three pinches of mixed herbs, until they are tender and nicely golden on both sides. This will take about 20 minutes.

COURGETTES WITH HERBS

Cooked in this way, the courgettes retain their fresh taste and crisp texture. They are particularly good served with fish or light meat. Any of the herbs mentioned below will enhance their flavour.

1 lb (450 g) fresh courgettes	*tarragon, basil or dill*
2 oz (50 g) butter	*salt and pepper*
a good squeeze of lemon juice	

Grate the courgettes coarsely, sprinkle liberally with salt, and leave to drain in a sieve or colander for at least one hour.

Melt the butter in a sauté pan, add the lemon juice and cook the courgettes over a moderate heat for no more than three or four minutes, stirring all the time so that they cook evenly. Add the finely chopped herbs and season to taste.

To serve immediately: serve hot or at room temperature.

To freeze: cool and freeze.

To serve after freezing: melt a little butter or oil over a low heat and add the frozen courgettes. Break up the frozen mass with a fork and heat thoroughly. Test for seasoning before serving.

~

COURGETTES AU GRATIN

This recipe is useful if you have forgotten to pick all your baby courgettes in time and they have grown into marrows, as it can be made equally well with either.

approx. 1¹/₂ lb (675 g) courgettes, fresh or frozen blanched	salt and pepper
2 oz (50 g) butter	2 oz (50 g) grated cheese

If you are using frozen courgettes, allow to thaw for 15 to 20 minutes, until just soft enough to cut, but do not then freeze the dish.

Halve the courgettes lengthwise. If you are using marrows, peel and cut lengthwise, take out the pith and seeds, and cut into 1-in (2-cm) slices.

Season – be generous with the pepper – and sauté gently on both sides in the butter until golden brown and tender.

To serve immediately: place the slices in a shallow ovenproof dish, sprinkle the grated cheese on top, and brown under the grill.

To freeze: cool and freeze.

To serve after freezing: place the frozen courgettes in an ovenproof dish, sprinkle on the grated cheese, and heat through in a medium oven (375°F/190°C/gas 5) for 45 minutes or until hot.

COURGETTES PROVENÇALES

1½ lb (675 g) courgettes, fresh   *¼ pt (150 ml) stock*
*   or frozen blanched*   *salt and pepper*
1 tbsp flour
2 tbsp olive oil   *2 oz (50 g) grated*
12 oz (350 g) onions   *   cheese*
1 lb (450 g) tomatoes, fresh or   *1 tsp chopped basil or*
*   frozen raw*   *   tarragon (optional)*

Frozen vegetables should be allowed to thaw until just soft enough to slice. Tomatoes will take about three-quarters of an hour and courgettes 15 to 20 minutes. If you are using frozen vegetables do not freeze the dish.

Cut the courgettes into ½-in (1-cm) slices, dip into the seasoned flour, and sauté in the olive oil until golden. Frozen courgettes may need an extra spoonful of oil. Take out of the pan and gently sauté the sliced onions until tender.

Meanwhile skin and slice the tomatoes. Put alternate layers of courgettes, onions and tomatoes in an ovenproof dish and pour over the stock.

To serve immediately: sprinkle on the basil and grated cheese. Cook in a medium oven (375°F/190°C/gas 5) for about three-quarters of an hour.

To freeze: cool and freeze.

To serve after freezing: put the frozen casserole in a medium oven (375°F/190°C/gas 5) for half an hour. Sprinkle on the basil and the cheese. Continue to cook for another hour, adding a little more stock if necessary.

~

COURGETTE SOUFFLÉ

These quantities will serve four people as a starter.

1 lb (450 g) courgettes, fresh   *1 oz (25 g) grated Gruyère or*
*   or frozen blanched*   *   Parmesan cheese*
1 oz (25 g) butter   *2 whole eggs*
2 tbsp flour   *2 extra whites*
¼ pt (150 ml) milk   *salt and pepper*

Frozen courgettes should be allowed to thaw until they are just soft enough to slice. Frozen egg whites must be allowed to thaw to room temperature.

Cut the courgettes into ½-in (1-cm) slices and cook gently in a tablespoon of water until tender. Strain very thoroughly and blend.

Make a sauce with the butter, flour and milk, and when it is smooth add the courgette purée. Cook for a minute or two. Add the cheese and the beaten egg yolks, season well and allow to cool. Beat the whites to soft peaks and fold in.

Pour into a well-buttered 2-pt (1-litre) soufflé dish, stand in a baking tin containing an inch or so of water, and cook in the middle of a medium oven (350°F/175°C/gas 4) for about 40 minutes, until the soufflé has set. It will never become as firm as a cheese soufflé, but it has a pleasantly creamy texture and a delicate taste.

~

COURGETTE CAKE

Like the carrot cake on p. 61, this has the merit of keeping well, and of having a pleasantly moist texture and an unusual taste. It is a good way of using up courgettes which will insist on growing too fast.

8 oz (225 g) courgettes	2 oz (50 g) chopped nuts
5 oz (150 g) butter	2 tsp vanilla essence
12 oz (350 g) sugar	
4 eggs	ICING
11 oz (300 g) self-raising	4 oz (100 g) butter
flour	4 oz (100 g) cream cheese
2 tsp ground cinnamon	2 tbsp honey or icing sugar
3 oz (75 g) seedless raisins	a little grated lemon or
(optional)	orange rind

Butter two 1-lb (450-g) loaf tins and line with baking paper.

Grate the unpeeled courgettes and set aside.

Cream the butter with the sugar until light and fluffy. Beat the eggs well and add alternately with the flour, beating in a little at a time and making sure that each is well mixed in before the next addition. Beat in the cinnamon and the courgettes, and finally the raisins (if you are using them), the chopped nuts and the vanilla essence.

Divide equally between the prepared tins, and bake in the centre of a medium oven (350°F/175°C/gas 4) for about one hour, or until a skewer inserted into the centre comes out clean. Turn the cakes on to a wire rack and leave to cool completely.

To serve immediately: beat the icing ingredients together until very light and fluffy, then spread thickly over the tops of the cakes.

To freeze: wrap and freeze.

To serve after freezing: unwrap and leave to thaw at room temperature for three to four hours. Ice as above.

Cucumber

The high water content of cucumbers makes them unsuitable for freezing raw, but they can be frozen very successfully in cooked dishes.

Peel the cucumber, cut in quarters lengthwise, discard the core, and cut into cubes. Place in a colander and sprinkle with plenty of salt, a few drops of wine vinegar and a pinch of sugar. (The salt will extract the water, and the vinegar and sugar help to retain the flavour.) Leave for at least half an hour to drain.

The cucumber can now be used for any of the following recipes.

CREAM OF CUCUMBER SOUP

2 cucumbers	2 tbsp cream
1 onion	salt and pepper
1¹/₂ pt (900 ml) stock	
1 oz (25 g) butter	**a little chopped mint or fine**
1 oz (25 g) flour	**sticks of cucumber**
2 egg yolks	**(optional)**

Prepare the cucumber as described above. Simmer with the chopped onion in the stock for about 20 minutes until soft. Blend.

Melt the butter in a pan, add the flour and cook for about three minutes over a gentle heat, stirring all the time. Add the blended mixture, season and simmer for a further three minutes.

Take the soup off the heat, lightly beat the egg yolks with the cream, and add to the soup. Heat gently until the soup thickens a little, but do not allow to boil.

To serve immediately: serve hot or chilled, with the mint or the cucumber sticks.

To freeze: cool and freeze.

To serve after freezing:

To serve hot – thaw at room temperature for several hours. Reheat gently, and on no account allow to boil. Serve as above.

To serve cold – thaw at room temperature for five to six hours. Serve as above.

BAKED CUCUMBER

Baked cucumber has a very distinctive taste (quite different from that of raw cucumber), though it retains some of the crispness of the fresh vegetable. It makes an excellent accompaniment to egg or fish dishes, and also combines particularly well with mushrooms.

2 cucumbers	*2 oz (50 g) butter*
1 tbsp chopped parsley, chives	*salt and pepper*
or basil, or a combination of	
all three	

Prepare the cucumber as described on p. 66. Put the drained pieces in an ovenproof dish. Sprinkle with the herbs and dot with the butter. Season. Place in a hot oven (425°F/220°C/gas 7) for half an hour, turning the cucumber occasionally so that the pieces become evenly coated with the butter. At the end of this time the cucumber should taste cooked, but should still be quite crisp.

To serve immediately: serve hot, either alone or mixed with sautéed mushrooms.

To freeze: cool and freeze.

To serve after freezing: tip the frozen cucumber into a saucepan and heat gently. Serve as above.

~

CUCUMBER RAGOUT

This is excellent served hot with meat or with a strongly flavoured fish, such as mackerel. It can also be eaten cold as an accompaniment to cold meat, especially if it is topped with a little yoghurt.

1 cucumber	*8 oz (225 g) new carrots*
1 onion	*1 green pimento*
1 tbsp olive oil	*salt and pepper*

Prepare the cucumber as described on p. 66. Fry the finely sliced onion in the oil for a few minutes. Add the cucumber, the carrots cut into thin slivers, and the pimento cut into rings (make sure that all the seeds have been removed). Season and cook gently for about 20 minutes. Serve hot or cold.

To freeze: cool and freeze.

To serve after freezing:

To serve hot – tip the frozen vegetables into a pan and heat very gently.

To serve cold – thaw at room temperature for four to five hours.

Lettuce

LETTUCE SOUP

This is a good way of using up lettuces which have started to bolt.

1 large lettuce	*³/₄ pt (450 ml) stock*
1 medium onion	*salt and pepper*
1 oz (25 g) butter	
2 level tbsp flour	*³/₄ pt (450 ml) milk*

Slice the onion and sweat in the butter for a few minutes. Shred the lettuce leaves coarsely, add to the pan, cover, and cook for five more minutes. Stir in the flour and pour on the boiling stock. Continue to stir until the soup comes to the boil, season, cover, and simmer for about 15 minutes. Blend.

To serve immediately: return the soup to the pan and add the milk. Bring back to the boil, test for seasoning and serve.

To freeze: cool and freeze.

To serve after freezing: tip the frozen soup into a pan and add the milk. Heat through gently, stirring from time to time. Test for seasoning and serve.

Marrow

The water content of marrow is high, so they are unsuitable for freezing raw, but the ragout in the following recipe, which keeps very well in the freezer, makes a pleasing accompaniment to meat.

MARROW RAGOUT

1 medium marrow	1 clove garlic
1 oz (25 g) butter	6–8 tomatoes, fresh or
2 tbsp olive oil	frozen raw
2 large onions	salt and pepper

Frozen tomatoes can be used straight from the freezer.

Peel the marrow, take out the seeds and pith and cut into cubes. Melt the butter and oil in a heavy pan and sweat the onions (cut into fine rings) and the finely chopped garlic. When these are transparent, add the marrow and the skinned tomatoes and sauté for about 20 minutes, or until all the vegetables are soft. Season liberally.

To serve immediately: serve hot.

To freeze: cool and freeze.

To serve after freezing: tip the frozen ragout into a pan, warm through gently and serve as above.

NOTE To make a lunch or supper dish, lightly beat four or five eggs with a fork, pour over the ragout and continue to cook over a gentle heat, stirring all the time, until the eggs begin to set to a creamy consistency. Triangles of fried bread go well with this dish.

Onions

Small pickling or button onions, usually only available in the summer and autumn, make all the difference in stews and casseroles, and are well worth freezing.

To freeze blanched: peel the button onions and blanch for three minutes, drain, cool and freeze. Frozen onions should be stored in airtight containers.

CREAMED ONION SOUP

1¹/₂ lb (675 g) onions	salt and pepper
2 oz (50 g) butter	
1 oz (25 g) fresh white	1 pt (600 ml) milk
breadcrumbs or rolled oats	fried croûtons or small pieces
1 pt (600 ml) stock	of diced cheese (optional)

Slice the onions. Heat the butter in a heavy pan and cook the onions very gently for one hour, with the pan covered, being careful to see that they do not colour at all. Add the breadcrumbs or rolled oats and the stock, season, and continue to cook for another three-quarters of an hour. Blend.

To serve immediately: return to the pan, add the milk and bring back to boiling point. Test for seasoning and serve. The croûtons or cheese can be added to the soup just before serving.

To freeze: cool and freeze in airtight containers to avoid cross-smells.

To serve after freezing: tip the frozen soup into a pan, add the milk and bring gently to the boil. Test for seasoning and serve as above.

~

FRENCH ONION SOUP

1¹/₂ lb (675 g) onions	2¹/₂ pt (1.5 litres) stock
3 oz (75 g) butter	salt and pepper
¹/₂ tsp sugar	
French bread (1 slice per	grated Gruyère or Cheddar
person)	1 clove garlic

Slice the onions finely into rings. Melt the butter in a heavy pan and cook the onions gently for at least 30 minutes, until they become creamy and butter-yellow. Stir from time to time, especially towards the end, so that they do not stick to the bottom of the pan. Add the salt and pepper and the sugar, which will help the onions to brown. Raise the heat a little, and, stirring constantly, cook for a further five minutes, by which time the onions should be a rich, golden colour. Add the stock, stir well and simmer for half an hour.

To serve immediately: dry the bread slowly under a grill or in the oven, rub with a cut clove of garlic, pile grated cheese on each slice and quickly melt under a hot grill. Test the soup for seasoning and pour, very hot, into soup bowls. Float one piece of the toasted bread in each bowl.

To freeze: cool and freeze in airtight containers.

To serve after freezing: tip the frozen soup into a pan and heat, stirring constantly at first, over a gentle heat. Bring to the boil and serve as above.

~

COQ-AU-VIN

4 lb (2 kg) chicken, jointed	*2 oz (50 g) flour*
2 oz (50 g) butter	*1 tbsp concentrated tomato*
2 tbsp oil	*purée*
4 oz (100 g) streaky bacon	*2 tbsp brandy*
1 lb (450 g) button onions,	*¹/₂ bottle full-bodied red wine*
fresh, or frozen blanched or	*thyme, bayleaf*
en compôte (see p. 72)	*8 oz (225 g) button mushrooms*
2 cloves garlic, chopped	*salt, pepper and 1 lump sugar*

Frozen chicken must be allowed to thaw before cooking, but onions may be used straight from the freezer.

Heat the butter and oil in a flameproof casserole and sauté the diced bacon, onions and garlic until they are golden. (If you are using frozen onions en compôte do not add yet.) Lift out and set aside. Roll the pieces of chicken in the well-seasoned flour and brown in the casserole. Lift out and set aside also. Stir in the remains of the flour and the tomato purée and cook for two minutes.

Warm the brandy, pour into the casserole and set alight. Leave to burn for a moment and douse the flames with the wine. Stir and allow to bubble for a few minutes. Return the chicken, onions, garlic and bacon to the casserole, add the herbs, seasoning and sugar, cover, and simmer for half an hour.

Add the whole mushrooms and the onions frozen blanched or en compôte, and cook for another half an hour. Test for seasoning and serve.

To freeze: cool and freeze.

To serve after freezing: thaw overnight in the refrigerator, or for at least five to six hours at room temperature. Return to the casserole and warm through over a very gentle heat for 45 minutes to one hour.

ONION COMPÔTE

These sweet-sour onions make an excellent relish for serving with meat or vegetarian dishes, and especially with braised artichokes (see p. 182). A little time-consuming to prepare, they are worth making in quantity.

2 lb (1 kg) button onions, fresh	*2 tbsp wine vinegar*
or frozen blanched	*2 tsp sugar*
2 oz (50 g) butter	*salt and pepper*

Frozen onions can be used straight from the freezer, but may need a little longer cooking time.

Blanch fresh onions for 15 seconds and peel as soon as they are cool enough to handle. Put the onions into a pan or casserole large enough to hold them in a single layer and add the butter and enough water to come halfway up the onions. Cook slowly for half an hour, turning occasionally.

When they begin to soften, add the other ingredients and simmer very gently for at least one hour, turning the onions and adding a little more water from time to time if necessary. When done, the onions should be quite soft but should have kept their shape; they should be a dark golden brown, and a rich, thick syrup should have formed.

To serve immediately: serve with the syrup.

To freeze: cool and freeze with the syrup in airtight containers.

To serve after freezing: tip the frozen onions into a pan, add a tablespoon of water if necessary, and heat through gently. Serve as above.

NOTE This onion compôte also makes a delicious filling for shortcrust or filo pastry tartlets.

~

ONIONS IN CIDER

8 fairly large onions	*bouquet garni*
2 tbsp olive oil	*salt and pepper*
1/4–1/2 pt (150–300 ml) cider	

Peel the onions and put in a pan large enough to hold all of them on the bottom. Add the olive oil and place over a moderate heat. When the oil starts to sizzle, pour in enough warmed cider to half-cover the onions. Add the bouquet garni and season. Cover and cook steadily for three-quarters of an hour. Uncover the pan and cook for another 20 minutes or so, until the onions are very tender and pale gold. Remove the bouquet garni.

To serve immediately: transfer the onions to a hot dish. Reduce the liquid in the pan until it thickens to a syrupy consistency and pour over the onions.

To freeze: allow the onions to cool in the cooking liquid. Freeze in a rigid container so that they keep their shape.

To serve after freezing: put the frozen onions and liquid into a heavy pan and heat gently. Finish off as for immediate eating.

~

ONIONS À LA GRECQUE

These make a very good hors d'oeuvre.

1 lb (450 g) button onions,	*2 tbsp tomato purée*
fresh or frozen blanched	*1 tbsp sugar*
¹/₄ pt (150 ml) water	*sprig of rosemary*
¹/₄ pt (150 ml) white wine	*salt and pepper*
juice of ¹/₂ lemon	
4 tbsp olive oil	*1 tbsp chopped parsley*

Frozen onions can be used straight from the freezer, but may need a little longer cooking time.

Blanch fresh onions for 15 seconds and peel as soon as they are cool enough to handle. Put the fresh or frozen onions in a pan with all the other ingredients. Bring slowly to the boil and simmer for about half an hour, when the onions should be soft. Lift out carefully with a slotted spoon and put in a bowl. Boil the cooking liquid rapidly for 5 to 10 minutes, or until it has reduced by nearly a half. Pour over the onions and leave to cool.

To serve immediately: sprinkle with the chopped parsley before serving.

To freeze: freeze with the liquid in a rigid, airtight container so that the onions keep their shape.

To serve after freezing: allow to thaw at room temperature for five to six hours. Serve as above.

NOTE Leeks à la Grecque can be made in the same way. Choose short, not too fat, leeks of the same size, fresh or frozen. They will cook in less time than the onions – 15 to 20 minutes – and should not be overcooked.

ONION TART

The quantities given below are enough for two 8-in (20-cm) tarts.

2 lb (1 kg) onions   *4 eggs*
10 oz (275 g) shortcrust pastry   *1 tsp French mustard*
  (see p. 218)   *¹/₂ pt (300 ml) single cream*
3¹/₂ oz (100 g) butter   *salt and pepper*
3 bacon rashers (optional)

Line one 10-in (25-cm) or two 8-in (20-cm) buttered flan tins with the pastry.

Slice the onions, not too finely, and cook gently until soft in most of the butter. Cool and spread on the pastry cases. If you are using the bacon, cut into dice and cook gently for about three minutes in the rest of the butter. Beat the eggs with the cream and mustard, season and pour over the onions. Sprinkle the bacon on top. Bake in a medium oven (375°F/190°C/gas 5) for 30 minutes.

To serve immediately: cook for another 10 to 15 minutes, until the pastry is golden brown. Serve very hot.

To freeze: cool and freeze.

To serve after freezing: put the frozen tart into a hot oven (425°F/220°C/gas 7). After 20 minutes turn the oven down to 375°F/190°C/gas 5, and cook for a further 20 to 30 minutes, until the tart is hot right through.

~

ONIONS IN WHITE SAUCE

A useful stand-by to keep in the freezer for flavouring and thickening stews and blanquettes, or to serve as a vegetable.

1 lb (450 g) button onions,   *¹/₂ pt (300 ml) stock*
  fresh or frozen blanched   *¹/₄ pt (150 ml) milk*
1 oz (25 g) butter   *salt and pepper*
1 oz (25 g) cornflour

Frozen onions can be used straight from the freezer.

Blanch fresh onions for two minutes. Put the onions in fresh water, bring to the boil and simmer until they are just tender but have not lost their shape (about 20 minutes). Drain well.

In a separate pan make a sauce with the butter, cornflour, stock and milk. Add the onions and test for seasoning before serving.

To freeze: cool and freeze in airtight containers. It is useful to package the onions in small quantities for use in other dishes.

To serve after freezing: heat the frozen onions gently, stirring carefully. For use in casseroles or other dishes add the frozen onions half an hour before the end of the cooking time, and stir well until they have thawed and become amalgamated with the dish.

Peas

Home-grown peas are so delicious that they should be enjoyed straight away. But if you have a real glut it is worth freezing some, for, though commercially frozen peas are excellent, home-frozen ones are even better.

To freeze blanched: shell the peas and blanch for one to two minutes. Drain, cool and freeze.

To freeze cooked: shell the peas and put them in a pan. To each 1 lb (450 g) of peas add 1 or 2 tbsp of water, a knob of butter and a little salt and sugar. Add three or four sprigs of mint. After they have come to the boil cook very gently for about three minutes. Remove the mint, cool the peas as quickly as possible, and freeze with their liquid.

To serve after freezing blanched: put the frozen peas in a heavy pan with 2 or 3 tbsp of water, a knob of butter, a little salt and sugar and three or four sprigs of mint. Cook very gently until the peas are tender, breaking up the frozen mass carefully with a fork from time to time. Test for seasoning, and add a little more salt and sugar if necessary.

Frozen blanched peas can also be cooked à la française. Sweat an onion in a generous knob of butter, add a few shredded lettuce leaves, and then the peas. Stir in some light stock or, at a pinch, water – 1/4–1/2 pt (150–300 ml) for each 1 lb (450 g) peas – together with a little sugar. Cover, and simmer gently until the peas are soft. Test for seasoning and serve.

To serve after freezing cooked: put the frozen peas in a heavy pan and warm gently until they are heated through, breaking up the frozen mass carefully with a fork as it thaws. They will probably be ready almost as soon as the cooking liquid has come to the boil. Test for seasoning, and add a little more salt and sugar if necessary.

PEA SOUP

This is a good way of using up peas that are past their best.

2 lb (1 kg) peas	*pinch of mixed herbs*
1 medium onion	*salt and pepper*
knob of butter or chicken fat	
1½ pt (900 ml) light stock	*2 tbsp cream*
1 tsp sugar	

Pod the peas. Slice the onion and cook gently in the butter or fat (chicken fat is very good for this soup). When it is golden, add the rest of the ingredients, season, and cook until the peas are soft. Blend.

To serve immediately: reheat, stir in the cream, test for seasoning and serve.

To freeze: cool and freeze.

To serve after freezing: tip the frozen soup into a pan and bring gently to the boil. Add the cream, test for seasoning and serve.

~

GREEN PEA PILAF

8 oz (225 g) peas, frozen blanched	*1 tbsp pine kernels or chopped hazelnuts*
12 oz (350 g) cooked long grain rice, preferably brown	*1 tbsp currants (optional)*
1 oz (25 g) butter	*1 tbsp finely chopped dried apricots (optional)*
1 tbsp oil	*1 tbsp chopped coriander or*
1 onion	*parsley leaves (optional)*
1 clove garlic	*yoghurt*
1 tsp coriander seeds, crushed	

Frozen peas and frozen cooked rice can be used straight from the freezer.

Cook the peas until just done and drain. Melt the butter and oil in a large sauté pan and cook the finely sliced onion and finely chopped garlic till quite brown. Add the coriander seeds, the pine kernels or hazelnuts, the currants and the apricots. Mix all well together, blend in the rice and heat through thoroughly. Finally add the peas and season to taste. Sprinkle on the coriander or parsley leaves and serve very hot with lightly seasoned yoghurt.

Turnips

It is only worth freezing turnips while they are still young and tender.

To freeze blanched: wash and trim the turnips and blanch whole for three minutes. Drain, cool and freeze.

GLAZED TURNIPS

1 lb (450 g) baby turnips, fresh
or frozen
1/2 pt (300 ml) water

1 oz (25 g) butter
1 oz (25 g) sugar
salt and pepper

Allow frozen turnips to thaw until they are just soft enough to cut.

Cut the turnips in half, unless they are very small, and make a criss-cross incision in the cut surface to ensure even cooking. Simmer very slowly in the water, butter, sugar and seasoning, turning from time to time, until they are cooked and the water has almost all been absorbed, leaving a rich golden glaze. Test for seasoning and serve.

To freeze: cool and freeze.

To serve after freezing: tip the frozen turnips into a pan and heat gently, stirring from time to time.

Apricots

Apricots can be frozen in sugar or syrup, as a purée, or cooked. The fruit should be really ripe, especially if it is to be frozen uncooked.

With sugar: wash, halve and stone the fruit, and dip for a few seconds in a solution of water and lemon juice, using the juice of half a lemon to 1 pt (600 ml) water. Mix the fruit with sugar in the proportion of 4 oz (100 g) sugar to 1 lb (450 g) fruit (weighed before stoning). Freeze.

In syrup: wash, halve and stone the fruit, and dip in the lemon solution. Put in a rigid container, and cover with cold syrup made in the proportion of 7 oz (200 g) sugar to 1 pt (600 ml) water.

Cooked: this is a useful way of freezing fruit which is not quite ripe. Wash, halve and stone the apricots. Put into a pan with syrup made in the proportion of 7 oz (200 g) sugar to 1 pt (600 ml) water. A generous ¼ pt (150 ml) syrup should be sufficient for 1 lb (450 g) apricots (weighed before stoning). Cook gently until the fruit is soft. Cool, and freeze in a rigid container.

Purée: wash, halve and stone the fruit. Blend with sugar in the proportion of 4 oz (100 g) sugar to 1 lb (450 g) fruit (weighed before stoning). To prevent discoloration, add about 1 tsp lemon juice for every 1 lb (450 g) fruit. The purée is likely to darken a little, but the taste should not be affected. Freeze in a rigid container.

APRICOT TART

6 oz (175 g) sweetened   4 oz (100 g) sugar
  shortcrust pastry (see p. 219)   ½ oz (12 g) butter
1 lb (450 g) apricots, fresh, or
frozen with sugar

Do not freeze this tart if it has been made with frozen fruit.

To make with fresh apricots
Line a buttered 8-in (20-cm) flan tin with the pastry. Bake blind for 10 minutes in a hot oven (425°F/220°C/gas 7).

Sprinkle half the sugar on the pastry case, halve the stoned apricots and place domed side up on the pastry, as close together as possible. Sprinkle on the rest of the sugar, and dot each half-fruit with a small knob of butter. Put in a moderate oven (375°F/190°C/gas 5) and bake for 30 minutes or until the fruit is cooked. The pastry should be a rich golden brown and a thick syrup will have formed.

To serve immediately: serve hot or cold.

To freeze: cool and freeze.

To serve after freezing: place the frozen tart in a hot oven (425°F/220°C/gas 7) for half an hour. Serve hot or cold.

To make from apricots frozen with sugar
Make as above, using the fruit as soon as it has thawed enough to separate, and omitting the sugar from the list of ingredients.

NOTE Plum tart can be made in the same way.

~

APRICOT ICE-CREAM

To make with fresh apricots

1 lb (450 g) apricots	*½ pt (300 ml) double or*
6 oz (175 g) sugar	*whipping cream*
1 tsp lemon juice	

Purée the stoned apricots with the sugar and the lemon juice. Whip the cream lightly and fold into the purée. Freeze for one to two hours or until the mixture has reached a mushy state. Beat well and return to the freezer. Remove from the freezer at least half an hour before serving, and leave in the refrigerator.

To make from frozen apricots

1 lb (450 g) apricots frozen	*2 oz (50 g) castor sugar*
with sugar or ½ pt	*½ pt (300 ml) double or*
(300 ml) apricot purée	*whipping cream*

Allow the fruit to thaw to a mushy state. Purée if necessary. Add the sugar and fold in the whipped cream. Complete the recipe as above.

FROZEN APRICOT MOUSSE

To make with fresh apricots

1 lb (450 g) apricots	3 eggs
6 oz (175 g) castor sugar	1/4 pt (150 ml) double or
1 tsp lemon juice	whipping cream

Purée the stoned apricots with 4 oz (125 g) of the sugar and the lemon juice.

Beat the eggs with the remaining 2 oz (50 g) sugar until they are thick and almost white. Gradually add the purée and fold in the lightly whipped cream Test for sweetness. Pour into a dish and freeze for at least three to four hours.

Remove from the freezer 10 to 15 minutes before serving, as the mousse should be eaten still almost frozen.

To make from frozen apricots

1 lb (450 g) apricots frozen	3 eggs
with sugar or	2 oz (50 g) castor sugar
1/2 pt (300 ml) apricot	1/4 pt (150 ml) double or
purée	whipping cream

Allow the fruit to thaw to a mushy state, and then proceed as above.

Cherries

Cherries, either red or black, can be frozen with sugar, in syrup or cooked. Only ripe fruit should be used. It is best to remove the stones before freezing, since the cherries are then easier to use in recipes afterwards. Also, if they are frozen unstoned they may acquire an almond-like flavour.

With sugar: wash and stone the fruit. To every 1 lb (450 g) fruit (weighed before stoning) allow 4 oz (100 g) sugar. Mix the fruit and sugar together and freeze.

In syrup: wash and stone the fruit and put in rigid containers. Cover with cold syrup made in the proportion of 7 oz (200 g) sugar to 1 pt (600 ml) water.

Cooked: this is a particularly good method of freezing cherries. Wash and stone the fruit and cook gently in syrup made with 7 oz (200 g) sugar to 1 pt (600 ml) water. About 1/2 pt (300 ml) syrup should be sufficient for 1 lb (450 g) fruit (weighed before stoning). When the fruit is soft, cool and pour into rigid containers before freezing.

Morello cherries are particularly good used in recipes, but you will need more sugar.

CHERRY PIE

1 lb (450 g) cherries, fresh or   *2 oz (50 g) ground almonds*
  frozen with sugar   *3–4 oz (75–100 g) sugar*
10 oz (275 g) sweetened
  shortcrust pastry (see p. 219)

Frozen cherries should be allowed to thaw partially. If you are using them you will not need any sugar, but do not then freeze the pie.

Line a floured 8-in (20-cm) flan tin with two-thirds of the pastry. Sprinkle on the ground almonds and arrange the stoned cherries on top. Add the sugar and cover with the rest of the pastry. Seal well.

To serve immediately: cook in a medium oven (375°F/190°C/gas 5) for about 50 minutes. Serve warm or cold.

To freeze: freeze uncooked.

To serve after freezing: put the frozen pie into a hot oven (425°F/220°C/gas 7) for 30 minutes. Turn the oven down to 375°F/190°C/gas 5, and cook for a further 45 minutes (1¼ hours in all).

~

HOT CHERRY SAUCE AND ICE-CREAM

This is a quick and easy dessert. The quantities given below will provide enough sauce for 8 to 10 people.

1 lb (450 g) cherries, frozen   *2 tbsp kirsch*
  cooked or in syrup   *vanilla ice-cream*
¼ pt (150 ml) brandy

Turn the frozen cherries into a saucepan and warm gently. If they have been frozen uncooked, continue to simmer until they are soft. Strain off the syrup, and continue to warm the cherries until they are very hot. Pour over the brandy and set alight. When the flames have died down, add the kirsch. Serve at once, poured over the individual helpings of ice-cream.

CHERRY ICE-CREAM

To make with fresh cherries

8 oz (225 g) cherries
1/4 pt (150 ml) water
4 oz (100 g) sugar

1/2 pt (300 ml) double or
whipping cream

These quantities make a very delicate ice-cream. If you want the taste of cherries to be more emphatic, use another 2 or 3 oz (50 to 75 g) cherries and add a little more sugar and water.

Stone the cherries. Make a syrup with the water and sugar and stew the fruit gently until soft.

Cool and blend briefly, as the ice-cream is more interesting if there are bits of cherry in it. Fold in the lightly whipped cream and freeze.

To serve after freezing: take out of the freezer about one hour before serving and leave in the refrigerator.

To make from frozen cherries

8 oz (225 g) cherries, frozen
cooked or in syrup

1/2 pt (300 ml) double or
whipping cream

Cooked cherries should be allowed to thaw until they are soft enough to blend. If they are not already cooked, stew gently in their syrup until they are soft. Complete the recipe as above, adding a little sugar to taste.

Currants: Black, White and Red

BLACKCURRANTS

These can be frozen with sugar, as a purée, or cooked.

With sugar: as blackcurrants are quite sour, you will need at least 6 oz (175 g) sugar to 1 lb (450 g) fruit. Strip the berries off the stalks and mix with the sugar before freezing.

Purée: strip the berries off the stalks, blend with 6 oz (175 g) sugar to 1 lb (450 g) fruit, put through a nylon sieve and freeze. This purée is excellent for making ice-cream, a cold drink in summer or a hot one in winter.

Cooked: simmer the berries gently with a very little water – just enough to stop them from sticking to the saucepan – and sugar in the proportion of 6 oz (175 g) sugar to 1 lb (450 g) blackcurrants. When they are soft, cool and freeze.

RED AND WHITE CURRANTS

These can be frozen in sugar or syrup or as a purée. White currants have a very delicate flavour, and make a pleasant mixture when combined with the red.

With sugar: strip the fruit off the stalks and mix with sugar in the proportion of 4 oz (100 g) sugar to 1 lb (450 g) fruit. Freeze.

In syrup: strip the fruit off the stalks and cover with cold syrup made in the proportion of 7 oz (200 g) sugar to 1 pt (600 ml) water. Freeze.

Purée: strip the fruit off the stalks and blend with 4 oz (100 g) sugar to 1 lb (450 g) fruit. Freeze.

BLACKCURRANT ICE-CREAM

To make with fresh blackcurrants

1 lb (450 g) blackcurrants	*¹/₂ pt (300 ml) double or*
8 oz (225 g) sugar	*whipping cream*
¹/₄ pt (150 ml) water	

Blend the blackcurrants and pass through a nylon sieve.

Boil the sugar and water together for three minutes and leave to cool. Whip the cream lightly. Stir the syrup into the fruit purée and fold in the lightly beaten cream. Freeze.

To serve: remove from the freezer one hour before serving and leave in the refrigerator.

To make from frozen blackcurrants

1 lb (450 g) blackcurrants	*3 oz (75 g) sugar*
frozen with sugar or	*¹/₄ pt (150 ml) water*
¹/₂ pt (300 ml) blackcurrant	*¹/₂ pt (300 ml) double or*
purée	*whipping cream*

Allow the fruit to thaw at room temperature for three to four hours, until it is soft enough to blend, and pass through a sieve. If you are using frozen purée it should be allowed to thaw for two to three hours. Complete as above.

BLACKCURRANT WATER-ICE

To make with fresh blackcurrants

1 lb (450 g) blackcurrants   *½ pt (300 ml) water*
8 oz (225 g) sugar

Blend the currants and pass through a nylon sieve. Boil the water and sugar for five minutes and leave to cool.

Stir the cold syrup into the currant purée and freeze for one to two hours, or until the mixture has reached a mushy state. Take out of the freezer and beat well. Freeze.

To serve: remove from the freezer 10 to 15 minutes before serving.

To make from frozen blackcurrants

1 lb (450 g) blackcurrants   *3 oz (75 g) sugar*
frozen with sugar or ½ pt   *¼ pt (150 ml) water*
(300 ml) blackcurrant purée

Allow the fruit to thaw at room temperature for three to four hours, until it is soft enough to blend, and pass through a nylon sieve. If you are using frozen purée, it should be allowed to thaw for two to three hours.

Make a syrup with the water and sugar and complete as above.

~

REDCURRANT ICE-CREAM

To make with fresh redcurrants

1 lb (450 g) redcurrants   *½ pt (300 ml) double or*
5 oz (150 g) sugar   *whipping cream*
¼ pt (150 ml) water

To make from frozen redcurrants

1 lb (450 g) redcurrants frozen   *2 oz (50 g) sugar*
with sugar or   *¼ pt (150 ml) water*
½ pt (300 ml) redcurrant   *½ pt (300 ml) double or*
purée   *whipping cream*

Make as for blackcurrant ice-cream (see p. 83).

REDCURRANT WATER-ICE

To make with fresh redcurrants

 1 lb (450 g) redcurrants   ¹/₂ pt (300 ml) water
 5 oz (150 g) sugar

To make from frozen redcurrants

 1 lb (450 g) redcurrants frozen 2 oz (50 g) sugar
  with sugar or ¹/₂ pt (300 ml) ¹/₂ pt (300 ml) water
  redcurrant purée

Make as for blackcurrant water-ice (see p. 84).

Gooseberries

Gooseberries freeze extremely well in a variety of ways. Since they have tough skins, they do not need sugar if frozen raw: just wash if necessary and freeze in polythene bags for use in mousses, fools and ice-cream.

In syrup: top and tail the fruit and put in waxed or plastic containers. Cover with cold syrup made in the proportion of 9 oz (250 g) sugar to 1 pt (600 ml) water.

Cooked: gooseberries frozen in this way are excellent served as a compôte. Top and tail the fruit and stew very gently in a syrup made in the proportion of 9 oz (250 g) sugar to 1 pt (600 ml) water. About ¹/₂ pt (300 ml) should be sufficient for 1 lb (450 g) gooseberries. Cool and freeze.

Purée: wash the fruit, but do not bother to top and tail it. Add sugar in the proportion of 4 oz (100 g) sugar to 1 lb (450 g) gooseberries and simmer gently with 2 or 3 tbsp of water – just enough to stop the fruit from catching. When it is soft, pass through a nylon sieve. Cool and freeze.

GOOSEBERRY TART

This tart is particularly good served with elderflower sorbet (see p. 48).

> *1 lb (450 g) gooseberries, fresh*   *2 egg yolks*
>   *or frozen raw*   *3 oz (75 g) sugar*
> *6 oz (175 g) sweetened*   *¹/₄ pt (150 ml) single cream*
>   *shortcrust pastry (see p. 219)*

Frozen gooseberries can be used straight from the freezer, but the tart should not then be frozen.

Line a buttered 8-in (20-cm) flan tin with the pastry and bake blind for 10 minutes in a hot oven (425°F/220°C/gas 7).

Top and tail the gooseberries. Pack them into the pastry case as closely as possible – if you stand them on end you can get more into the space.

Beat the egg yolks lightly with the sugar and cream and pour over the gooseberries. Return to the oven and bake for a further 30 to 40 minutes at 375°F/190°C/gas 5 until the eggs and cream have set. If you are using frozen gooseberries, the cooking time should be about 10 minutes longer.

To freeze: cool and freeze.

To serve after freezing: place the frozen tart in a hot oven (425°F/220°C/gas 7) for half an hour. Serve warm or cold.

~

GOOSEBERRY MOUSSE

To make from fresh gooseberries

> *1 lb (450 g) gooseberries*   *2 egg whites*
> *4–6 oz (125–175 g) sugar*   *¹/₄ pt (150 ml) double or*
> *¹/₂ oz (12 g) gelatine*   *whipping cream*
> *a squeeze of lemon juice*

Frozen egg whites should be allowed to thaw to room temperature before whisking.

Do not bother to top and tail the gooseberries. Simmer gently with the sugar and 2 tbsp of water for about 15 minutes, or until the fruit is soft. Pass through a nylon sieve.

Soak the gelatine in 2 tbsp water and stir immediately into the hot purée, so that it dissolves completely. Add the lemon juice, test for sweetness, and stir in a little more castor sugar if necessary. Cool.

Whisk the egg whites till they are stiff but not dry and fold into the purée. Beat the cream lightly and fold this in also. Pour into a dish. Chill before serving or cool and freeze.

To serve after freezing: allow to thaw at room temperature for five to six hours, or overnight in the refrigerator.

To make from frozen gooseberry purée

½ pt (300 ml) gooseberry purée	*2 egg whites*
½ oz (12 g) gelatine	*¼ pt (150 ml) double or*
a squeeze of lemon juice	*whipping cream*

Heat the frozen purée gently and complete the recipe as above.

~

GOOSEBERRY ICE-CREAM

To make from fresh gooseberries

1 lb (450 g) gooseberries	*½ pt (300 ml) double or*
6 oz (175 g) sugar	*whipping cream*

Make a purée with the gooseberries as described on p. 85, but using 6 oz (175 g) sugar instead of 4 oz (100 g). Allow to cool. Whip the cream lightly and fold into the purée. Freeze.

To serve: remove from the freezer one hour before serving and leave in the refrigerator.

To make from frozen gooseberry purée

½ pt (300 ml) frozen	*½ pt (300 ml) double or*
gooseberry purée	*whipping cream*
2 oz (50 g) castor sugar	

Allow the purée to thaw to a mushy state. Whip the cream lightly with the sugar, and fold into the purée. Freeze. Serve as above.

GOOSEBERRY FOOL

1 lb (450 g) frozen gooseberries ⎫ or ½ pt (300 ml) frozen
4 oz (100 g) sugar ⎬ gooseberry purée
½ pt (300 ml) double or
  whipping cream

If you are using gooseberries frozen whole, stew gently in a little water. Add the sugar when the fruit begins to soften. Blend, pass through a nylon sieve and cool. Fold in the lightly whipped cream and chill before serving.

Allow frozen purée to thaw before completing as above.

Melons

Melons are often cheap in August and September, and though they lose a little of their taste when they are frozen it is worthwhile putting some in the freezer for later use in fruit salad. The dark-fleshed Italian or Charentais melons are best.

Peel the melon, take out the seeds and cut the fruit into cubes or scoop into balls. Mix with sugar in the proportion of 4 oz (100 g) sugar to 1 lb (450 g) melon. Freeze.

MELON ICE-CREAM

2 small ripe melons – approx.   4 egg yolks
  1 lb (450 g) melon flesh   4 oz (100 g) sugar
½ pt (300 ml) single cream

Heat the cream to near boiling point, pour on to the yolks beaten lightly with the sugar and return to the pan. Stir over a gentle heat until the custard thickens, but do not allow to boil. Strain if necessary and leave to cool.

Halve or quarter the melons, remove the pips and scoop out the flesh. Blend. Add the custard and blend for a few more seconds until smooth. Taste for sweetness and freeze.

To serve: remove from the freezer 15 minutes before serving.

Peaches and Nectarines

Peaches and nectarines are delicious frozen. The skins should be removed first; if they do not come off easily, pour boiling water over the fruit, leave for 15 seconds or more and plunge immediately into cold water. Halve and stone. The methods of freezing are the same as for apricots (see p. 78). Peaches and nectarines discolour very quickly, so they should be prepared for freezing as quickly as possible.

PEACH AND RASPBERRY COMPÔTE

6 peaches or nectarines
approx. 4 oz (100 g) sugar
½ pt (300 ml) water

8 oz (225 g) raspberries
Alpine strawberries

2 tbsp kirsch, brandy or
*   peach brandy*

½ oz (12 g) flaked almonds
whipped cream

The strawberries are not essential, but even a few make a great difference to the taste.

To make from fresh fruit
Skin the peaches or nectarines (see above) but leave whole. Make a syrup with the sugar and water, and poach the fruit gently until soft. Leave in the syrup until the fruit is cold and slice thickly. Add the raspberries and the strawberries.

To serve immediately: add the flaked almonds, pour on the kirsch or brandy and chill for two to three hours. Serve with lightly whipped cream.

To freeze: freeze in a waxed or plastic container.

To serve after freezing: thaw for three to four hours. Add the almonds and kirsch or brandy, and leave for at least half an hour before serving with whipped cream.

To make from frozen fruit
This is a good dessert to make from frozen fruit. Use peaches or nectarines which have been frozen either cooked or in sugar, and raspberries frozen in sugar. Thaw the fruits separately before mixing in a bowl. Add the almonds and brandy or kirsch, and leave for about half an hour before serving.

SPICED PEACHES OR NECTARINES

This is an unusual alternative to chutney for serving with cold ham, pork, duck or pheasant, and a good way of using slightly underripe fruit.

2 lb (900 g) peaches or nectarines	*1 tsp ground cloves*
1 lb (450 g) sugar	*1/2 tsp ground nutmeg*
2 tsp each ground cinnamon, allspice and coriander seeds	*1/2 pt (300 ml) cider or wine vinegar, or a combination of the two*

Peel the fruit (see p. 89) and halve and stone it. Mix the remaining ingredients in a large pan and bring slowly to simmering point, stirring until the sugar has dissolved. Add the fruit and simmer gently for about five minutes, or until it is soft. Lift the fruit out with a slotted spoon and continue to boil the syrup for about 10 minutes, until it thickens. Strain over the fruit and cool.

To freeze: freeze in small quantities.

To serve after freezing: allow to thaw for three to four hours before serving.

~

PEACH OR NECTARINE TART

This is made in exactly the same way as apricot tart (see p. 78), and is if anything more delicious. You will need five or six peaches or nectarines, according to size. The fruit should be peeled before it is put into the pastry case (see p. 89).

Pineapple

Pineapples freeze excellently with sugar or in syrup.

With sugar: peel the pineapples, remove the eyes and the core, and cut into slices or chunks. Mix with sugar in the proportion of 4 oz (100 g) sugar to 1 lb (450 g) fruit.

In syrup: peel the pineapples, remove the eyes and the core, and cut into slices or chunks. Put in waxed or plastic containers and cover with cold syrup made in the proportion of 7 oz (200 g) sugar to 1 pt (600 ml) water.

> NOTE Pineapple and mint go well together, and this is a good way of serving pineapple frozen with sugar. Allow to thaw and sprinkle some finely chopped mint over the top before serving.

PINEAPPLE WATER-ICE

1 medium pineapple (approx.	*³/4 pt (450 ml) water*
2 lb/ 900 g)	*4–6 oz (125–175 g) sugar*

Peel the pineapple, cut out the eyes and core and blend the flesh (there should be approx. ³/4 pt (450 ml) purée). Boil the water and sugar together for three minutes – it is difficult to give exact quantities of sugar, as pineapples vary greatly in sweetness. Allow to cool. Mix the syrup with the pineapple purée and freeze for one to two hours, until it has reached a mushy state. Blend again and return to the freezer.

To serve: remove from the freezer 10 to 15 minutes before serving.

Plums

Choose ripe, firm plums and stone before freezing, as they may otherwise acquire an almond-like flavour. Avoid the varieties with tough skins, which tend to become even tougher in the freezer. Victorias and greengages are both excellent.

Plums are best frozen either in syrup or cooked. Like peaches and apricots, they are inclined to become discoloured, so if you are freezing them raw, dip briefly in a solution of the juice of half a lemon to 1 pt (600 ml) water.

In syrup: halve and stone the plums and dip in the lemon solution. Put in waxed or plastic containers and cover with cold syrup made in the proportion of 7 oz (200 g) sugar to 1 pt (600 ml) water.

Cooked: stone the plums and cook gently in syrup made with 7 oz (200 g) sugar to 1 pt (600 ml) water. About ½ pt (300 ml) syrup should be sufficient for 1 lb (450 g) fruit (weighed before stoning). When the plums are soft (after about 10 minutes) cool and freeze.

PLUM TART

Make in the same way as apricot tart (see p. 78), using 1 lb (450 g) plums to 6 oz (175 g) pastry.

~

ZWETSCHGEN TART

Zwetschgen are the very dark plums with a strong bloom and deep-yellow flesh. Their sweet flesh and tart skins make them ideal for this recipe.

approx. 1 lb (450 g) plums   2–4 oz (50–100 g) sugar
6 oz (175 g) sweetened   ¼ tsp cinnamon
    shortcrust pastry (see p. 000)   1 oz (25 g) flaked almonds
1 tbsp biscuit or sponge cake
    crumbs

Line a buttered 8-in (20-cm) flan tin with the pastry. Bake blind in a hot oven (425°F/220°C/gas 7) for 10 minutes. Sprinkle on the biscuit or cake crumbs, which will help to absorb the plum juice and prevent the pastry from getting soggy. Halve and stone the plums and lay tightly on the pastry, skin side upwards. If you have a lot of plums, you can pack them in close ranks, so that they are virtually standing on their sides. Sprinkle on 2 oz (50 g) sugar combined with the cinnamon and the almonds. Bake in a hot oven (425°F/220°C/gas 7) for 40 minutes or until the plums are cooked and very slightly charred at the edges.

To serve immediately: taste a little piece of plum for sweetness and sprinkle on more sugar if necessary. Serve warm or cold.

To freeze: cool and freeze.

To serve after freezing: place the frozen tart in a hot oven (425°F/220°C/gas 7) for half an hour. Serve warm or cold.

~

PLUM ICE-CREAM

To make from fresh plums

1 lb (450 g) plums	*2 tbsp (or more) gin*
4–5 oz (125–150 g) sugar	*1/4 pt (150 ml) double or*
1/4 pt (150 ml) water	*whipping cream*

Halve and stone the plums.

Bring the water and sugar to the boil, stir until the sugar has dissolved, and boil for three to five minutes to reduce. Add the plums to the syrup and simmer until soft. Blend and pass through a nylon sieve. Add the gin. (Sloe gin or slivoviz may be used instead.)

Lightly whip the cream till bulky but not stiff. Fold in the plum purée and taste for sweetness – the ice-cream should be tart but not sour. Stir in a little icing sugar if necessary. Freeze.

To serve after freezing: remove from the freezer 15 minutes before serving and, if you like, pour a little more of the spirits over each helping.

To make from frozen plums

1/2 pt (300 ml) plums, frozen	*1/4 pt (150 ml) double or*
cooked or in syrup	*whipping cream*
2 tbsp (or more) gin	

Allow the cooked plums to thaw or gently cook the plums frozen in syrup. Blend and proceed as above, adding a little sugar to taste.

Raspberries

Raspberries are one of the most successful fruits to freeze, since they can be used for a great number of dishes. They keep their flavour best if they are frozen with sugar, but it is worth freezing a few without sugar for use as decoration.

With sugar: to 1 lb (450 g) fruit allow 4 oz (100 g) sugar. Mix the fruit and sugar gently together before freezing.

Without sugar: lay the raspberries on a tray in a single layer and freeze. Put into waxed or plastic containers and return to the freezer.

Purée: blend with 4 oz (100 g) sugar to 1 lb (450 g) fruit. Put through a nylon sieve and freeze in waxed or plastic containers.

FUOCO NELLA NEVE

This is a delicious way of amalgamating meringue, fruit and whipped cream, and is a good dish for a party. The exact quantities of fruit are not important. Raspberries or red and white currants, or a combination of the two, are best for the filling.

FILLING	MERINGUE CASES
about 8 oz (225 g) soft fruit, fresh, or frozen in sugar	*3 egg whites, fresh or frozen*
castor or icing sugar	*6 oz (175 g) castor or icing sugar*
2 tbsp brandy or kirsch	
1/2–3/4 pt (300–450 ml) double or whipping cream	

Make the meringue mixture as described on p. 230. Line three trays with baking parchment. Make three circles of diminishing size – about 8½, 7 and 5 in (22, 18 and 13 cm) in diameter – and spread the meringue mixture evenly over each. Cook in a very low oven. Start at about 125°F/52°C/gas ½, and after half an hour or so turn the heat down to 100°F/38°C/gas ¼. They will take at least two hours.

To prepare the filling: if fresh fruit is being used, mix the fruit, sugar and brandy or kirsch together and leave to stand for an hour or so to draw the juice out of the fruit. The quantity of sugar depends on individual tastes and the type of fruit used. If fruit frozen in sugar is used, allow it to thaw for three to five hours before testing for sweetness, and add more sugar if necessary. Pour over the brandy or kirsch, and leave for a little while so that the liqueur is absorbed by the fruit.

This sweet should be finished off at the last possible moment. Put the largest meringue case on a big dish and spread about two-thirds of the fruit and juice on top. Repeat with the medium-sized meringue case and the rest of the fruit. Top with the smallest meringue case.

Whip the cream lightly – enough to give it a fluffy consistency – and pile on before bringing the dish to the table.

~

LINZER TORTE

This tart can be made with raspberries or redcurrants, or with a mixture of the two.

PASTRY
4 oz (100 g) butter
4 oz (100 g) castor sugar
1 egg yolk
grated rind of ¹/₂ lemon or
  ¹/₂ orange
7 oz (200 g) flour
1¹/₂ tsp cinnamon
¹/₂ tsp ground cloves

4 oz (100 g) ground almonds
pinch of salt

FILLING
8–10 oz (225–275 g)
  raspberries
2 oz (50 g) sugar
or 8–10 oz (225–275 g)
  raspberries frozen in sugar

If you are using frozen fruit, do not freeze the tart.

Cream the butter and sugar, add the egg yolk and the grated rind. Sift together the flour and spices and add gradually. Add the ground almonds and knead well together. Or you can put all the ingredients into a food processor and process until they form a ball. Chill for at least one hour before using.

Line a buttered 10-in (25-cm) flan tin with the pastry, leaving aside enough to make strips for the top. Spread the fruit over the pastry and sprinkle on sugar to taste. If you are using frozen fruit spread it on when it has only slightly thawed. Cut the remains of the rolled-out pastry into strips about ¹/₂ in (1 cm) wide and criss-cross them diagonally over the fruit, or make a basket-work lattice.

To serve immediately: bake in a moderate oven (350°F/175°C/gas 4) for 40 to 50 minutes. Serve warm or cold.

To freeze: cool and freeze.

To serve after freezing: place the frozen tart in a hot oven (425°F/220°C/gas 7) for half an hour, then turn the heat down to 350°F/175°C/gas 4, and cook for a further 40 minutes.

SUMMER PUDDING

This pudding is delectable fresh or frozen. It can be made from a mixture of whatever soft fruit happens to be available, and everyone has their own favourites, including strawberries, cherries, currants and gooseberries. However, raspberries and blackcurrants should predominate to give the authentic flavour.

To make from fresh fruit

approx. 4 oz (100 g) stale white bread
1½ lb (675 g) mixed fruit
6–8 oz (175–225 g) sugar

¼ pt (150 ml) water

whipped cream for serving

Use a basin or soufflé dish which holds about 1½ pt (1 litre). Cut the bread into thin slices, remove the crusts, and completely line the basin with the slices, leaving enough to cover the top.

Make a syrup with the sugar and water (the exact quantity of sugar will depend on what fruit you are using). Gently stew the fruit until soft, and pour into the prepared dish while still hot. Cover with a thin layer of bread. Put a plate or saucer on top, exactly fitting the basin, and a weight on top of this, so that the pressure will cause the juice to soak into the bread (but see that it doesn't overflow above the rim of the plate).

If there is any excess juice, keep on one side for serving with the pudding. Refrigerate for several hours.

To serve immediately: turn on to a dish and serve with cream.

To freeze: wrap the basin and freeze.

To serve after freezing: leave at room temperature for about six hours. Serve as above.

To make with frozen fruit

approx. 4 oz (100 g) stale white bread

1½ lb (675 g) mixed fruit
whipped cream

Use mixed fruit that has been frozen in sugar. Line a basin with the bread as above. Tip the frozen fruit into a saucepan and gently stew until it is soft. There will probably be enough juice, but if necessary add a little water. Complete as above.

RASPBERRY ICE-CREAM

To make with fresh raspberries

1 lb (450 g) raspberries	1/2 pt (300 ml) double or
5 oz (150 g) sugar	whipping cream
1/4 pt (150 ml) water	

To make with frozen raspberries

1 lb (450 g) raspberries frozen	1/4 pt (150 ml) water
with sugar or 1/2 pt (300 ml)	1/2 pt (300 ml) double or
raspberry purée	whipping cream
2 oz (50 g) sugar	

Make as for blackcurrant ice-cream (see p. 83).

NOTE This ice-cream is very refreshing made with 12 oz (350 g) raspberries and 4 oz (100 g) redcurrants.

~

RASPBERRY WATER-ICE

To make with fresh raspberries

1 lb (450 g) raspberries	1/2 pt (300 ml) water
6 oz (175 g) sugar	

To make with frozen raspberries

1 lb (450 g) raspberries frozen	3 oz (75 g) sugar
with sugar or 1/2 pt (300 ml)	1/2 pt (300 ml) water
raspberry purée	

Make as for blackcurrant water-ice (see p. 84).

NOTE As with raspberry ice-cream, redcurrants are excellent substituted for some of the raspberries.

Strawberries

The best way of freezing strawberries is to purée them: frozen whole they tend to become mushy and tasteless when they thaw. Mousses and ice-creams made with frozen purée, however, have the taste and fragrance of the freshly picked fruit. It is also useful to have a few whole strawberries frozen in sugar to add to fruit salad.

Purée: hull the strawberries and blend with sugar in the proportion of approximately 3–4 oz (75–100 g) sugar to 1 lb (450 g) fruit.

With sugar: hull the fruit and leave whole or slice. To 1 lb (450 g) fruit allow 3–4 oz (75–100 g) sugar. Mix the fruit and sugar gently together before freezing.

STRAWBERRY MOUSSE

To make from fresh strawberries

2 lb (1 kg) strawberries	juice of 2 lemons
4 tbsp cold water	3 egg whites
1 oz (25 g) gelatine	1/2 pt (300 ml) double or
10 oz (275 g) castor sugar	whipping cream

Tie a collar of double thickness of greaseproof paper round one 2-pt (1 litre) soufflé dish or two 1-pt (500 ml) dishes, so that it rises about 2 in (4 cm) above the top of the rim. Tie the paper very tightly, or else the soufflé mixture will leak away between the paper and the rim.

Blend the strawberries, but if the mousse is to be eaten straight away, keep back a few for decoration.

Put the water into a small saucepan, sprinkle in the gelatine, and leave for five minutes. Add the sugar and the lemon juice and stir over a low heat until the sugar and the gelatine have dissolved. Do not allow to boil. Take off the heat, stir into the strawberry purée, test for sweetness, and if necessary add a little more castor sugar.

Whisk the whites until they stand in soft peaks, beat the cream lightly, and fold both into the purée. Pour into the prepared soufflé dish.

To serve immediately: put into the refrigerator or a cool place until the mousse is firm. (This will take several hours.) Just before serving run a knife carefully round the top of the mousse and remove the paper collar. Serve decorated with the reserved strawberries.

To freeze: wrap and freeze.

To serve after freezing: thaw at room temperature for six to eight hours, or overnight in the refrigerator.

To make from frozen strawberries

This is an excellent dish to make from frozen strawberry purée (see p. 98), but do not then freeze the mousse.

> 1 pt (600 ml) strawberry purée   juice of 2 lemons
> 4 tbsp cold water   3 egg whites
> 1 oz (25 g) gelatine   1/2 pt (300 ml) double or
> 3–4 oz (75–100 g) sugar   whipping cream

Allow the purée to thaw, and complete the recipe as above.

~

STRAWBERRY ICE-CREAM

This is lighter than most ice-creams – more a cross between ice-cream and water-ice. The exact proportion of cream to fruit is therefore not important.

To make with fresh strawberries

> 1 lb (450 g) strawberries   1 tbsp orange juice
> 5 oz (150 g) sugar   approx. 1/2 pt (300 ml) single
> 1/8 pt (75 ml) water   cream or 1/4 pt (150 ml)
> 1 tbsp lemon juice   double or whipping cream

Blend the strawberries and pass through a nylon sieve.

Boil the water with the sugar for three minutes, leave to cool and stir into the strawberry purée, together with the lemon and orange juice. If you are using single cream pour it into the mixture; if you are using double or whipping cream beat very lightly and fold in. Test for sweetness and add a little more castor sugar if necessary. Freeze for one to two hours, or until the mixture has reached a mushy state. Take out of the freezer, beat well, and replace in the freezer.

To serve: remove from the freezer one hour before serving and leave in the refrigerator.

To make from frozen strawberry purée

> 1/2 pt (300 ml) strawberry purée   1 tbsp orange juice
> 2 oz (50 g) sugar   approx. 1/2 pt (300 ml) single
> 1/8 pt (75 ml) water   cream or 1/4 pt (150 ml)
> 1 tbsp lemon juice   double or whipping cream

Allow the strawberry purée to thaw to a mushy state and complete as above.

STRAWBERRY WATER-ICE

To make from fresh strawberries

1 lb (450 g) strawberries   *½ pt (300 ml) water*
5 oz (150 g) sugar

Blend the strawberries and pass through a nylon sieve. Boil the water and sugar for five minutes and leave to cool.

Stir the cold syrup into the strawberry purée and freeze for one to two hours, or until the mixture has reached a mushy state. Take out of the freezer, beat well, and return to the freezer.

To serve: remove from the freezer 10 to 15 minutes before serving.

To make from frozen strawberries

½ pt (300 ml) strawberry   *3 oz (75 g) sugar*
*   purée*   *½ pt (300 ml) water*

Allow the purée to thaw to a mushy state. Make a syrup with the water and sugar and complete as above.

Autumn

SCALLOPS • GROUSE • VENISON • AUBERGINES • BRUSSELS SPROUTS
RED CABBAGE • CELERY • MUSHROOMS • PARSNIPS • PIMENTOS
SWEET CORN • TOMATOES • APPLES • BLACKBERRIES
PEARS • QUINCES • NUTS

Scallops

FRUITS DE MER IN CREAM SAUCE

This mixture may be used as a filling for vol-au-vents, or as a stuffing for crêpes de fruits de mer. The proportions of fish given are approximate. It is a particularly useful recipe if you have some cooked white fish, since any combination of white fish and shellfish may be used.

4 large scallops, fresh or frozen
8 oz (225 g) any cooked white
  fish
1/4 pt (150 ml) prawns
  (preferably with the shells)
1/2 pt (300 ml) white wine
1/2 pt (300 ml) water
1 onion
a strip of lemon peel

6 peppercorns
a little fennel or thyme
1 oz (25 g) flour
1/2 oz (12 g) butter
small glass of dry sherry or
  vermouth or a dash of
  Pernod
1/4 pt (150 ml) cream
salt and pepper

Frozen scallops and prawns should be allowed to thaw thoroughly, but if you are using them do not freeze this dish.

Make a court-bouillon by boiling the white wine and water, together with the shells of the prawns and the roughly chopped onion, the lemon peel, the peppercorns and the fennel or thyme. When the liquid has reduced by half, strain and gently poach the scallops in it for 10 minutes. Lift out, slice fairly thinly and mix with the flaked white fish and the prawns.

Make a beurre manié by working the flour into the butter and drop this into the cooking liquid. Heat gently, stirring until the beurre manié has dissolved, and continue to simmer until the sauce has thickened. Season, add the sherry, vermouth or Pernod and the cream and fold the fish mixture into the sauce.

To serve immediately: either spoon the mixture into hot vol-au-vent cases and serve; or, for crêpes de fruits de mer, make some pancakes with a batter using half milk and half beer, and adding a good pinch of curry powder. Roll each pancake round a spoonful of the hot mixture and serve.

To freeze: cool and freeze.

To serve after freezing: allow to thaw for at least one hour. Tip the frozen mixture into a pan and heat through very gently. You may need to add an extra spoonful of cream at this stage. Serve as above.

SCALLOPS AU GRATIN

6–8 large scallops (one per
   person), fresh or frozen
approx. ¹/₂ pt (300 ml) white
   wine
approx. ¹/₂ pt (300 ml) water
1 onion
strip of lemon peel
bouquet garni
8 oz (225 g) button
   mushrooms
squeeze of lemon juice

1 oz (25 g) butter
1 oz (25 g) flour
a dash of dry sherry
¹/₄ pt (150 ml) double cream or
   crème fraîche
1 tbsp chopped parsley
1 shallot
2 oz (50 g) fresh white
   breadcrumbs

approx. 1 oz (25 g) butter

Frozen scallops should be allowed to thaw thoroughly, but if you are using them do not freeze this dish.

Detach fresh scallops from the shells and wash both in cold water. Make a court-bouillon by boiling together the wine, water, roughly chopped onion, lemon peel and bouquet garni until the liquid has reduced by about half. Add the scallops and poach for 5 to 10 minutes or until they are just cooked. Drain, and strain the cooking liquid into a clean pan. Meanwhile simmer the mushrooms briefly in a little water with a squeeze of lemon juice.

Make a beurre manié by working together the butter and flour, add to the cooking liquid and simmer gently, stirring, until the sauce is smooth and thick. Season and add a dash of sherry. Add the cream or crème fraîche gradually.

Slice the scallops and arrange evenly on the shells or in ramekins. Add the mushrooms and pour over the sauce. Sprinkle with a mixture of finely chopped parsley, shallot and breadcrumbs.

To serve immediately: dot with a little butter and place under a hot grill until the top is lightly browned.

To freeze: cool and freeze.

To serve after freezing: allow to thaw for at least one hour. Dot with butter and place under a medium grill until the scallops are heated through. This will take between 15 and 20 minutes.

Grouse

If you have grouse that you do not want to cook immediately, they can be stored in the freezer raw. Pluck and draw the birds, wrap individually and freeze in a polythene bag. They can later be roasted or casseroled.

To roast after freezing: allow the frozen grouse to thaw and wipe inside and out. Place a large lump of butter inside each bird and wrap in a slice of bacon. Roast in a moderately hot oven (400°F/200°C/gas 6) for 30 minutes. Place a piece of toast underneath each bird to absorb the juice, dredge with a little flour, baste, and return to the oven for a further 10 minutes. Serve on the toast.

CASSEROLE OF GROUSE

Older, tougher or slightly higher birds may be used for this casserole.

2 brace of grouse, fresh or frozen	1/2 pt (300 ml) red wine
	bouquet garni
1 oz (25 g) butter	12 button onions or 8 oz
1 tbsp oil	(225 g) onion compôte
2 medium onions	(see p. 72)
2 carrots	8 oz (225 g) button mushrooms
1 clove garlic	juice of 1/2 lemon
2 tbsp flour	1 tbsp redcurrant jelly
1/2 pt (300 ml) stock	salt and pepper

If you are using frozen grouse, allow to thaw. Onion compôte can be used straight from the freezer.

Melt the butter and oil in a flameproof casserole, wipe the birds and brown on all sides. Remove from the casserole and brown the diced onions, carrots and garlic. Sprinkle on the flour and continue to cook, stirring constantly, for two minutes. Slowly stir in the stock, add the wine, the bouquet garni and the seasoning and replace the grouse. Cover and simmer gently on top of the stove, or place in a moderate oven (350°F/175°C/gas 4) for about one hour, or until the birds are tender – the time will vary according to their age.

If you are using fresh button onions, blanch for 10 minutes.

Add the button onions or onion compôte and the whole mushrooms to the casserole 10 to 15 minutes before the end of the cooking time, stirring in well.

When the birds are cooked, remove from the casserole and cut in half. Add the lemon juice and the redcurrant jelly to the sauce, and test for seasoning.

To serve immediately: return the birds to the casserole and heat thoroughly before serving.

To freeze: cool and freeze.

To serve after freezing: allow to thaw at room temperature for five to six hours or overnight in the refrigerator. Heat through gently either on top of the stove or in a moderate oven.

Venison

Venison is tender, extremely tasty – there is hardly any waste – and relatively inexpensive. It has very little fat, so if you are going to roast it, it will be much improved if you lard it liberally first.

To freeze: make sure the meat has been well hung, and if necessary hang it in a cool, airy place for a few days. Wash in cold water, scraping off any of the damp sticky substance that may have formed on the outside (use the back of a knife for this) and dry. Rub all over with flour, to keep the surface dry, wrap well, and freeze in an extra-thick polythene bag so that the smell does not contaminate any of the other contents of your freezer.

BRAISED VENISON

One of the nicest ways of cooking venison is to marinate the meat for a few days and then braise it in the marinating juices. This is also the best method if you are going to freeze the whole joint or part of it, as it produces a generous amount of richly flavoured sauce in which the venison can be frozen and subsequently reheated. As with all meat, the larger the joint the better the results. Onion compôte (see p. 72) and braised chestnuts (see p. 192) are excellent accompaniments.

¹/₄ *haunch of venison*	*bay leaf, thyme, rosemary*
(approx. 5 lb/ 2¹/₂ kg), fresh	*6 crushed peppercorns*
or frozen	*6 crushed juniper berries*
2 onions	*2 oz (50 g) butter*
2 cloves garlic	*1 tbsp flour*
2 carrots	*1 glass port or Madeira*
3 tbsp olive oil	*2 tbsp redcurrant jelly*
1 bottle red wine	*salt and pepper*

Frozen venison can be used straight from the freezer and allowed to thaw in the marinade.

Roughly chop the onions, garlic and carrots and put in a large bowl. Place the venison on top, pour over 2 tbsp of olive oil and the wine, add the herbs, the peppercorns and the juniper berries and allow the meat to soak in this marinade for two or three days, turning it occasionally so that all sides are kept evenly moist.

When you are ready to cook the venison (the longer you leave it in the marinade the gamier it will be), take out and dry well. Heat 1 oz of the butter with the remaining tablespoon of oil in a large flameproof casserole or roasting tin, and sear the meat quickly on all sides. Strain the marinade into a saucepan and bring to a rapid boil to reduce by almost half. Pour over the venison and cover the casserole or, if you are using a roasting tin, cover with a double layer of foil folded firmly over the edges. Cook in a low oven (300°F/150°C/gas 2) for anything between two and four hours, depending on the size of the joint (a 5-lb/2½-kg joint will take roughly 2½ hours). When the meat is tender remove from the casserole and keep warm.

Bring the sauce to the boil and reduce by nearly half. Make a beurre manié with the rest of the butter and the flour, stir this into the sauce and continue to cook until it thickens. Add the port or Madeira and the redcurrant jelly and test for seasoning. Carve the meat, return to the casserole and serve.

To freeze: allow to cool and freeze the meat, whole or sliced, with the sauce.

To serve after freezing: tip the frozen meat into a flameproof casserole or saucepan and heat gently on top of the stove for about 40 minutes.

> NOTE The bones can be used as the basis of an excellent venison soup, cooked with root vegetables and onions which have been briefly braised in butter or oil. Any leftover scraps of the meat and sauce can be put in as well, and perhaps another dash of port or Madeira.

Aubergines

Aubergines are best frozen cooked, as in any of the recipes that follow. It used to be thought advisable to get rid of any bitterness or excess moisture by sprinkling the aubergine slices lightly with salt and leaving for about half an hour, before rinsing thoroughly and drying. However, with modern methods of cultivating aubergines, especially if they are young and fresh, this no longer seems to be necessary.

MOUSSAKA

This rich Mediterranean mixture of lamb and aubergines is a considerable trouble to prepare but a great pleasure to eat. So make a large quantity at a time. The amounts given here will fill two 2-pt (1-litre) dishes.

2 lb (900 g) minced lamb,
  fresh or frozen
3 lb (1½ kg) aubergines
8 oz (225 g) onions
2 cloves garlic
approx. ½ pt (300 ml) olive
  oil
herbs – preferably a little of
  each of the following: thyme,
  rosemary, marjoram
spices – a pinch each of ground
  coriander, mace, allspice and
  (optional) cinnamon

2 tbsp concentrated tomato
  purée
salt and pepper

SAUCE
2 pt (1 litre) milk
6 egg yolks
3 tsp cornflour
2 oz (50 g) grated cheese
salt, pepper and a little grated
  nutmeg

Frozen lamb must be allowed to thaw at least partially.

To make the sauce, scald the milk, beat the egg yolks with the cornflour and gradually add the milk, stirring all the time. Season with salt, pepper and nutmeg. Leave this mixture in a double pan or a bowl set in a pan of simmering water at the back of the stove, stirring from time to time. It should thicken to a rich smooth custard. Stir in the cheese towards the end.

Slice or chop the onions and garlic very finely and cook slowly in 2 tbsp of the olive oil in a heavy frying pan until they are soft and transparent, but do not allow to brown. Add the meat, herbs, spices and seasoning, and continue to cook gently until all the meat has changed colour. Add the tomato purée. Set the mixture aside.

Slice the aubergines thinly. Heat some olive oil in a heavy frying pan and cook the aubergine slices very gently, a few at a time – they should become a translucent golden yellow but not be allowed to brown. Take each batch out when it is ready and drain on absorbent paper. This will take longer, absorb more oil and use more kitchen paper than you will believe possible.

When all the aubergine slices have been cooked, assemble the moussaka. Line the bottom of an ovenproof dish with aubergines. Follow with a layer of the meat mixture, and continue to alternate the two until both mixtures have been used up, ending with a layer of aubergines. Pour the sauce over the top.

To serve immediately: bake in a moderate oven (350°F/175°C/gas 4) for about one hour and serve.

To freeze: moussaka can be frozen cooked or uncooked. Wrap the dish well.

To serve after freezing: cook the frozen moussaka in a hot oven (425°F/220°C/gas 7) for 20 minutes and then turn the oven down to 350°F/175°C/gas 4. If it was frozen cooked, bake for a further 20 to 30 minutes. If it was frozen uncooked, bake for a further 40 to 50 minutes.

~

AUBERGINE CASSEROLE

2 lb (1 kg) aubergines	*flour*
2 lb (1 kg) tomatoes, fresh or	8 oz (225 g) Mozzarella or
frozen raw	Bel Paese cheese
1 onion	salt, pepper, sugar
1 carrot	
olive oil	**2 oz (50 g) grated Parmesan**
2–3 sprigs basil	**cheese**
a few sprigs parsley	

Frozen tomatoes should be skinned and then allowed to thaw until they can be chopped.

Chop the onion and carrot finely, and cook briskly in 2 tbsp oil with the basil and parsley. When the onion is golden add the skinned and roughly chopped tomatoes. Season with salt and pepper and a little sugar to taste, cover the pan and simmer until the sauce has reduced to a thick paste.

Slice the aubergines, dust lightly with flour and fry gently in olive oil until golden brown. Spread each batch on kitchen paper so that any surplus oil will drain off. It is impossible to specify the exact quantity of olive oil you will need, so start by generously covering the bottom of your frying pan and add more as necessary.

Put a little olive oil – just enough to coat the bottom – in a shallow baking dish and arrange in it a layer of aubergines. Slice the Mozzarella or Bel Paese thinly and put some of this on top. Spread with tomato sauce. Continue with more layers of aubergine, cheese and tomato sauce until all are used up, finishing with sauce.

To serve immediately: sprinkle on the Parmesan and dot the surface with a few drops of olive oil. Bake in a moderate oven (350°F/175°C/gas 4) for 40 minutes or so, until the top is golden brown and bubbling.

To freeze: cool and freeze.

To serve after freezing: sprinkle the frozen dish with the Parmesan. Bake in a hot oven (400°F/200°C/gas 6) for 45 minutes to one hour.

AUBERGINES PROVENÇALES

1½ lb (675 g) aubergines	salt and pepper
1½ tbsp flour	
¼–½ pt (150–300 ml) olive oil	¼–½ pt (150–300 ml) light stock
1½ lb (675 g) onions	1 tbsp chopped basil
2 lb (900 g) tomatoes	4 oz (100 g) grated cheese

Slice the aubergines quite thickly. Dip in the flour and sauté in the olive oil in a heavy pan until they are golden brown all over. It is difficult to judge exactly how much oil they will take, so start with about 4 tbsp and add more as you need it. Take the aubergines out of the pan and put on absorbent paper to soak up excess oil.

Gently fry the sliced onions in the pan until they are quite tender, adding a little more oil if necessary. Skin the tomatoes and slice them.

Put a layer of aubergines in an ovenproof dish, then one of onion, and then one of tomato, and continue until the vegetables are finished. Season each layer.

To serve immediately: pour over the stock and sprinkle on the basil and finally the grated cheese. Cook in a moderate oven (375°F/190°C/gas 5) for about one hour. Serve.

To freeze: cool and freeze.

To serve after freezing: heat the frozen dish in a moderate oven (375°F/190°C/gas 5). Check the quantity of liquid after about half an hour and add a little stock if necessary. Sprinkle on the basil and cheese, and continue to cook for about another hour.

~

RATATOUILLE

This colourful medley of Mediterranean vegetables can be eaten hot or cold. It goes particularly well with a robust meat dish, or with grilled mackerel or mullet.

2 medium aubergines	2 pimentos (red or green)
2 tbsp olive oil	8 oz (225 g) tomatoes
2 Spanish onions	salt, pepper and a pinch of sugar
2 cloves garlic	

Heat the oil in a flameproof casserole or heavy pan. Sauté the finely sliced onions and garlic over a low heat until they become transparent, and add the thickly sliced aubergines. When the aubergines become translucent add the pimentos, cut into strips and with the seeds taken out, and finally, after another 10 minutes' cooking, the skinned tomatoes cut into quarters. Season and continue to cook over a low heat for 30 to 40 minutes, until all the vegetables are soft, but have not lost their individual colour and identity. Test for seasoning and serve.

To freeze: cool and freeze.

To serve after freezing:

To serve hot – return the frozen ratatouille to a pan or casserole, heat gently and serve.

To serve cold – allow to thaw for at least six hours at room temperature or overnight in the refrigerator.

~

PIPÉRADE

Served in this way, ratatouille can be turned into a pleasant light supper dish. The pipérade can be eaten by itself or with fried croûtons or fried bacon or ham.

> *ratatouille (the quantity given on p. 110)*
> *1 tbsp olive oil*
> *4–6 eggs*
> *salt and pepper*

Frozen ratatouille can be used straight from the freezer.

Warm the olive oil in a deep frying or sauté pan or in a flameproof earthenware dish. Add the ratatouille and heat through gently. Beat the eggs lightly with a fork, and when the ratatouille is quite hot pour them into the pan and stir gently until they have just set but are still creamy. Test for seasoning and serve at once.

STUFFED AUBERGINES

4 aubergines
4 tbsp olive oil
2 large onions
2 cloves garlic
8 oz (225 g) mushrooms, fresh
  or frozen sautéed
2 tbsp fresh breadcrumbs
1 egg

2 tbsp chopped herbs (parsley,
  marjoram, thyme)
4 oz (100 g) Mozzarella or
  soft goat cheese (optional)
salt and pepper

tomato sauce (see p. 130)

Frozen sautéed mushrooms can be used straight from the freezer.

Place the aubergines on a rack in a medium-hot oven (400°F/200°C/gas 6) with a baking tray underneath to catch any drips. After 20 to 30 minutes, depending on the size of the aubergines, they should be soft to the touch and the skins should be wrinkly. Meanwhile chop the onions and garlic and cook in the oil in a large sauté pan until soft.

Remove the aubergines from the oven, and as soon as they are cool enough to handle cut in half lengthwise, place cut-side down on a board and peel off the skins, starting from the broad end. Lay the skins side by side on an oiled baking dish.

Add the chopped aubergine flesh and the chopped raw mushrooms, if you are using fresh ones, to the onions and the garlic. Cook until the mixture is soft and amalgamated. If you are using frozen sautéed mushrooms add them at this point. Over a low heat stir in the breadcrumbs and herbs and the lightly beaten egg. Taste for seasoning and spoon the mixture into the aubergine skins. Top with sliced cheese.

To serve immediately: place in a moderate oven (350°F/175°C/gas 4) for 20 to 30 minutes. Serve with the tomato sauce.

To freeze: cool and freeze.

To serve after freezing: place in a moderate oven (350°F/175°C/gas 4) for one hour, and serve as above.

TURKISH STUFFED AUBERGINES

This is a spicier variation of the previous recipe.

4 aubergines	*1 tsp allspice*
4 tbsp olive oil	*1 tsp pine kernels (optional)*
8 oz (225 g) onions	*salt and pepper*
2 cloves garlic	

Follow the previous recipe, omitting the mushrooms, breadcrumbs, egg, herbs and cheese. Add the allspice and pine kernels to the mixture before stuffing the aubergines.

Brussels Sprouts

These are extremely easy to freeze, and it is a joy to have several bags in the freezer in late winter. Red Brussels sprouts are an interesting variation: they have a special nutty flavour, and their great virtue for gardeners is that pigeons don't eat them.

To freeze blanched: trim off any coarse or discoloured leaves. Wash and blanch for two to three minutes, depending on size. Drain, cool and freeze.

To serve after freezing: tip the frozen sprouts into boiling water – about 1 in (2 cm) in the pan should be enough – and cook fairly briskly until they are soft, which will take about 10 minutes. Break up the mass of sprouts gently with a fork from time to time. Serve with a generous knob of butter.

They are also excellent mixed with braised chestnuts (see p. 192).

Red Cabbage

Red cabbage freezes excellently cooked and, if anything, improves with reheating. It should be frozen in expendable containers, since it is difficult to eradicate the smell of the cabbage afterwards.

2½–3 lb (1¼–1½ kg) red cabbage	2 cloves (optional)
1 large onion	approx. ¼ pt (150 ml) red wine or a mixture of wine vinegar and water
1 clove garlic	1–2 tbsp brown sugar
1 oz (25 g) butter	1 large potato
1 tbsp olive oil	salt and pepper
2 large cooking apples	

Slice the onion and garlic and soften in the butter and olive oil in a large pan for about 10 minutes. Add the cabbage, cut into ¼-in (½-cm) slices and, when this has cooked down in the pan (after about 15 minutes), add the peeled, cored and sliced apples, the cloves, the wine and a tablespoon or so of sugar. Season and cook gently for about three hours either on top of the stove or in a fairly slow oven (325°F/160°C/gas 3). Towards the end of the cooking time add the coarsely grated potato. Test for seasoning and, if necessary, add more salt or sugar. The dish is now ready to serve.

To freeze: cool and freeze.

To serve after freezing: turn the frozen cabbage into a heavy pan and cook gently until it is hot all through (which will take half an hour at least, unless the quantity is small). Add a little wine, water or stock if necessary.

~

RED CABBAGE WITH ORANGE

Follow the previous recipe for red cabbage but, about a quarter of an hour before the end of the cooking time, add the juice and finely grated peel of an orange.

RED CABBAGE WITH CHESTNUTS

Prepare 1 lb (450 g) chestnuts (see p. 191) and add to the cabbage for the last two hours of the cooking. If you are using dried chestnuts, they should first be boiled for 30 minutes or so in plenty of water before they are added to the cabbage.

~

PORK WITH RED CABBAGE

3-lb (1¹/₂-kg) piece of boned pork for roasting
2¹/₂–3 lb (1¹/₄–1¹/₂ kg) cooked red cabbage, fresh or frozen
1 tsp salt
¹/₄ tsp pepper

2 generous tsp chopped fresh herbs or 1 tsp dried herbs
1 clove garlic
8 oz (225 g) chestnuts (optional)
1 tbsp olive oil

Start by marinating the pork. This is not essential, but it is quick and easy to do and gives the meat a spicy taste.

Mix together the salt, pepper, crushed garlic and herbs (use any you have available). Spread all over the pork. Leave in a covered bowl for several hours, turning over from time to time so that the herbs blend into the meat juice.

Tip the red cabbage into a flameproof casserole and warm through gently, stirring from time to time, until it is hot. Add the chestnuts if you are using them.

Brown the pork on all sides in the oil. Place on the cabbage, cover the casserole and put in a fairly slow oven (325°F/160°C/gas 3) for about 2¹/₄ hours, by which time the meat should be well cooked. Lift the pork out, put on a large warmed dish and arrange the cabbage round it, together with the cooking liquid. You may not need all the liquid, but be generous with it as there is no gravy.

NOTE Any leftovers can be frozen.

Celery

Celery cannot be frozen for subsequent use in salads, but blanched celery is excellent as a vegetable.

To freeze blanched: quarter the heads or cut the individual sticks into 2- or 3-in (5- or 8-cm) pieces. Wash thoroughly and blanch for four to five minutes for the heads, or three minutes if the celery has been cut into pieces. Drain, cool and freeze.

To serve after freezing: put the frozen celery in boiling water and cook for about 15 minutes from the time it comes to the boil. Serve with a béchamel sauce made with milk and a little of the celery liquid. Or put the celery in a shallow heatproof dish, cover with dry breadcrumbs, small pieces of butter and grated cheese, and put under the grill for a few minutes until a golden crust has formed.

CELERY SOUP

1 lb (450 g) celery, fresh or
   frozen
1 large onion
1 oz (25 g) butter
1¼ pt (750 ml) light stock
bouquet garni
½ oz (12 g) cornflour

¼ pt (150 ml) milk
2 tbsp cream
1 egg yolk
salt and pepper

chopped parsley (optional)

Frozen celery can be used straight from the freezer.

Cut the celery into 1-in (2-cm) pieces. You can use the outside stalks and some of the green leaves as well. Chop the onion roughly. Sauté the celery and the onion in the butter for a few minutes, but do not let them brown. Add the stock, the bouquet garni and the seasoning, cover the pan and simmer for about 20 minutes, until the vegetables are soft. Blend and return to the pan. Mix the cornflour with the milk and add to the soup. Bring to the boil and simmer for a few minutes, stirring all the time. Stir the cream into the yolk, add and heat through, but do not allow to boil.

To serve immediately: test for seasoning, and serve with a little finely chopped parsley or celery leaves sprinkled over each helping.

To freeze: cool and freeze.

To serve after freezing: tip the frozen soup into a pan and heat through gently. Do not allow the soup to boil. Serve as for immediate eating.

Mushrooms

Mushrooms freeze excellently sautéed, and are one of the best stand-byes to have in the freezer. They can also be frozen raw for a short time in cellophane-wrapped punnets for use in emergencies.

To freeze sautéed: wash or wipe the mushrooms, slice, and sauté in butter until soft, allowing approximately 1 oz (25 g) butter to 1 lb (450 g) mushrooms. Cool and freeze with the cooking liquid.

MUSHROOM SOUP

*8 oz (225 g) mushrooms, fresh
or frozen sautéed
1/2 oz (12 g) butter
1 medium onion
1 stick celery (optional)
1 tbsp olive oil
1 level tbsp flour*

*3/4 pt (450 ml) light stock
3/4 pt (450 ml) milk
squeeze of lemon juice
salt and pepper*

chopped parsley

Frozen sautéed mushrooms can be used straight from the freezer, but in this case you will not need the butter.

Slice fresh mushrooms finely and cook gently in the butter. In another pan, sweat the finely chopped onion and celery in the oil until quite soft. Add the flour and stir for a minute or two. Pour in the stock and milk and bring to the boil, continuing to stir. Add the mushrooms and leave to simmer for a few minutes over a very gentle heat. (If you are using frozen mushrooms it may take a little longer.) Blend. Add a squeeze of lemon juice and season.

To serve immediately: serve with a sprinkling of parsley over each helping.

To freeze: cool and freeze.

To serve after freezing: tip the frozen soup into a pan and heat gently. Serve as above.

CHICKEN BREASTS WITH MUSHROOMS AND CREAM

1 lb (450 g) mushrooms, fresh
or frozen sautéed
4–6 boned chicken breasts, fresh
or frozen
2 medium onions
2 oz (50 g) butter

¹/₃ pt (225 ml) dry white
wine
squeeze of lemon juice
¹/₃ pt (225 ml) double cream
or crème fraîche
salt and pepper

Frozen chicken breasts must be allowed to thaw. Frozen sautéed mushrooms can be used straight from the freezer, but do not then freeze the dish.

Skin the breasts and cut in half if they are very large.

Chop the onions finely and cook gently in half the butter in a large flameproof casserole until soft and golden. Remove from the pan and set aside. Heat the remaining butter in the pan and brown the chicken breasts on both sides. Remove from the pan and set aside. Add the wine and cook briskly until it has reduced by about half.

Return the chicken breasts and onions to the pan, add the sliced mushrooms, season and add the lemon juice. Stir in the cream and heat slowly until the sauce has almost come to the simmer, but do not let it boil. Cover and cook in a low oven (275°F/140°C/gas 1) for two hours.

Serve with rice.

NOTE A lovely way of serving this dish is to skin five or six tomatoes, scoop out the middle and leave them upside down to drain. When you are ready to serve the chicken breasts, make a ring of rice round the edge of a big dish and pile the chicken breasts and their sauce in the middle. Spoon a little rice into each tomato, decorate with a sprig of watercress or parsley, and arrange on top of the rice.

MUSHROOMS IN CREAM SAUCE

This simple concoction of cream and mushrooms makes a delicate accompaniment to chicken or fish. A little of the mixture placed in a ramekin, topped with an egg and a spoonful of cream and baked briefly in a moderate oven, is a delicious start to a meal or a light supper dish. It can also be served on toast or used as an omelette or vol-au-vent filling. Made with fresh mushrooms it freezes excellently.

8 oz (225 g) mushrooms,
  frozen sautéed
2 onions
1 oz (25 g) butter
squeeze of lemon juice

approx. ⅛ pt (75 ml) double
  cream, crème fraîche or sour
  cream
salt and pepper

Frozen mushrooms can be used straight from the freezer.

Sauté the finely chopped onions in the butter. Add the frozen mushrooms and heat through gently. When they are warm add a squeeze of lemon juice, stir in the cream and test for seasoning. Bring briefly to the boil and serve.

~

MUSHROOM RISOTTO

8 oz (225 g) mushrooms, fresh
  or frozen sautéed
1 onion
1–1½ oz (25–40 g) butter
8 oz (225 g) risotto rice

approx. 1¼ pt (750 ml)
  chicken or light stock
4 oz (100 g) grated cheese
salt and pepper

Frozen mushrooms can be used straight from the freezer.

Chop the onion and sweat in 1 oz (25 g) butter for five minutes. Add the rice and mix well. Stir in the boiling stock and simmer very gently, covered, for about 15 minutes. Meanwhile, if you are using fresh mushrooms, slice and cook in the remaining butter until soft. Frozen sautéed mushrooms should be heated gently and will not need any added butter. When the rice is cooked, stir in the mushrooms and half the cheese, and season. This dish should be quite moist, so add a little more hot stock if necessary.

Transfer to a warm dish, sprinkle with the remaining cheese and serve very hot.

MUSHROOM RAMEKINS

A rich and delicious starter.

12 oz (350 g) mushrooms,
*   fresh, or frozen sautéed*
1 oz (25 g) butter
¹/₂ oz (12 g) cornflour
3 eggs
¹/₄ pt (150 ml) double or
*   whipping cream or crème*
*   fraîche*
parsley or chervil to garnish
salt, pepper, nutmeg

CREAM SAUCE
2 shallots
1 oz (25 g) butter
6 tbsp (100 ml) dry white wine
¹/₄ pt (150 ml) double or
*   whipping cream or crème*
*   fraîche*
salt and pepper

If you are using frozen sautéed mushrooms, you will not need the butter.

Chop fresh mushrooms finely and squeeze in a cloth to extract the water. Sweat in the butter for 5 to 10 minutes. If you are using frozen ones, heat gently and blend. Mix well together the cornflour, the eggs and the cream, stir in the mushrooms, and season with salt, pepper and freshly grated nutmeg.

Butter six ramekin dishes generously. Put the mixture into them within ¹/₂ in (1 cm) of the top. Cook in a bain-marie in a low oven (250°F/120°C/gas 1) for 1–1¹/₄ hours, or until they are firm to the touch.

While they are cooking, make the sauce.

Sauce: chop the shallots finely and sweat in the butter. When they are soft add the wine and reduce until there is only about 1 tbsp left. Add the cream or crème fraîche, season, and simmer for about 10 minutes.

When the ramekins are ready, remove from the oven and leave in the bain-marie for 10 minutes. Turn out on to a warmed serving dish or individual plates, pour the sauce over the top, and garnish each ramekin with a little sprig of parsley or chervil.

Parsnips

o freeze blanched: peel the parsnips and cut into quarters. Blanch for two
inutes. Drain, cool and freeze.

To freeze cooked: boil the parsnips for 10 minutes or so, until they are just
nder. Drain well and cook in a covered pan with plenty of butter for another 10
inutes. Cool and freeze.

To serve after freezing blanched:

1 Cook the frozen parsnips in boiling water until they are just tender. Drain
ell, add plenty of butter, cover the pan and leave over a gentle heat for a few
inutes. Serve with plenty of ground pepper.

2 Bake the frozen parsnips in a hot oven, sprinkled with olive oil and herbs, or
ace round the joint and roast.

To serve after freezing cooked: tip the frozen parsnips into a pan and heat through
ntly. Add a little more butter if necessary and serve with freshly ground pepper.

PARSNIP, APPLE AND GINGER SOUP

ople either love or hate parsnips and ginger. This is for lovers of both.

2 lb (1 kg) parsnips, fresh	*salt and pepper*
or frozen blanched	
4 oz (100 g) butter	*2 pt (1 litre) stock or water*
2 onions	*cream*
2 apples	*parsley*
2 oz (50 g) root ginger	

ozen parsnips can be used straight from the freezer.
Peel fresh parsnips and cut into rings or chunks. Melt the butter in a large
n, and cook the chopped onions until translucent. Add the peeled, cored and
ughly chopped apples, the parsnips, and the peeled and chopped ginger. Cover
d cook over a gentle heat until all the ingredients are quite soft. Blend.

To serve immediately: return to the pan, add the stock or water, season and heat
rough. Serve with a swirl of cream and a sprinkling of chopped parsley on each
ving.

To freeze: cool and freeze.

To serve after freezing: tip the frozen purée into a pan, add the stock or water
d heat through gently. Serve as above.

Pimentos: Red, Green and Yellow

Pimentos freeze best blanched. Freeze in small quantities, as you are not likely to nee *more than two or three at a time. It is a good idea to mix the colours.*

To blanch: wash the pimentos, cut in half, remove the seeds and slice. Blanch.

BEEF GOULASH WITH PIMENTOS

This is a good hearty dish. It has a much stronger flavour than the veal goulas on p. 24, and is considerably less expensive. It is easy to make in large quantitie and is ideal for parties.

3 lb (1¹/₂ kg) braising beef, fresh or frozen	*3 tbsp flour*
1 lb (450 g) pimentos, fresh or frozen	*1 tbsp paprika (or more)*
	1 pt (600 ml) stock
¹/₄ lb (100 g) paprika speck or streaky bacon	*8 oz (225 g) tomatoes*
	bay leaf, pinch of oregano and thyme
1 lb (450 g) onions	*salt and pepper*
2 cloves garlic	
1 tbsp caraway seeds (optional)	*1 lb (450 g) potatoes*
	¹/₄ pt (150 ml) sour cream

Frozen beef should be allowed to thaw until it is soft enough to cut. Froz pimentos can be used straight from the freezer.

Cut the speck or bacon into small cubes and fry gently in a flamepro casserole. Add the sliced onions and garlic, the chopped caraway seeds and t meat cut into bite-sized cubes, and sauté until the vegetables are golden brow Sprinkle on the flour and paprika (exactly how much paprika you use depends your taste and how fresh the paprika is, as it loses some of its pungency wi time). Cook gently for two more minutes, stirring well. Add the stock, the pee and roughly chopped tomatoes, the pimentos cut into strips and with the see taken out, and the herbs and seasoning. Simmer on a low heat for about 1 hours or until the meat is tender.

To serve immediately: peel the potatoes, cut into ¹/₂-in (1-cm) slices and parb for six to eight minutes. Add to the goulash, simmer for another 10 minutes until they are cooked but not mushy, gently stir in the sour cream, heat through and serve.

To freeze: cool and freeze.

To serve after freezing: if possible, allow to thaw for at least three to four hours. Return to the casserole and heat gently. When the meat is warmed through (allow about three-quarters of an hour), continue as for immediate eating. If the sauce is too thick, add a little more water to the goulash before adding the potatoes.

~

BRAISED BEEF WITH PIMENTOS

3 lb (1½ kg) braising beef in
  one piece
1 lb (450 g) pimentos
1 oz (25 g) butter
1 tbsp olive oil

1 clove garlic
2 onions
2 tomatoes
1 wine glass red or white wine
salt and pepper

If you are using frozen beef it should be allowed to thaw at least partially before cooking. Frozen pimentos can be used straight from the freezer.

Melt the butter and oil in a flameproof casserole. Wipe the meat and rub with the cut clove of garlic, salt and pepper it and sear quickly on all sides. Remove from the casserole, add the chopped onions and garlic and fry gently for five minutes. Return the meat to the casserole and add the peeled and chopped tomatoes, the pimentos cut into strips and with the seeds taken out, and the wine. Bring to the boil and allow to bubble for a few moments, then cover the casserole and leave on a very low heat or in a low oven (300°F/150°C/gas 2) for 1½–2 hours.

To serve immediately: remove the meat from the casserole and carve. Reduce the sauce by quick boiling if necessary, and serve with the meat.

To freeze: cool and freeze.

To serve after freezing: return the frozen meat to a flameproof casserole and heat through gently on top of the stove. Proceed as for immediate eating.

CHICKEN CASSEROLE WITH PIMENTOS

4-lb (2-kg) chicken, jointed, fresh or frozen	2 onions
2 pimentos, fresh or frozen	1 clove garlic
1 oz (25 g) butter	8 oz (225 g) tomatoes
1 tbsp olive oil	1/4 pt (125 ml) white wine
	salt and pepper

Frozen chicken must be allowed to thaw before cooking, but pimentos can be used straight from the freezer.

Wipe the pieces of chicken and season well. Melt the butter and oil in a flameproof casserole, sear the chicken pieces quickly on all sides and lift out. Lower the heat and sauté the sliced onions and chopped garlic for 10 minutes. Replace the chicken joints, add the pimentos, cut into strips and with the seeds taken out, and the peeled and roughly chopped tomatoes. Add the wine and seasoning, bring to the boil and leave to simmer, covered, over a very low flame for 45 minutes to one hour, by which time the chicken should be cooked and the vegetables soft and amalgamated into a thick sauce. If after one hour the sauce still seems rather watery, leave the lid off for the last half hour.

To serve immediately: check for seasoning and serve hot with rice or noodles.

To freeze: cool and freeze.

To serve after freezing: allow to thaw for at least three to four hours. Return to the casserole and heat slowly, stirring gently from time to time. Allow about 45 minutes. Serve as above.

~

CHICKEN PAPRIKA

4-lb (2-kg) chicken, fresh or frozen, cut into serving pieces	1 lb (450 g) tomatoes, fresh or frozen raw
2 pimentos, preferably 1 red and 1 green, fresh or frozen	1/2 pt (300 ml) stock
1–2 tbsp flour	1 tbsp concentrated tomato purée
2 tbsp olive oil	salt and pepper
2 onions	bay leaf
1 or 2 cloves garlic	
approx. 1 tsp paprika	1/2 pt (300 ml) sour cream

Frozen chicken must be allowed to thaw thoroughly before cooking. Frozen pimentos can be used straight from the freezer, but frozen tomatoes should be allowed to thaw until they are soft enough to chop.

Season the flour well and coat the pieces of chicken in it. Fry in the oil over a good heat in a flameproof casserole for 10 minutes. Add the chopped onion, the crushed garlic, and the pimentos, sliced and with the seeds taken out. Stir in the paprika. It is impossible to give exact quantities, as the strength varies so greatly, but be careful not to put in too much at the beginning, and taste as you go. Cook for another 10 minutes or so before adding the skinned and roughly chopped tomatoes, the stock, the concentrated tomato purée, the seasoning and the bay leaf. Bring to the boil, cover, and simmer for about 45 minutes to one hour either on top of the stove over a gentle heat or in a moderate oven (350°F/175°C/gas 4).

To serve immediately: 10 minutes before the chicken is ready, add the sour cream. Stir in well and test for seasoning before serving.

To freeze: cool and freeze.

To serve after freezing: allow to thaw for at least three to four hours. Return to the casserole and heat slowly for about 45 minutes, stirring gently from time to time. Add the sour cream, test for seasoning and serve.

~

PEPERONATA

A pleasantly pungent and unusual dish which can be served on its own or as a side dish and is especially good as an accompaniment to pasta.

2 lb (1 kg) red pimentos, fresh or frozen	1 large onion
	1 clove garlic
2 lb (1 kg) ripe tomatoes, fresh or frozen raw	3–4 tbsp olive oil
	salt and pepper

Frozen pimentos can be used straight from the freezer, but frozen tomatoes should be allowed to thaw until they are soft enough to chop.

Slice the onion and garlic and cook in the olive oil until golden brown. Add the sliced and seeded pimentos, cover, and continue to cook gently for 15 minutes. Skin the tomatoes, chop roughly and put in the pan. Season, and cook for a further 30 to 40 minutes, until the tomatoes have turned into a thick sauce and the peppers are quite soft. The liquid should all be absorbed by the peppers, so if the dish is too runny towards the end of the cooking leave the lid off for the last few minutes.

To freeze: cool and freeze.

To serve after freezing: tip the frozen peperonata into a pan and heat gently.

STUFFED PIMENTOS

These can be served hot as a main course, with tomato sauce, or cold as an hors d'oeuvre.

8 pimentos	*1 tbsp concentrated tomato*
1 lb (450 g) minced beef or	*purée*
lamb	*1 tbsp currants (optional)*
2 onions	*a sprinkling of chopped*
1–2 cloves garlic	*rosemary leaves*
4 tbsp olive oil	*salt and pepper*
8 oz (225 g) cooked	
long-grain rice (approx.	***1 pt (600 ml) tomato sauce***
3 oz/75 g raw)	***(optional, see p. 130)***

Frozen meat should be allowed to thaw at least partially.

Sauté the chopped onions and garlic in 2 tbsp of the olive oil, add the meat and stir over a gentle heat until the meat has changed colour. Add the rice, the tomato purée, the currants, the rosemary and the seasoning, and heat well through.

Meanwhile cut the tops off the pimentos and take out the cores. Remove the pith, preferably with a grapefruit knife or spoon, being careful not to injure the pimento cases. Rinse out the insides and tops.

Stuff the cases with the meat mixture, place them upright in an ovenproof dish and replace the tops. Sprinkle the remains of the olive oil over and round the pimentos, cover the dish with a lid or foil, and bake in a moderate oven (375°F/190°C/gas 5) for 40 minutes.

To serve immediately: serve hot with tomato sauce, or leave to cool and serve as an hors d'oeuvre.

To freeze: cool and freeze.

To serve after freezing: place the frozen pimentos in a medium oven (350°F/175°C/gas 4) and heat through. Allow 40 minutes for this. Serve as above.

PIMENTO AND TOMATO TART

2 red pimentos, fresh or frozen
1 green pimento, fresh or
  frozen
1 lb (450 g) tomatoes
10 oz (275 g) shortcrust pastry
  (see p. 218)
1 large onion
2 cloves garlic
1 oz (25 g) butter

2 tbsp olive oil
3 eggs
1/3 pt (225 ml) milk
2 oz (50 g) fresh breadcrumbs
2 tbsp grated cheese, preferably
  Parmesan
4 oz (100 g) goat cheese
  (optional)
salt and pepper

Frozen pimentos can be used straight from the freezer.

Line a 10-in (25-cm) buttered flan tin, or two 7-in (18-cm) tins, with the pastry.

Chop the onion and the garlic finely and fry gently in the butter and oil in a large frying pan. After a few minutes add the sliced and seeded pimentos and cook for another 15 minutes until soft. Beat the eggs and milk together, and stir in the breadcrumbs. Add the peeled and roughly chopped tomatoes and the pimentos and mix well together. Stir in the cheese and season. Pour into the pastry cases and top with sliced goat cheese if you are using it. Cook in a medium oven (375°F/190°C/gas 5) for about 45 minutes, until the filling has set. Serve hot.

To freeze: cool and freeze.

To serve after freezing: put the frozen tart in a hot oven (425°F/220°C/gas 7) for 20 minutes, then turn down the oven to 375°F/190°C/gas 5, and cook for another 20 to 30 minutes, depending on the size of the tart, until it is hot right through.

Sweet Corn

Sweet corn are excellent frozen, but they should be allowed to thaw before they are cooked, as otherwise they lose their crispy texture.

To freeze blanched: remove the husks and silk and trim the ends. Blanch for four to eight minutes, according to size. Drain, cool and freeze.

To serve after freezing: thaw before cooking. This will take a full three or four hours. Plunge into a pan of salted boiling water and simmer for 12 to 15 minutes. Drain and serve with lots of butter, or with lemon juice, salt and pepper.

SWEET CORN FRITTERS

These are good on their own, and are an excellent accompaniment also to cold meat, especially ham. They can be varied by adding a little minced or chopped ham to the mixture before frying.

1 sweet corn, fresh or frozen	*2 eggs*
1 tbsp flour	*oil for frying*
1/2 tsp baking powder	*salt*
1/4 tsp paprika	

Frozen corn should be allowed to thaw before cooking.

Boil the corn in water until tender, which will take 10 to 15 minutes. Drain and cut the corn off the cob. Chop coarsely and mix with the dry ingredients. Stir in the beaten egg yolks and fold in the stiffly beaten whites. Heat some oil in a large frying pan until smoking hot, put the sweet corn mixture into the pan in small spoonfuls, and cook quickly on both sides. Drain on kitchen paper and serve very hot.

Tomatoes

If you grow tomatoes, and have a glut, they are well worth freezing. Although they are available in the shops all the year round, the price fluctuates considerably, and they have the best flavour at this time of year, so it pays to freeze as many as you can. Since the water content is high, they are not suitable for later use in salads. However, they are excellent, either whole or puréed, for subsequent cooking.

To freeze raw: choose firm, ripe tomatoes. Cover with very hot water for a few seconds, drain, and skin. Freeze.

You can also freeze the tomatoes unskinned. When you come to use them, drop into boiling water for a few seconds, and the skins will come off easily.

To freeze cooked (puréed): imperfect or slightly overripe tomatoes can be used for this. Cut up roughly, take out any imperfect bits (there is no need to skin them) and put in a heavy pan with a little salt, pepper and sugar. Stew gently for about 15 minutes and put through a nylon sieve. Cool and freeze.

Tomato purée is excellent as a flavouring for soups, stews and sauces, and is delicious mixed with winter vegetables such as artichokes or celeriac.

TOMATO SOUP (1)

1 lb (450 g) tomatoes, fresh or frozen raw (skinned)	1¹/₂ pt (900 ml) water or stock
1 medium onion	2 oz (50 g) rice
4 oz (100 g) bacon	salt, pepper and sugar
¹/₂ oz (12 g) butter	
1 tsp flour	*chopped parsley (optional)*

Frozen tomatoes should be allowed to thaw until they are soft enough to chop.

Skin the tomatoes. Slice the onion finely, dice the bacon, and fry both gently in a pan in the butter until the onion is lightly browned. Sprinkle in the flour and stir until blended. Chop the tomatoes roughly and add to the pan, together with the boiling water or stock. Season and add a little sugar. Bring to the boil and add the rice. Simmer, covered, for about 20 minutes, stirring occasionally.

To serve immediately: test for seasoning and serve with chopped parsley sprinkled over each helping.

To freeze: cool and freeze.

To serve after freezing: tip the frozen soup into a pan and heat slowly. Test for seasoning and serve with parsley as above.

TOMATO SOUP (2)

This is a creamier, lighter soup than the previous one.

> 2 lb (1 kg) tomatoes, fresh or frozen raw (skinned)
> 1 oz (25 g) butter
> 1 tbsp olive oil
> 2 medium potatoes
> 2 onions
> 2–3 sprigs parsley
> a little basil
>
> 1 pt (600 ml) water or light stock
> salt, pepper, 2 tsp sugar
>
> 1/2 pt (300 ml) milk
> cream (optional)
> parsley (optional)
> basil (optional)

Frozen tomatoes can be used straight from the freezer.

Skin the tomatoes. Melt the butter and oil in a heavy pan, add the peeled and diced potatoes and the sliced onions and cook gently for five minutes. Stir in the tomatoes and the herbs, sugar and seasoning, and continue to cook gently until the vegetables have softened. Add the water or stock and simmer until all the vegetables are well cooked. Blend.

To serve immediately: add the milk and reheat, but do not allow to boil. Test for seasoning and serve with a spoonful of cream and a sprinkling of chopped parsley or basil in each bowl.

To freeze: cool and freeze.

To serve after freezing: turn the frozen soup into a pan, reheat gently, and proceed as above.

~

TOMATO SAUCE (1)

These quantities will make about 2½ pt (1½ litres) of sauce.

> 2 lb (1 kg) tomatoes, fresh or frozen raw
> 4 medium onions
> 4 cloves garlic
> 4 tbsp olive oil
>
> 4 tbsp concentrated tomato purée
> 1/2 pt (300 ml) red wine
> basil (optional)
> salt, pepper and sugar

If you are using frozen tomatoes there is no need to wait for them to thaw.

Skin the tomatoes. Chop the onions and garlic finely and sauté in the olive oil in a heavy pan until the onion is transparent. Add the tomatoes and all the other ingredients. Cover the pan and let the sauce simmer for two to three hours over a very low heat, stirring from time to time. Test for seasoning. By the time the sauce is ready to serve it should be quite thick, but if it is too runny, uncover and raise the heat for a few minutes.

To freeze: cool, and freeze in convenient quantities. It is difficult to remove the smell of tomato sauce from the container, so use pots that are expendable.

To serve after freezing: tip the frozen sauce into a pan and heat very gently, stirring from time to time. Test for seasoning before serving.

~

TOMATO SAUCE (2)

This sauce, which is quick and easy to make, is lighter than the previous one. It can be used not only with spaghetti, but also to give flavour to other dishes. It is excellent for freezing.

2 lb (1 kg) very ripe tomatoes	several sprigs parsley
1 onion	2 tbsp olive oil
1 carrot	salt, pepper, sugar
1 celery stalk	

Chop the onion, carrot, celery stalk and parsley fairly finely. Put in a pan with the olive oil and cook over a brisk heat until golden. Skin the tomatoes, chop roughly and add. Season (be generous with the pepper), and sprinkle in sugar to taste. Cover the pan and simmer for 20 minutes. Blend and test for seasoning.

To serve immediately: return to the pan and reheat.

To freeze: cool and freeze in airtight, expendable containers, as the smell is very strong.

To serve after freezing: tip the frozen sauce into a pan and reheat gently.

SAUCE BOLOGNESE

2 lb (1 kg) tomatoes, fresh or frozen raw or puréed	¼ pt (150 ml) stock or red wine
1 lb (450 g) minced beef	4 tbsp concentrated tomato purée
2 onions	
2 cloves garlic	thyme and basil
1 carrot	salt and pepper
4 tbsp olive oil	

Frozen meat should be allowed to thaw for two to three hours if possible. Tomatoes can be used straight from the freezer.

Skin the tomatoes. Sauté the finely chopped onions, garlic and carrot in the oil for 10 minutes. Add the meat and continue to cook very gently until it changes colour. Add the tomatoes and all the other ingredients. Simmer very slowly, without a lid, stirring from time to time, until the sauce has reduced to a thick purée. Test for seasoning.

To freeze: cool and freeze in convenient quantities in airtight, expendable containers, as the smell is very strong.

To serve after freezing: tip the frozen sauce into a pan and heat very gently, stirring from time to time. Test for seasoning before serving.

~

TOMATOES PROVENÇALES

1 lb (450 g) tomatoes	2 tbsp breadcrumbs
2 medium onions	1 tbsp olive oil
2 cloves garlic	salt and pepper
parsley and basil	

Cut the tomatoes in half. Score each cut surface with a sharp knife, sprinkle on a little salt and pepper, and leave upside down to drain. Chop the onions, garlic and herbs very finely, mix with the breadcrumbs, and put a good teaspoon of the mixture on to each tomato, pressing it in as much as possible. Sprinkle over a little olive oil and grill for 15 to 20 minutes, by which time the tomatoes should be cooked and the tops a little charred.

To serve immediately: serve hot as a vegetable dish or as a starter.

To freeze: cool and freeze.

To serve after freezing: place the frozen tomatoes in a medium oven (350°F/175°C/gas 4) and heat through for half an hour. Serve as above.

PIZZA

This is a quickly made pizza which does not need yeast. The basic cheese and tomato topping can be added to in any number of ways, such as with black olives, anchovies, bacon, ham, sliced mushrooms, or sliced pimentos.

8 oz (225 g) flour	*12 oz (350 g) tomatoes*
¼ pt (150 ml) milk	*6–10 anchovy fillets (optional)*
4 tbsp olive oil	*4 oz black olives (optional)*
1 tsp baking powder	*1 tsp chopped marjoram*
6 oz (175 g) cheese	*salt and pepper*

Oil a baking tin about 11 in (28 cm) in diameter, or two 8-in (20-cm) tins. Stir together the flour, milk, oil and baking powder, and season generously. Spread this mixture thinly and evenly over the tin – it will be quite springy. Grate or slice the cheese on top, and over this put the sliced tomatoes. Arrange the anchovy fillets and the olives on the tomatoes, and sprinkle over the marjoram.

Cook in a hot oven (450°F/230°C/gas 8) for about 25 minutes, or until the dough is cooked through and the cheese is melting and bubbly.

To freeze: take out of the oven about five minutes before you would do if you were going to eat the pizza at once. Cool and freeze.

To serve after freezing: put the frozen pizza in a hot oven (450°F/230°C/gas 8) and heat through for 45 minutes to one hour.

NOTES
1 It is useful to have a supply of small individual pizzas in the freezer. These will take only 20–25 minutes to heat through.
2 If you like crunchy food, any pizza that is left over will warm up splendidly next day. Sprinkle generously over the top a layer of any garnish available (grated cheese, sliced tomatoes, an anchovy fillet or two), finish with a spoonful of olive oil, and bake in a moderate oven (350°F/175°C/gas 4) for about 20 minutes.

STUFFED TOMATOES

This dish is best made with large Mediterranean tomatoes.

4 oz (125 g) long-grain   *parsley and marjoram*
cooked rice (1½–2 oz/   *peel of 1 lemon*
40–50 g raw)   *1 tbsp olive oil*
3 shallots   *salt and pepper*

Cut the tops off the tomatoes and scoop out the pulp. Mix with the cooked rice, add the finely chopped shallots and herbs, and the grated lemon peel. Season, and fill the tomatoes with the mixture. Arrange on a shallow baking dish, dribble a little olive oil over each tomato and bake in a moderate oven (350°F/175°C/gas 4) for about half an hour, or until the tomato cases are soft.

To serve immediately: serve hot as a vegetable with meat or fish or cold as an hors d'oeuvre, sprinkling on a little more olive oil before serving.

To freeze: cool, and put in single layers on a foil-covered baking tray. Freeze for 24 hours, wrap well and return to the freezer.

Apples

Apples freeze wonderfully, provided they are cooked first.

To freeze puréed:

1 Peel, core and slice the apples and put in a pan with just enough water to keep them from burning: 2 or 3 tbsp should be enough. Cover, and cook steadily until they are soft and frothy. Stir in sugar or honey to taste, cool, and freeze.

2 This method saves time if you have a lot of small apples. It makes a tarter purée, more suitable for apple sauce. Halve or quarter the apples and take out any bad pieces, but do not peel or core. Cook with a little water until soft and pass through a nylon sieve. Sweeten to taste with sugar or honey, cool and freeze.

APPLE CHEESECAKE

1 large cooking apple　　　　*2 oz (50 g) butter*
6 oz (175 g) shortcrust pastry　*1 egg*
　(see p. 218)　　　　　　　*1 lemon*
4 oz (100 g) castor sugar

Line a buttered 8-in (20-cm) flan tin with the pastry. Cook blind in a hot oven (425°F/220°C/gas 7) for 10 minutes.

Cream the sugar and butter. Add the beaten egg, the apple (peeled and coarsely grated) and the rind and juice of the lemon. Spread the filling over the flan case and bake in a hot oven (400°F/200°C/gas 6) for 20 to 25 minutes. Turn the oven down to 325°F/160°C/gas 3, and cook for a further 25 minutes or so (about 50 minutes in all) until the filling has set.

To serve immediately: serve warm or cold.

To freeze: cool and freeze.

To serve after freezing: place the frozen tart in a hot oven (400°F/200°C/gas 6) for half an hour. Serve warm or cold.

~

CREAMY APPLE FLAN

1 lb (450 g) cooking apples　　*3–4 oz (75–100 g) sugar*
6 oz (175 g) sweetened　　　*1/4 pt (150 ml) double cream*
　shortcrust pastry (see p. 219)

Line a buttered 8-in (20-cm) flan tin with the pastry and bake blind for 10 minutes in a hot oven (425°F/220°C/gas 7). Peel, core and quarter the apples and cut into thin slices. Arrange these very close together, standing upright, in the pastry case. Sprinkle on the sugar, pour on the cream and cook in a moderate oven (375°F/190°C/gas 5) for 40 minutes.

To serve immediately: this flan can be served hot or cold, but is best hot.

To freeze: cool and freeze.

To serve after freezing: place the frozen flan in a hot oven (425°F/220°C/gas 7) for half an hour. Serve hot or cold.

APPLES IN THEIR DRESSING GOWNS

8 medium cooking apples   *1 oz (25 g) butter*
1 lb (450 g) shortcrust pastry   *raisins (optional)*
  (see p. 218)
approx. 4 oz (100 g)   *icing or castor sugar*
  demerara sugar

Peel the apples and core them, but leave whole. Roll out the pastry, cut into eight squares, and place an apple on each. Stuff the centre of each apple with as much sugar as it will hold and perhaps a few raisins, and dot with a small knob of butter. Pinch together the four corners of each square to meet at the top of the apple, and then pinch together the edges of the pastry, to make a neat parcel.

To serve immediately: place the parcels on a buttered baking tray and bake in a hot oven (425°F/220°C/gas 7) for 15 minutes. Turn the oven down to 375°F/190°C/gas 5, and bake for a further half an hour. Serve hot or cold, dredged with a little icing or castor sugar.

To freeze: place on a baking tray and freeze. When frozen, take out, wrap individually and return to the freezer.

To serve after freezing: place the frozen apples on a buttered baking tray and bake in a hot oven (425°F/220°C/gas 7) for half an hour. Lower the oven to 375°F/190°C/gas 5, and cook for a further half an hour. Serve as for immediate eating.

NOTE You can also freeze the apples after they have been cooked. In that case, when you take them out of the freezer they will only need 20 minutes in a hot oven, and a further 20 minutes after you have turned the oven down.

APPLE TART

8 oz (225 g) cooking apples	*2 oz (50 g) sugar*
6 oz (175 g) shortcrust pastry	*1 tbsp apricot jam*
(see p. 218)	*1 tbsp water*

Line a buttered 8-in (20-cm) flan tin with the pastry and bake blind in a hot oven (425°F/220°C/gas 7) for 10 minutes.

Peel, quarter and core the apples and cut into very fine slices. Arrange overlapping in rounds on the pastry, sprinkle on the sugar and bake in a hot oven (425°F/220°C/gas 7) for half an hour. By this time the apples should be soft, and a little browned at the edges.

When the tart has cooled make the glaze by boiling the jam and water together for one minute, strain, cool, and brush over the flan.

To serve immediately: allow the glaze to set and serve.

To freeze: wrap and freeze.

To serve after freezing: place the frozen tart in a hot oven (425°F/220°C/gas 7) for half an hour. Serve warm or cold.

~

COVERED APPLE TART

1 lb (450 g) cooking apples	*grated rind of 1 lemon*
10 oz (275 g) shortcrust pastry	
(see p. 218)	*icing sugar*
3–4 oz (75–100 g) sugar	

Line a buttered 8-in (20-cm) flan tin with two-thirds of the pastry. Peel, core and quarter the apples and cut into thin slices. Fill the flan case with these, sprinkle on the sugar and the grated lemon rind and cover with the remaining pastry. Seal the edges well.

To serve immediately: bake in a hot oven (425°F/220°C/gas 7) for 20 minutes, lower the temperature to 350°F/175°C/gas 4, and continue baking for another half an hour or until the pastry is golden brown. Turn the tart out and serve hot or cold, liberally dredged with icing sugar.

To freeze: wrap and freeze.

To serve after freezing: put the frozen tart in a hot oven (425°F/220°C/gas 7) for 30 minutes, turn the oven down to 375°F/190°C/gas 5, and bake for a further 40 to 50 minutes. Serve as above.

TOFFEE APPLE TART

1¹/₂ lb (675 g) tart eating   *4 oz (100 g) sugar*
  apples   *1 oz (25 g) butter*
5 oz (150 g) shortcrust pastry   *1 tbsp water*
  (see p. 218)

Melt the sugar with ¹/₂ oz (12 g) of the butter and the water in a small pan until it turns a golden toffee colour. (This will not work with a non-stick pan.) Pour quickly into a buttered 8-in (20-cm) flan tin, turning the tin so that the whole surface becomes coated with the toffee.

Peel, core and quarter the apples, and arrange closely on the toffee. Dot with the remaining butter and cover with the pastry, sealing the edges down well. Prick the pastry and bake in a hot oven (425°F/220°C/gas 7) for 40 minutes.

To serve immediately: allow to cool for a few minutes, then put a large plate on top of the tin and turn the tart out carefully, so that the toffee is on top. Be careful not to spill any juice. Serve hot or cold.

To freeze: cool and freeze.

To serve after freezing: place the frozen tart in a hot oven (425°F/220°C/gas 7) for 20 minutes. Serve as for immediate eating.

~

APFELKUCHEN

These quantities will make one very large cake – excellent for a party – or two smaller ones.

2 lb (1 kg) cooking apples   *2 or 3 drops vanilla essence*
1 lb (450 g) butter   *¹/₂ tsp cinnamon (optional)*
8–10 oz (225–275 g) sugar
2 eggs   *whipped cream*
12 oz (350 g) flour

Butter a shallow rectangular baking tin, measuring about 12 x 8 in (30 x 20 cm), or two 8-in (20-cm) flan tins, and line with baking paper.

Cream the butter with 4 oz (100 g) of the sugar. Add the well-beaten eggs, the flour and the vanilla essence. Spread the mixture in the tin.

Peel, core and quarter the apples, and cut into very thin slices – about ¹/₈ in (¹/₂ cm) thick at the outer edge. Press them, rounded side upwards, into the cake mixture. Every inch should be covered, and in the end you should have a pattern of half-moons sticking up cheek by jowl. Dredge the rest of the sugar on top (you can if you like mix ½ tsp cinnamon with this), and bake in a hot oven (400°F/200°C/gas 6) until the apples are pale brown and juicy, and the cake mixture is well cooked. This will take at least one hour. When the cake has cooled a little, turn on to a cake rack and leave until cold.

To serve immediately: serve with whipped cream.

To freeze: freeze on the cake rack for 24 hours. Wrap and return to the freezer.

To serve after freezing: place the frozen apfelkuchen in a moderate oven (350°F/175°C/gas 4) for 15 to 20 minutes before leaving to thaw for another hour at room temperature. Serve as above.

~

SWEDISH APPLE CAKE

This can be served as a cake, or with whipped cream as a dessert. If it is not being made for the freezer it should if possible be stored in a tin for 3 or 4 days before eating to bring out the flavour.

3 large cooking apples	*8 oz (225 g) flour*
3 oz (75 g) butter	*1 tbsp chopped candied orange*
6 oz (175 g) castor sugar	*peel*
2 eggs	*1 tsp grated fresh orange peel*
2 tbsp milk	*2 oz (50 g) chopped almonds*

Grease a shallow baking tin about 10 in (25 cm) square, and line with baking parchment. Cream the butter and sugar until fluffy. Add the beaten eggs and the milk. Sieve in the flour and add the candied peel, orange peel and almonds. Peel and core the apples, cut into very small dice and mix in well. Put into the tin and bake in a moderate oven (350°F/175°C/gas 4) for 40 to 50 minutes. Turn on to a cake rack and cool.

To freeze: wrap and freeze.

To serve after freezing: thaw at room temperature for about four hours.

APPLE STRUDEL

This traditional Austrian dish is not difficult to make, but it takes rather a long time, so it is a good idea to make a number of strudels at once. As an alternative to making the pastry yourself, you can use filo or strudel pastry. The following quantities will make four medium-sized strudels.

PASTRY
1 lb (450 g) flour
1/2 tsp salt
2 small eggs
4 tbsp olive oil
approx. 1/4 pt (150 ml) warm
   water

FILLING
3 lb (1 1/2 kg) cooking apples
4 oz (100 g) fresh
   breadcrumbs

2 oz (50 g) butter
6 oz (175 g) castor or
   demerara sugar
squeeze of lemon juice
a handful of raisins
   (optional)
2 oz (50 g) chopped blanched
   almonds (optional)

a little melted butter
icing sugar

To make the pastry, sift the flour and salt into a bowl. Whisk the eggs and oil together and pour into a well in the middle of the flour. Work this gradually into the flour, together with as much warm water as is needed to form a stiff dough which comes away clean from the sides of the bowl. Flour a pastry board and knead the dough until it begins to form bubbles. Leave to rest in a warm place for half an hour.

Meanwhile fry the breadcrumbs in the butter to a crisp golden colour. Peel, core and quarter the apples and cut into paper-thin slices.

Divide the dough into four equal parts and make one strudel at a time. Spread a clean tea towel on a flat surface, sprinkle liberally with flour and on this roll out the first quarter of pastry until it is about the same shape and size as the tea towel, very thin indeed and transparent. It is important to use the rolling pin from the centre outwards, as otherwise you are likely to end up with thin pastry at the edges but a thick section in the middle. You can also pull and stretch it by hand, but this is best done by two people.

Sprinkle on 1 oz (25 g) breadcrumbs and cover the whole surface closely with about a quarter of the apple slices, leaving a 1-in (2-cm) margin at the edges. Sprinkle on about 1 1/2 oz (40 g) sugar, a squeeze of lemon juice, and a few raisins and almonds if you are using them. Lift up one end of the tea towel and gently allow the strudel to roll itself up as it falls away from the towel. Have a greased baking tin ready at the other end, with the tea towel just overlapping on to it, so that the strudel will finally roll on to the tin. Seal the edges with a little water.

Make three more strudels the same way.

To serve immediately: brush a little melted butter over the top of the strudel and bake in a hot oven (450°F/230°C/gas 8) for 15 minutes. Turn the oven down to 375°F/190°C/gas 5, for another 40 minutes. Sprinkle liberally with sieved icing sugar before serving hot or cold.

To freeze: put the uncooked strudel into the freezer on the baking tin and leave for about 24 hours. It is important that it should go into the freezer straight away, before the apples begin to ooze their juice. When it is frozen, wrap and replace in the freezer.

To serve after freezing: brush the frozen strudel with a little melted butter and cook in a hot oven (450°F/230°C/gas 8) for half an hour, then turn the oven down to 375°F/190°C/gas 5, and cook for another 45 minutes to one hour. Serve as for immediate eating.

To make with bought filo or strudel pastry: allow frozen filo pastry to thaw completely before using. Once you have opened the packet and unfolded the contents, keep covered with a damp cloth, taking off the pastry sheets one by one as needed.

As the sheets are quite small, you will need six to eight for each strudel. Lay them out on a tea towel, allowing plenty of overlap and brushing each with melted butter before adding the next one. Roll up as above and seal all the edges well.

Any leftover sheets can be returned to the freezer, well wrapped, provided they have not been allowed to dry out.

~

DANISH APPLE PUDDING

3/4 pt (450 ml) apple purée,
  fresh or frozen
4 oz (100 g) coarse fresh
  breadcrumbs
1 oz (25 g) sugar or 1 tbsp
  honey

2 oz (50 g) flaked almonds
3 oz (75 g) butter
2 tbsp sherry
1/4 pt (150 ml) double or
  whipping cream

Allow frozen purée to thaw.

Test the purée for sweetness and add more sugar or honey if necessary. Mix the breadcrumbs with 1 oz (25 g) sugar and the almonds and fry gently in the butter. When they are crisp and golden leave to cool.

Arrange a layer of the apple purée in a glass bowl, cover with a layer of the crumbs and repeat until both crumbs and apple have been used up, finishing with a layer of crumbs. Sprinkle on the sherry and top with the whipped cream.

FRIAR'S OMELETTE

½ pt (300 ml) apple purée,	1 egg and 1 yolk
fresh or frozen	2 oz (50 g) butter
1 oz (25 g) flour	grated rind of 1 lemon
1 tsp sugar	approx. 2 tbsp rum or calvados
⅛ pt (75 ml) milk	castor sugar

Allow frozen apple purée to thaw.

Make a batter with the flour, sugar, milk and the whole egg. Beat well and leave for at least one hour. When you are ready to make the omelette, gently warm the apple purée and beat into it the egg yolk, the lemon rind and 1 oz (25 g) butter. Taste for sweetness and add more sugar if necessary. Keep the mixture hot. Melt the rest of the butter in a large frying pan (about 10 in/25 cm in diameter), beat the batter once more, pour into the pan and cook gently. When the first side is done, turn the omelette over and, while the second side is cooking, spread the apple mixture over the top. When the omelette is thoroughly cooked, fold over and sprinkle with the rum or calvados and plenty of castor sugar. Serve very hot.

You can if you like flambé the omelette, in which case the sugar should be sprinkled on before the rum or calvados.

~

APPLE SNOW

This is a favourite recipe with children, and with the addition of sherry makes a pleasant pudding for adults too.

¾ pt (450 ml) apple purée,	2 eggs
fresh or frozen	approx. 2 tbsp sugar or 1 tbsp
5–6 trifle sponges	honey
1 pt (600 ml) milk	4–5 tbsp sherry (optional)
1 tbsp custard powder	

Allow frozen apple purée to thaw. Test for sweetness and add more sugar or honey if necessary.

Slice each of the sponges into about six pieces and put in a dish. Make a custard with the milk, the custard powder and the egg yolks, and sweeten to taste.

If the pudding is for adults add 2 or 3 tbsp sherry to the custard, and sprinkle the rest over the sponge. Pour the hot custard over the sponge and leave to get cold. An hour or two before eating, beat the egg whites very stiffly and fold into the apple purée. Pile on top of the sponge, and chill before serving.

Blackberries

Blackberries freeze extremely well, and preserve their fresh, hedgerow taste almost indefinitely. Freeze the best berries with sugar and purée the less perfect ones.

With sugar: mix the berries gently with sugar in the proportion of 3–4 oz (75–100 g) sugar to 1 lb (450 g) fruit. Freeze.

Purée: blend the blackberries with 3–4 oz (75–100 g) sugar to 1 lb (450 g) fruit, and rub through a nylon sieve. Freeze.

BLACKBERRY FLUFF

1 lb (450 g) blackberries	*a little castor sugar (optional)*
frozen with sugar	*3 egg whites*
¹/₂ oz (12 g) gelatine	
juice of ¹/₂ lemon	**whipped cream for serving**
2 tbsp water	**(optional)**

Frozen egg whites should be allowed to thaw to room temperature before whipping.

Simmer the frozen blackberries until they are soft – about 15 to 20 minutes – and put through a nylon sieve. Sprinkle the gelatine over the lemon juice and water, leave for a few minutes, and heat gently until the gelatine has dissolved. Add to the purée, test for sweetness, and stir in a little castor sugar if necessary. Leave in a cool place until the mixture thickens and begins to set. Fold in the stiffly beaten egg whites. Chill for three to four hours and serve with whipped cream.

BLACKBERRY ICE-CREAM

To make with fresh blackberries

1 lb (450 g) blackberries *½ pt (300 ml) double or*
5 oz (150 g) sugar   *whipping cream*
¼ pt (150 ml) water

To make from frozen blackberries

1 lb (450 g) blackberries *2 oz (50 g) sugar*
frozen with sugar or   *¼ pt (150 ml) water*
½ pt (300 ml) blackberry *½ pt (300 ml) double or*
purée   *whipping cream*

Make as for blackcurrant ice-cream (see p. 83).

~

BLACKBERRY WATER-ICE

To make with fresh blackberries

1 lb (450 g) blackberries *½ pt (300 ml) water*
5 oz (150 g) sugar   *a good squeeze of lemon juice*

To make with frozen blackberries

1 lb (450 g) blackberries *2 oz (50 g) sugar*
frozen with sugar or ½ pt *½ pt (300 ml) water*
(300 ml) blackberry purée

Make as for blackcurrant water-ice (see p. 84).

Pears

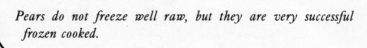

Pears do not freeze well raw, but they are very successful frozen cooked.

To freeze cooked: peel and halve the pears and take out the cores. Drop at once into slightly salted water to prevent discoloration. Make a syrup with ½ pt (300 ml) water and 4 oz (100 g) sugar – this is enough for 2 lb (1 kg) pears. Rinse the pears and poach gently in the syrup for about 30 minutes or until they are quite soft. Cool and freeze in the syrup.

PEARS IN RED WINE

This is the simplest possible dessert, and one of the most refreshing.

2 lb (1 kg) dessert pears	*1 stick cinnamon (optional)*
¼ pt (150 ml) water	*4–5 cloves (optional)*
4 oz (100 g) sugar	
¼ pt (150 ml) red wine	*whipped cream or ice-cream*

Make a syrup with the water and sugar and boil for three minutes. Peel the pears but leave whole and with their stalks on. Put in a pan which will hold them all on the bottom, and pour over the syrup and wine. Add the cinnamon and cloves if you are using them. Cover, and poach gently until the pears are quite soft. Lift out of the pan and put in a bowl. Boil the juice hard, with the lid off, until it has reduced by about half, then pour over the pears and leave to cool, turning them over from time to time so that each side absorbs the syrup. Serve with whipped cream or ice-cream.

To freeze: freeze the pears and juice together.

To serve after freezing: thaw at room temperature for five to six hours. Serve as above.

PEAR FRANGIPANE TART

4–5 ripe pears, depending on
    size
6 oz (175 g) shortcrust pastry
    (see p. 218)
2 tbsp apricot jam or any other
    jam or jelly

4 oz (100 g) butter
4 oz (100 g) sugar
2 eggs
4 oz (100 g) ground almonds
2 tbsp flour

Line an 8-in (20-cm) flan tin with the pastry and bake blind in a hot oven (425°F/220°C/gas 7) for 10 to 15 minutes.

Melt the jam or jelly with 2 tbsp water and bring just to the boil, stirring until smooth. Strain if necessary, and use half to brush over the base of the pastry case.

Beat the butter with the sugar until pale and fluffy. Beat in the eggs one by one and fold in the ground almonds and the flour. Spread the mixture in the pastry case.

Peel and halve the pears and take out the stalks and cores. Press the halves, cut-side down, into the frangipane mixture, stalk ends towards the centre, and quickly slice downwards across each pear six or seven times, so that they keep their shape but are thinly sliced. Bake in a moderate oven (375°F/190°C/gas 5) for 40 to 50 minutes, or until the frangipane has completely set.

To serve immediately: brush with the remaining glaze, sprinkle with a little castor sugar and return to the oven for five minutes to produce a slightly crunchy finish. Serve warm.

To freeze: cool and freeze.

To serve after freezing: put the frozen tart into a moderate oven (375°F/190°C/gas 5) and heat through for 30 to 40 minutes. Finish as above, or, if it is not convenient to make the glaze, dust with icing sugar.

Quinces

Quinces add a very special flavour to apple and pear desserts. They cannot be stored raw for more than a week or two, but they freeze well blanched, so if you like their taste keep some in the freezer for adding to apple pies, puddings and tarts. They also make the most delicious and surprising ices.

To freeze blanched: peel, quarter and core the quinces, being careful to take out all the hard pieces round the core. Cut into chunks and blanch for two minutes. Drain, cool and freeze in small quantities.

To freeze cooked: prepare as above and cook gently with a little sugar and a tiny bit of water - just enough to keep them from burning - until tender. Cool and freeze with the cooking liquid in small quantities, or purée before freezing.

QUINCE ICE-CREAM

¹/₂ pt (300 ml) quince purée   *¹/₄ pt (150 ml) double or*
5 oz (150 g) sugar   *whipping cream*
¹/₄ pt (150 ml) water

Allow frozen purée to thaw.

Boil the sugar and water for five minutes. Cool and add to the purée. Whip the cream lightly, fold into the purée. Freeze.

To serve after freezing: remove from the freezer one hour before serving and leave in the refrigerator.

~

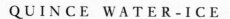

QUINCE WATER-ICE

¹/₂ pt (300 ml) quince purée   *6 oz (175 g) sugar*
¹/₂ pt (300 ml) water

Allow frozen purée to thaw.

Boil the water with the sugar for five minutes. Cool, and stir into the quince purée. Strain and freeze for one to two hours, until the mixture has reached a mushy state. Remove from the freezer, beat well, and replace in the freezer.

To serve: remove from the freezer 10 to 15 minutes before serving.

Nuts

NUT ROAST WITH TOMATO SAUCE

This nut roast is best frozen cooked. If you are in a hurry, ready-chopped mixed nuts can at a pinch be substituted for the whole ones.

1¹/2 oz (40 g) butter	*4 oz (100 g) cashew nuts*
1 medium onion	*4 oz (100 g) fresh brown*
4 oz (100 g) cheese	* breadcrumbs*
1 tsp thyme	*1–2 tbsp chopped parsley*
2 oz (50 g) hazelnuts, skinned	*2 eggs*
2 oz (50 g) almonds, skinned	*salt and pepper*

Grease a 1 lb (450 g) loaf tin with ¹/2 oz (12 g) butter. Melt the remaining butter in a pan and sweat the finely chopped onion until soft and slightly brown. Transfer to a bowl. Grate the cheese into the bowl and add the thyme, finely chopped nuts, breadcrumbs, parsley and beaten eggs. Mix well and season. Press into the tin and bake at 350°F/175°C/gas 4 for 45 minutes, or until golden brown.

To serve immediately: leave to cool for three minutes and turn on to a warm serving dish. Cut into slices and serve with spicy tomato sauce.

To freeze: cool and freeze.

To serve after freezing: allow to thaw for five to six hours at room temperature. Dot with butter, cover with foil and heat in a moderate oven (350°F/175°C/gas 4) for 1¹/2 hours. Serve as above.

SPICY TOMATO SAUCE

1 large onion	*2 tbsp tomato purée*
1 stick celery	*1 tsp sugar*
2 cloves garlic	*1 tbsp red wine vinegar*
2 tsp olive oil	*pinch of mixed herbs*
¹/4 tsp mild curry powder	*tabasco sauce (optional)*
2 lb (900 g) tomatoes, fresh or	*salt and pepper*
* frozen raw, or 1 large tin*	
* tomatoes*	

Frozen tomatoes can be used straight from the freezer.

Sweat the chopped onion, celery and garlic in the oil until soft and stir in th curry powder. Add the skinned and chopped tomatoes (if you are using frozen ones, there is no need to chop them), tomato purée, sugar, vinegar and herbs. Season. Simmer for one hour, blend, and add a few drops of tabasco sauce to taste.

~

CHARLOTTE MALAKOFF

This is a rich dessert, and is particularly delicious served with a rather tart fruit, such as raspberry or redcurrant purée.

4 oz (100 g) ground almonds	*4 oz (100 g) unsalted butter*
2 tbsp Grand Marnier	*4 oz (100 g) castor sugar*
1 tbsp water	*¹/₄ pt (150 ml) double or*
4 oz (100 g) sponge fingers	*whipping cream*
(or more)	

Mix 1 tbsp of the Grand Marnier with the water in a plate and dip the smooth sides of the sponge fingers briefly in the liquid. Line a charlotte mould or pudding basin with the biscuits, standing them round the sides, sugar side outwards, and trim to size.

Cream the butter and sugar until white and fluffy and add the rest of the Grand Marnier and the ground almonds. Whip the cream lightly and fold in. Pour the mixture into the mould and tap sharply on the table two or three times to get rid of any air bubbles.

To serve immediately: chill for three to four hours, turn out of the mould and serve.

To freeze: wrap and freeze.

To serve after freezing: thaw at room temperature for about six hours before serving.

WALNUT CHARLOTTE MALAKOFF

Make as for Charlotte Malakoff, substituting finely ground walnuts for the ground almonds. This is only for those with a passion for walnuts, as the taste is quite strong. For a slightly milder version, substitute pecans.

~

CHOCOLATE CHARLOTTE MALAKOFF

Add 2 oz (50 g) plain chocolate to the basic ingredients, and substitute strong coffee for the water. You can also use Tia Maria instead of Grand Marnier. Dip the sponge fingers in a mixture of the liqueur and coffee. Melt the chocolate in a double saucepan or a basin set over a pan of simmering water, and add to the well-beaten butter and sugar mixture.

~

FROZEN ALMOND OR HAZELNUT CREAM

This is not exactly an ice-cream but more what the Italians call a semi-freddo, which never becomes quite hard. It should be eaten within three or four days, and is particularly good served with a fruit purée.

4 oz (100 g) blanched almonds	*4 tbsp water*
or skinned hazelnuts	*4 tbsp Marsala*
4 egg whites	*1/2 pt (300 ml) double or*
4 oz (100 g) sugar	*whipping cream*

Frozen egg whites should be allowed to thaw to room temperature.

Roast the nuts in a hot oven or under a grill until they are dark brown but not burnt. Leave to cool and crush to a fine powder.

Whip the egg whites until they are stiff. Melt the sugar with the water and boil until it turns golden brown. (This does not work with a non-stick pan.) Pour in a thin thread into the egg whites, continuing to whisk until all has been amalgamated. Stir in the powdered nuts, keeping aside a little for decoration. Add the Marsala and finally fold in the whipped cream. Pour into small cocotte dishes or ramekins. Freeze.

To serve: remove from the freezer 15 minutes before serving.

PRALINE ICE-CREAM

This ice-cream is particularly good served with a fruit purée.

PRALINE
8 oz (225 g) blanched
  almonds
4 oz (100 g) sugar
2 tbsp water

ICE-CREAM
4 egg yolks
5 oz (150 g) sugar
1/2 pt (300 ml) milk or single
  cream
1/2 pt (300 ml) double or
  whipping cream

To make the praline: roast the almonds in a hot oven or under a grill until they are dark brown but not burnt. Melt the sugar with the water in a heavy pan and boil gently until golden brown. (This does not work with a non-stick pan.) Remove from the heat and add the almonds, stirring with a wooden spoon so that they become evenly coated. Pour on to a wooden board or baking tray and leave to cool.

To make the ice-cream: lightly beat the egg yolks with the sugar, heat the milk or single cream and add it, stirring well. Return the custard to the pan and stir over a gentle heat, or in the top of a double boiler, until it thickens. Do not allow to boil. Leave to cool.

Meanwhile crush the praline mixture to a powder. Stir into the cooled custard, whip the double or whipping cream lightly and fold in. Freeze.

To serve: remove from the freezer 15 minutes before serving.

~

HAZELNUT ICE-CREAM

4 oz (100 g) hazelnuts
1/2 pt (300 ml) single cream
4 egg yolks
4 oz (100 g) sugar

2 tbsp Marsala (optional)
1/2 pt (300 ml) double or
  whipping cream

Roast and skin the hazelnuts and grind finely. Put in a pan with the single cream and bring very slowly to simmering point. Lightly beat the egg yolks with the sugar and stir in the hot cream. Return to the pan and stir over a gentle heat or in the top of a double boiler until the mixture thickens, but do not allow to boil. Cool. Add the Marsala and fold in the lightly whipped double or whipping cream. Freeze.

To serve: take out of the freezer 15 minutes before serving.

CHOCOLATE HAZELNUT GÂTEAU

4 oz (100 g) hazelnuts	*1 tbsp strong coffee*
4 oz (100 g) butter	*1 tbsp rum*
4 oz (100 g) castor sugar	
4 eggs	*¼ pt (150 ml) double or*
4 oz (100 g) plain chocolate	*whipping cream (optional)*

Roast and skin the hazelnuts and grind finely. Beat the butter and sugar until light and fluffy, add the egg yolks one by one and then the hazelnuts. Melt the chocolate over a low heat with the coffee and beat into the mixture. Add the rum, and finally fold in the stiffly beaten whites of egg.

Pour into a buttered 8-in (20-cm) sponge or flan tin and bake in a moderate oven (350°F/175°C/gas 4) for 30 to 35 minutes, or until a skewer inserted into the cake comes out clean.

Allow to cool on a cake rack. Serve with whipped cream.

To freeze: freeze when quite cold.

To serve after freezing: thaw at room temperature for four to five hours.

~

HAZELNUT MERINGUES

4 egg whites	*½ pt (300 ml) double or*
6 oz (175 g) hazelnuts	*whipping cream*
8 oz (225 g) castor sugar	
finely grated rind of 1 lemon	

Frozen egg whites must be allowed to thaw to room temperature.

Heat the oven to 200°F/100°C/gas ¼.

Without removing the skins, roast the hazelnuts lightly in the oven for about 20 minutes. Blend or chop finely.

With the egg whites and sugar, make the meringue mixture as described on p. 230. Fold in the hazelnuts and the grated lemon rind. Line shallow trays with baking parchment. Shape the mixture into small meringues or large circles, and bake for two to three hours, until the meringues are firm but not coloured. Cool on a wire rack.

To serve immediately: serve sandwiched with lightly whipped cream. These meringues are particularly good eaten with raspberries or with raspberry sauce.

To freeze: freeze the meringues in tins or plastic containers so that they will not break.

To serve after freezing: the meringues can be served straight from the freezer. Serve as above.

Variation: walnuts or pecans can be substituted for the hazelnuts.

~

WALNUT SOUP

8 oz (225 g) walnuts	*2 pt (1 litre) light stock*
1 large clove garlic	*salt and pepper*
a little cream	**chopped parsley**

Blend the walnuts with the garlic and a little stock. Add the rest of the stock gradually, pour into a pan and heat gently. Season to taste.

To serve immediately: pour into bowls with a little swirl of cream and a sprinkling of parsley on each serving.

To freeze: cool and freeze.

To serve after freezing: tip the frozen soup into a pan, reheat very gently and serve as above.

WALNUT TOFFEE TART

8 oz (225 g) walnuts	*2 tbsp water*
14 oz (400 g) sweetened	*¹/₂ pt (300 ml) double cream*
shortcrust pastry (see p. 219)	
8 oz (225 g) sugar	*icing sugar*

Line one 10-in (25-cm) or two 7-in (18-cm) buttered flan tins with about two-thirds of the pastry rolled out thinly, keeping aside enough to make lids. Put the sugar and water in a heavy pan and boil, stirring continuously, until it is pale gold. (This will not work with a non-stick pan.) Remove from the heat and stir in the cream. Return to the heat and cook, stirring, until the mixture turns a rich golden brown. Stir in the roughly chopped walnuts, leave to cool a little and spread into the pastry-lined flan cases. Cover with the rest of the pastry, prick the top a few times with a fork and bake at 325°F/160°C/gas 3, for 30–45 minutes, until the pastry is cooked but not brown. Turn out of the tins and leave to cool.

To serve immediately: dredge with icing sugar and serve.

To freeze: cool and freeze.

To serve after freezing: put the frozen tart into a hot oven (425°F/220°C/gas 7) for 10 to 15 minutes and leave to thaw for one to two hours. Serve as above.

Winter

SMOKED HADDOCK • SMOKED MACKEREL • PHEASANT • PIGEON
HARE • BEEF • JERUSALEM ARTICHOKES • CELERIAC
LEEKS • POTATOES • CHESTNUTS
CITRUS FRUITS • CHRISTMAS

Smoked Haddock

Smoked haddock is particularly succulent now, especially if it has not been dyed. Stored in the freezer in a creamy sauce, as in the recipe given below, it can be used later to make impromptu supper dishes. It is especially good combined with eggs.

ARBROATH SMOKIES

These are young haddocks left whole and hot-smoked to a dark tarry colour; they are at their best and freshest at this time of year. The quantities given below are enough for a starter for six, or a supper dish for two.

2 Arbroath smokies
2 onions
8 oz (225 g) tomatoes
1 oz (25 g) grated cheese

¹/₂ pt (300 ml) single or
double cream
pepper

Flake the flesh of the smokies and set aside. Grate or finely chop the onions and put half into a small casserole. Pile the fish on top, add the remaining onions and season well with pepper. Cover with a single layer of sliced tomatoes, sprinkle the grated cheese over the top and pour on the cream. Place in a medium oven (375°F/190°C/gas 5) for 20 minutes.

To serve immediately: leave in the oven for a further 10 minutes, until the top is lightly browned.

To freeze: cool and freeze.

To serve after freezing: place the frozen smokies in a hot oven (425°F/220°C/gas 7) for 20 minutes lower the oven to 350°F/175°C/gas 4, and continue to cook for a further 30 to 40 minutes until the dish is hot right through.

SMOKED HADDOCK IN CREAM SAUCE

2 lb (1 kg) smoked haddock	*2 oz (50 g) flour*
1 pt (600 ml) milk	*pepper*
1 onion	
1 bay leaf	**parsley**
2 oz (50 g) butter	

Place the haddock in a large pan, skin side up to prevent it from sticking, cover with the milk, and add the onion cut in quarters and the bay leaf. Bring to the boil, cover closely and remove from the heat. Leave for half an hour, by which time the fish should be cooked and cool enough to handle. Lift out and flake, removing the skin and bones.

Make a sauce with the butter, the flour and the strained milk in which the fish was cooked. When the sauce has thickened add the fish.

To serve immediately: test for seasoning (this dish is very unlikely to need any salt) and add some finely chopped parsley. Serve with rice.

To freeze: cool and freeze. It is useful to divide the mixture into four equal quantities for making any of the recipes given below.

To serve after freezing: tip the frozen haddock into a pan, heat gently and proceed as for immediate eating.

~

SMOKED HADDOCK SOUFFLÉ

1/2 pt (300 ml) smoked haddock	*1/4 pt (150 ml) milk*
in cream sauce (1/4 of the	*1 oz (25 g) grated cheese*
quantity given above)	*2 whole eggs*
1 oz (25 g) butter	*2 egg whites*
1 oz (25 g) flour	*pepper*

rozen haddock in cream sauce can be used straight from the freezer. Frozen egg hites must be allowed to thaw to room temperature before whipping.

Make a sauce with the butter, flour and milk, stir in the frozen haddock and arm thoroughly. Stir in the grated cheese and the egg yolks. Add the pepper d test for seasoning, adding a little salt if necessary. Allow to cool while you hip the egg whites until stiff. Fold into the haddock mixture, pour into a ttered soufflé dish and cook in a moderate oven (375°F/190°C/gas 5) for 35 to minutes. The top should be well risen and browned and the inside still quite eamy. Serve at once.

SMOKED HADDOCK MOUSSE

1 lb (450 g) smoked haddock in cream sauce (half the quantity given in the recipe on p. 157)
1/2 oz (12 g) gelatine
1/8 pt (75 ml) water
1/4 pt (150 ml) mayonnaise
2 hard-boiled eggs

1/8 pt (75 ml) double or whipping cream or crème fraîche
pepper

2 hard-boiled eggs
parsley (optional)
1/2 pt (300 ml) aspic jelly

Frozen smoked haddock should be allowed to thaw, but if you are using it do not freeze the mousse.

Turn the creamed haddock into a large bowl. Melt the gelatine in the water, heat gently and, when it has dissolved, stir into the haddock. Add the mayonnaise and two hard-boiled eggs, finely chopped or mashed. Season. Lightly whip the cream or crème fraîche and fold into the mixture.

For immediate eating: turn the mixture into a soufflé dish and leave to set. Slice the remaining eggs and arrange on the top. A few tiny sprigs of parsley can be added to make the mousse look pretty. Make up 1/2 pt (300 ml) aspic jelly and, when it is cold, pour over enough to cover the eggs. Leave for a couple of hours for the aspic to set.

To freeze: turn into a soufflé dish and freeze.

To serve after freezing: allow to thaw overnight in the refrigerator and complete as for immediate eating.

~

OMELETTE ARNOLD BENNETT

For each omelette use:
2 eggs
2 tbsp smoked haddock in cream sauce (see p. 157)

1/4 oz (10 g) butter
pepper

Frozen haddock in cream sauce can be used straight from the freezer.

Tip the haddock into a pan and heat gently. Make an omelette in the usual way. Just as it is beginning to set, put 2 tbsp of the haddock mixture into the centre of the omelette, fold over and serve.

Smoked Mackerel

SMOKED MACKEREL PÂTÉ

This pâté is best eaten within a month or two of freezing.

2 medium smoked mackerel	1 tsp creamed horseradish
pinch of ground mace	(optional)
3 oz (75 g) butter, melted	freshly ground pepper
8 oz (225 g) curd cheese	
a little lemon juice	lemon wedges

Do not freeze this pâté if you have made it from frozen smoked mackerel.

Remove the skin and bones from the mackerel. Blend the flesh with the mace, butter and curd cheese until smooth. Add lemon juice and pepper to taste, and the horseradish if you are using it.

To serve immediately: put into a bowl or terrine and chill in the refrigerator for an hour or so before serving. Serve with lemon wedges.

To freeze: freeze in plastic containers, sealed very tightly so that the fishy smell does not penetrate the rest of the freezer.

To serve after freezing: thaw in the refrigerator overnight. Serve as above.

Pheasant

Pheasants freeze well raw. Pluck and draw each bird and wipe the inside. Wrap individually before freezing.

ROAST PHEASANT

If you have a plump young pheasant the simplest, and one of the most delicious, ways to cook it is to roast it. Frozen birds must be allowed to thaw thoroughly overnight in the refrigerator.

Cover the breast with slices of bacon and roast in a moderate oven (350°F/175°C/gas 4) for 50 to 60 minutes. About 10 minutes before serving remove the bacon, sprinkle a little flour over the breast, baste and return to the oven. Baste once or twice more to brown.

To serve immediately: traditionally roast pheasant is served with game chips, fried breadcrumbs, bread sauce, redcurrant jelly and gravy. Braised chestnuts and onion compôte are also excellent (see pp. 192 and 72).

~

PHEASANT À LA CRÈME

2 pheasants, fresh or frozen	a pinch of thyme and 1 bay leaf
1 oz (25 g) butter	2 tbsp brandy
1 tbsp olive oil	1/2 pt (300 ml) double cream
2 medium onions	or crème fraîche
2 carrots	salt and pepper

Frozen pheasants must be allowed to thaw thoroughly before cooking.

Melt the butter and oil in a flameproof casserole and brown the pheasants all over. Add the finely chopped onions and carrots, the thyme and the bay leaf. Cover the casserole and leave on a very low heat for 20 minutes. Warm the brandy, pour over the pheasants and set alight. Douse with the cream or crème fraîche. Season, cover the casserole again and continue to simmer until the pheasants are tender – probably another 30 minutes. Test for seasoning, remove the bay leaf and serve.

To freeze: cool and freeze.

To serve after freezing: thaw in the refrigerator overnight. Heat gently in the casserole on top of the stove or in a low oven (325°F/160°C/gas 3) for about 40 minutes.

~

PHEASANT WITH HERBS

This dish goes well with natural (brown) rice.

2 pheasants, fresh or frozen	*³/₈ pt (250 ml) white wine*
1 onion	*2 tbsp cream*
2 oz (50 g) butter	*salt and pepper*
8 cloves garlic	
6 bay leaves	*1 tbsp chopped parsley*
¹/₂ tsp thyme	

Frozen pheasants must be allowed to thaw thoroughly before cooking.

Cut the pheasants into serving pieces and make a stock with the carcasses and the onion. While this is simmering, season the pieces of pheasant and brown gently in the butter in a flameproof casserole. Add the whole cloves of garlic, bay leaves, thyme and wine. Cover the casserole and simmer until the pheasants are tender – about 30 minutes, but longer may be necessary. When they are done, take out and, for immediate eating, transfer to a serving dish and keep warm. Remove the garlic and bay leaves from the casserole and add ¹/₂–³/₄ pt (300–450 ml) of the stock, according to how much sauce you like. Add the cream, bring to the boil and stir until the sauce is smooth.

To serve immediately: test the sauce for seasoning, pour over the pheasants and serve, sprinkled with the chopped parsley.

To freeze: cool the pheasants and sauce, and freeze in a plastic container.

To serve after freezing: tip the frozen pheasants into a flameproof casserole or heavy pan and warm through over a very gentle heat, stirring from time to time. Allow at least 40 minutes for this. Sprinkle with chopped parsley before serving.

PHEASANT CASSEROLE WITH MUSHROOMS

2 pheasants, fresh or frozen	STUFFING
2 tbsp olive oil	4 oz (100 g) cooked ham
2 oz (50 g) butter	4 tbsp cooked rice (approx.
1 medium onion	1½ oz/40 g uncooked)
2 cloves garlic	1 tsp each thyme and
½ pt (300 ml) stock	marjoram, finely chopped
1 lb (450 g) button	2 tbsp brandy (optional)
mushrooms, fresh or frozen	1 egg
sautéed	salt and pepper

Frozen pheasants must be allowed to thaw thoroughly before cooking. Frozen mushrooms can be used straight from the freezer: if you use them you will only need 1 oz (25 g) butter.

Make the stuffing first. Chop the ham finely, add the rice and finely chopped herbs, season, and mix with the brandy and enough egg to make the mixture soft but not mushy.

Stuff the pheasants, truss firmly, and brown well in a flameproof casserole in the oil and 1 oz (25 g) butter, with the finely chopped onion and the garlic. Add the stock, cover the casserole and place in a slow oven (300°F/150°C/gas 2) until the birds are nearly cooked (about two hours). Meanwhile sauté the whole mushrooms in the rest of the butter or, if you are using frozen sautéed mushrooms, heat gently. Add to the casserole at the end of the cooking time. The dish is now ready to serve.

To freeze: cool and freeze.

To serve after freezing: thaw in the refrigerator overnight. Heat gently in the casserole on top of the stove or in a low oven (325°F/160°C/gas 3) for about 40 minutes.

If there is any left over, it is delicious cold.

NORMANDY PHEASANT

2 pheasants, fresh or frozen	1 small glass calvados or
2 oz (50 g) butter	brandy
1 tbsp oil	1/4 pt (150 ml) stock
1 onion	1/2 pt (300 ml) single cream
4 medium cooking apples	salt and pepper

Frozen pheasants must be allowed to thaw thoroughly before cooking.

Melt the butter and oil in a flameproof casserole and brown the birds on all sides. Lift out, and sauté the chopped onion and the peeled, cored and chopped apples until slightly soft. Replace the pheasants on top, pour over the calvados or brandy and set alight. Douse with the stock and cream. Season, cover the casserole and cook over a very low heat, or in a moderate oven (350°F/175°C/gas 4), for 40 to 50 minutes or until the birds are tender. Adjust the seasoning and, if the apples were very sour, add a little sugar.

The sauce should now be fairly smooth but, if you like, you can lift out the pheasants and pass through a sieve or blend.

To serve immediately: carve the pheasants, replace in the casserole with the sauce, warm through and serve.

To freeze: cool and freeze.

To serve after freezing: thaw in the refrigerator overnight. Heat gently in the casserole on top of the stove or in a low oven (325°F/160°C/gas 3) for about 40 minutes.

NOTE Chicken is also delicious cooked in this way.

Pigeon

Pigeons are a cheap source of meat and keep well in the freezer. Wrap individually before freezing.

PIGEONS À LA CRÈME

4 pigeons, fresh or frozen	a squeeze of lemon juice
2 oz (50 g) butter	salt and pepper
1 tbsp oil	
4 rashers bacon	1/2 pt (300 ml) single cream
1/2 pt (300 ml) white wine	2 egg yolks
1 tbsp brandy (optional)	

Frozen pigeons must be allowed to thaw thoroughly before cooking.

Melt the butter and oil in a large flameproof casserole and brown the pigeons on all sides. Place them breast-side up, cover each one with a rasher to keep the meat moist, pour on the wine and add the brandy, the squeeze of lemon juice, and the salt and pepper. Cover and simmer over a gentle heat for 30 to 40 minutes until tender.

Lift the pigeons out of the casserole and keep warm while you are making the sauce. Strain the liquid in the casserole. Whisk together the egg yolks and the cream and stir into the liquid. Cook over a gentle heat until the sauce thickens, but do not allow to boil.

To serve immediately: return the pigeons to the casserole and heat through. Test for seasoning and serve.

To freeze: cool and freeze the pigeons with the sauce.

To serve after freezing: allow to thaw overnight in the refrigerator or for at least four to five hours at room temperature. Heat through gently on top of the stove, making sure the sauce does not come to the boil.

NOTE This dish is particularly good served with a purée of artichokes (see p. 181).

CASSEROLE OF PIGEONS AND MUSHROOMS

4 pigeons, fresh or frozen
2 oz (50 g) streaky bacon
2 tsp flour
1/2 pt (300 ml) water
1/2 pt (300 ml) white wine
bouquet garni

8 oz (225 g) button onions,
  fresh or frozen blanched
8 oz (225 g) mushrooms, fresh
  or frozen sautéed
2 oz (50 g) butter
salt and pepper

Frozen pigeons must be allowed to thaw thoroughly before cooking. Frozen onions and frozen sautéed mushrooms can be used straight from the freezer.

Melt the diced bacon in a flameproof casserole and gently brown the pigeons on all sides. Remove from the casserole, sprinkle in the flour, and stir for a minute or two until brown. Add the water and wine and the bouquet garni. Season. Boil for a few minutes, replace the pigeons, cover the casserole and leave to simmer for about 40 minutes, until the pigeons are tender. Meanwhile brown the onions in the butter in a separate pan, add the sliced or chopped fresh mushrooms, and sauté gently. Add mushrooms and onions to the casserole for the last 15 minutes of cooking, stirring in well (this should be sufficient time for frozen mushrooms to thaw).

To serve immediately: take the pigeons out of the casserole and keep warm on a serving dish. Remove the bouquet garni. If the cooking liquid is too thin, thicken with a beurre manié made with 1 tbsp flour and 1/2 oz (12 g) butter. Test for seasoning, pour over the pigeons and serve.

To freeze: remove the bouquet garni, cool and freeze.

To serve after freezing: allow to thaw overnight in the refrigerator or for at least four to five hours at room temperature. Heat through gently on top of the stove or in a medium oven (350°F/175°C/gas 4), and complete as above.

PIGEONS IN RED CABBAGE

4 pigeons, fresh or frozen
2 oz (50 g) butter
4 rashers streaky bacon
2 onions
1 apple
1 medium red cabbage
1/4 pt (150 ml) red wine or a
  mixture of wine vinegar and
  water
2 tbsp brown sugar

6 juniper berries
juice of 1/2 lemon
salt and pepper

} or 2–2 1/2 lb (900–1 1/4 kg)
frozen red cabbage
(see p. 114)

Frozen pigeons should be allowed to thaw for at least three to four hours before cooking. Frozen red cabbage can be used straight from the freezer.

Melt the butter and the chopped bacon in a flameproof casserole and brown the pigeons on all sides. Remove from the casserole.

If you are using fresh red cabbage, brown the chopped onions and the chopped, peeled apple. Finely slice the red cabbage and add to the casserole, together with the remaining ingredients, stir, and heat through.

If you are using frozen cabbage, put in the casserole with a little water, the juniper berries and the lemon juice, and heat slowly. Season.

As soon as the cabbage is hot, place the pigeons on top, cover, and leave over a very low heat for 2 1/2–3 hours. Check from time to time to see that the cabbage is not catching, and if necessary add a little more liquid (water, stock or wine).

To serve immediately: when the cabbage is cooked, test for seasoning and serve.

To freeze: cool and freeze in a plastic container.

To serve after freezing: allow to thaw overnight in the refrigerator or for at least four to five hours at room temperature, and heat through gently on top of the stove. You may need to add a little water, stock or wine.

PIGEONS IN TOMATO SAUCE

4 pigeons, fresh or frozen	*¹/₄ pt (150 ml) water*
2 oz (50 g) streaky bacon	*bouquet garni*
1 onion	*1 tbsp brown sugar*
1 clove garlic	*8 oz (225 g) mushrooms, fresh*
2 lb (900 g) tomatoes, fresh or	*or frozen sautéed*
frozen raw	*salt and pepper*

Frozen pigeons should be allowed to thaw for at least three to four hours before cooking. Frozen tomatoes and frozen sautéed mushrooms can be used straight from the freezer.

Melt the diced bacon in a flameproof casserole, add the finely chopped onion and garlic and gently brown the pigeons. Add the skinned tomatoes (chopped if you are using fresh ones), the water and the bouquet garni. Season and add the sugar. Bring to the boil, cover the casserole, and cook in a medium oven (350°F/175°C/gas 4) for 1¹/₂ hours. The mushrooms should be added for the last half hour (chopped if you are using fresh ones). Test for seasoning and serve.

To freeze: cool and freeze.

To serve after freezing: allow to thaw overnight in the refrigerator or for at least four to five hours at room temperature. Heat through gently on top of the stove for about half an hour or in a medium oven (350°F/175°C/gas 4) for at least 45 minutes.

Hare

Hare is one of the cheapest varieties of meat, and it loses none of its characteristic flavour in freezing. If it is more convenient to freeze the hare raw, either joint it or leave it whole, but be sure to wrap it very well.

HARE SOUP

leftovers and bones of hare	*bouquet garni*
2 oz (50 g) butter	*approx. 4 pt (2 litres) water*
1 onion	*12 peppercorns*
1 carrot	*1 small glass port*
1 celery stalk	*salt*
1 tbsp cornflour	

Melt the butter in a large pan, and quickly fry the bones and pieces of hare and the roughly chopped vegetables. Stir in the cornflour, add the bouquet garni, the water, the peppercorns and some salt, put the lid on the pan and simmer gently for about two hours. Remove the meat and the bones from the pan, chop the meat roughly and return to the pan. Add the port, test for seasoning, reheat and serve.

To freeze: cool and freeze.

To serve after freezing: tip the frozen soup into a pan and heat slowly.

HARE CASSEROLE WITH FORCEMEAT BALLS

The marinating and slow cooking make this the richest and most aromatic of all the hare dishes, while the herbs in the forcemeat balls add a very pleasant freshness.

1 hare, fresh or frozen
6 cloves garlic
6 bay leaves
peel of 1 lemon
¼ pt (150 ml) olive oil
1 bottle red wine
3 oz (75 g) flour

10 cloves or 1 tsp powdered
cloves
2 rashers streaky bacon or
1 oz (25 g) butter and
1 tbsp olive oil
salt and pepper

Frozen hare must be allowed to thaw thoroughly before cooking.

Cut the meat off the bones and put into a large bowl. Add the roughly chopped garlic, the bay leaves, the thinly pared rind of lemon, the olive oil and as much of the wine as you have room for in the bowl, and leave to marinate overnight.

The next day drain the pieces of meat, dry well and roll in the seasoned flour, to which you have added freshly ground black pepper and the crushed or powdered cloves. Melt the chopped rashers of bacon or the oil and butter in a flameproof casserole. Quickly brown each piece of meat, add any of the seasoned flour that remains, stir well and cook for a few minutes. Pour on the strained marinating liquid and any remaining wine, raise the heat and bring to the boil. Put the lid on the casserole, place in a slow oven (300°F/150°C/gas 2) and cook for five to six hours, by which time the meat and sauce will have reduced to a rich stew. Test for seasoning.

To serve immediately: serve with forcemeat balls (see below), baked potatoes and, if possible, quince, medlar or crab-apple jelly.

To freeze: cool and freeze.

To serve after freezing: tip the frozen hare into a heavy pan or flameproof casserole and warm gently, stirring from time to time (allow at least 40 minutes for this). Serve as above.

FORCEMEAT BALLS

4 oz (100 g) fresh	*2 tbsp milk*
breadcrumbs	*1–2 oz (25–50 g) butter*
1 tsp chopped parsley	*1 tbsp oil*
1 tsp chopped marjoram	*salt and pepper*
½ tsp thyme	
finely grated rind of 1 lemon	*1 oz (25 g) butter*
1 egg	*1 tbsp oil*

Mix the breadcrumbs with the herbs, the seasoning and the lemon peel. Add the egg lightly beaten with the milk, and the just-melted butter. Mix all well together and roll the mixture into little balls about the size of a walnut.

To serve immediately: fry quickly in the butter and oil and drop into the hare casserole just before serving.

To freeze: wrap and freeze.

To serve after freezing: fry the frozen forcemeat balls in the butter and oil and drop into the hare casserole just before serving.

ROAST SADDLE OF HARE

1 saddle of hare, fresh or
 frozen
4 oz (100 g) sliced streaky
 bacon
2 oz (50 g) butter or 2 tbsp oil

$^1/_2$ pt (300 ml) red wine
1 tbsp port or Madeira
1 tbsp redcurrant jelly
salt and pepper

Frozen hare must be allowed to thaw thoroughly before cooking.

Wrap the saddle of hare in the bacon and place in a roasting tin with the butter or oil. Roast in a hot oven (425°F/220°C/gas 7) for half an hour. Take the meat off the bones, remove the skin, and carve into thick slices.

Add the red wine to the roasting pan together with the port or Madeira and the redcurrant jelly. Season. Return the meat to the pan and continue to cook in a moderate oven (350°F/175°C/gas 4) for a further 20 minutes or until the meat is completely cooked. The dish is now ready to serve.

To freeze: cool and freeze with the sauce.

To serve after freezing: tip the frozen meat into a flameproof casserole and warm through gently for at least half an hour or until the meat is hot right through.

ROAST SADDLE OF HARE IN CREAM

1 saddle of hare, fresh or frozen	*1 tsp finely chopped thyme*
1 tbsp olive oil	*2 oz (50 g) butter*
1 tsp wine vinegar	*¼ pt (150 ml) double cream*
1 tsp finely chopped rosemary	*or crème fraîche*
leaves	*salt and pepper*

Frozen hare must be allowed to thaw thoroughly before cooking.

Remove the iridescent skin from the saddle, place in a roasting tin, drizzle over the oil and vinegar and sprinkle on the salt, pepper and herbs. Leave to marinate for three to four hours, turning from time to time.

Melt the butter in a small pan and, when it starts to sizzle, pour over the hare. Roast in a moderate oven (375°F/190°C/gas 5) for 35–40 minutes, turning the meat occasionally. Take care not to allow the sediment in the pan to burn, as this would give a bitter taste.

When the meat is done, remove from the oven and carve into thick slices. Keep warm. Pour the cream or crème fraîche into the roasting pan and stir over a moderate heat, scraping up all the sediment in the bottom of the pan. Bring to the boil, test for seasoning, and add a few more drops of wine vinegar if the sauce does not have enough bite.

To serve immediately: pour the sauce over the hare and serve very hot.

To freeze: cool and freeze.

To serve after freezing: allow to thaw for at least three to four hours, turn into a casserole and heat gently on top of the stove. When the hare has completely thawed, bring just to the boil, add a little more cream and seasoning if necessary, and serve as above.

JUGGED HARE

When making this recipe, you may like to keep the saddle for roasting (see pp. 171–2). Preserve the blood carefully – ask your butcher to keep it for you if he is jointing the hare – as it is an essential part of this recipe.

1 hare	*bouquet garni*
2 oz (50 g) butter	*2 cloves*
4 oz (100 g) streaky bacon	*1 lb (450 g) button*
1 lb (450 g) button onions,	*mushrooms (optional)*
fresh, or frozen blanched	*1 tbsp redcurrant jelly*
2 oz (50 g) flour	*1 tbsp port or Madeira*
1 pt (600 ml) red wine	*salt and pepper*

Frozen hare must be allowed to thaw thoroughly before cooking, but button onions can be used straight from the freezer.

Joint the hare. Melt the butter in a heavy pan or flameproof casserole and brown the pieces of hare. Remove from the pan and fry the diced bacon and the onions until golden brown. Remove these also from the pan. Stir in the flour and, when slightly browned, slowly pour on the wine, stirring to prevent lumps. Add the salt, pepper, bouquet garni and cloves and return the meat, bacon and onions to the pan. Cover and simmer slowly for two hours or place in a low oven (300°F/150°C/gas 2). Add the whole mushrooms and continue to cook for a further 20 minutes or until the meat is tender.

Take out the meat and bring the sauce to a rapid boil for five minutes to reduce. Add the redcurrant jelly, the port or Madeira and, lastly, the blood, adding very slowly and taking care not to allow the sauce to boil, as the blood would then curdle.

To serve immediately: replace the meat in the casserole, test for seasoning and serve.

To freeze: allow to cool and strip the meat off the bones as far as possible, since they are quite large and take up a lot of freezer space. Freeze.

To serve after freezing: tip the frozen hare into a heavy pan or flameproof casserole and warm through gently for about 40 minutes or until the meat is hot. Do not allow to boil. Test for seasoning and serve.

Beef

BOEUF EN DAUBE

This dish is good served with ribbon noodles, boiled potatoes or polenta.

3 lb (1½ kg) braising beef
(chuck or skirt), fresh or
frozen
3 tbsp olive oil
1–1½ lb (450–675 g) onions
2 cloves garlic
1 carrot
3 tomatoes, peeled and roughly
chopped, or 1 tbsp
concentrated tomato purée

bouquet garni
2 cloves
thin strip of orange peel
piece of celery, sliced
1 pt (600 ml) red wine
(it doesn't matter how cheap
or old)
approx. 4 oz (100 g) black
olives (optional)
salt and pepper

Frozen beef should be allowed to thaw until it is soft enough to cut.

Trim the fat off the meat and cut into bite-sized pieces. Heat the oil in a flameproof casserole and brown the meat. Slice the onions and garlic, cut the carrot into strips, and add to the casserole. When they begin to brown, put in the rest of the ingredients (except for the olives), and season. The wine should three-quarters cover the contents of the casserole; if necessary, make up with stock or water. Bring to the boil, cover, and transfer to a very low oven (250°F/120°C/gas 1) for three to four hours. The liquid does not thicken, but remains of a gravy-like consistency. Add the olives about half an hour before the end of the cooking time.

To serve immediately: test for seasoning and serve.

To freeze: allow to cool, skim any fat from the top, and freeze.

To serve after freezing: allow to thaw for at least three to four hours. Heat very gently on top of the stove, stirring from time to time. Allow about one hour for this quantity.

BEEF AND ONION CASSEROLE

3 lb (1½ kg) braising beef,   *1 oz (25 g) butter*
fresh or frozen   *1 tbsp oil*
8 oz (225 g) button onions,   *bouquet garni*
fresh, or frozen blanched   *1½ pt (900 ml) stock*
1½ lb (675 g) carrots, fresh,   *2 tbsp concentrated tomato*
or frozen blanched   *purée*
3 oz (75 g) seasoned flour   *salt and pepper*

Frozen beef should be allowed to thaw until it is soft enough to cut, but onions and carrots can be used straight from the freezer.

Trim the meat and cut into 1-in (2-cm) cubes. Roll in the seasoned flour and brown evenly in the butter and oil in a large frying pan.

Transfer the meat to a casserole and add the onions, the carrots (cut into slices if they are large) and the bouquet garni.

Add the remaining flour to the frying pan, and cook over a moderate heat until it has browned. Draw off the heat and stir in the stock. Bring to the boil, stirring all the time. Season, and add the tomato purée. Strain into the casserole. Cover and cook in a slow oven (300°F/150°C/gas 2) for about 2½ hours, until the meat is tender.

To serve immediately: test for seasoning and serve.

To freeze: cool and freeze.

To serve after freezing: allow to thaw for at least three to four hours before warming very gently over a low heat, stirring from time to time.

BEEF OLIVES

2 lb (900 g) beef (topside,
  rump steak or best-quality
  braising steak), fresh or
  frozen
4 oz (100 g) fresh
  breadcrumbs
2 onions
8 oz (225 g) mushrooms, fresh,
  or frozen sautéed

zest of 1 lemon
large handful of parsley
1 egg
2 tbsp olive oil
1 tbsp flour
approx. ½ pt (300 ml) stock
1 clove garlic
1 tbsp French mustard
salt and pepper

If you are using frozen meat it is easiest to slice while it is still fairly hard at the centre. Frozen mushrooms should be allowed to thaw until they are soft enough to chop.

Trim the fat off the beef and slice very thinly. Beat out each piece with a rolling pin, season, and trim into squares or oblongs large enough to roll round a spoonful of stuffing.

Mix the breadcrumbs with the chopped onions and chopped mushrooms, add the thinly pared and finely chopped lemon zest and the parsley, season, and bind with the egg.

Place one dessertspoonful of the mixture on each piece of meat, roll into little sausage shapes and either secure with a toothpick or wind round with thread. In a flameproof casserole, brown each beef olive rapidly in the oil on all sides and remove. Sprinkle the flour into the casserole and allow to brown gently, then return the olives and cover with the stock, to which you have added the crushed clove of garlic. Simmer over a low heat, uncovered, for 45 minutes, by which time the meat should be cooked and the sauce thickened. Stir the French mustard into the sauce and test for seasoning – it should be fairly sharp to make a pleasant contrast with the fresh taste of the stuffing.

To serve immediately: remove the toothpicks or thread before serving.

To freeze: cool and freeze.

To serve after freezing: allow to thaw for two to three hours. Heat very gently on top of the stove. Allow about 40 minutes for this. You may need to add a little more stock or water. Serve as above.

POT-AU-FEU

This classic French dish will provide two courses for a family meal; the stock can be served first as a clear soup, and the meat and vegetables make up the main course. It should be cooked in as large a quantity as your biggest pan will hold. The meat is also excellent cold, and the stock may be used for any number of purposes later. Do not use less than the quantities given here, as a smaller piece of beef would probably disintegrate during the long cooking.

2–3 lb (1–1¹/₂ kg) beef bones
3-lb (1¹/₂-kg) piece topside
1 onion
1 carrot for stock
1 clove garlic
a large bouquet garni
a piece of lemon peel
1 lb (450 g) onions

1 lb (450 g) carrots, fresh, or
*   frozen blanched whole*
1 lb (450 g) leeks, fresh or
*   frozen blanched whole*
some slices of French bread
*   (optional)*
salt and pepper

For this recipe both meat and vegetables may be used straight from the freezer.

Put the bones in a very large pan and cover with cold water. If you have a chicken carcass in the freezer, put this in also. Bring the water very slowly to boiling point and, as it continues to simmer, skim off the scum that will form on top. When the water is clear add the topside, skim again and, when no more scum rises, add the onion, carrot, garlic, bouquet garni, lemon peel and seasoning, and continue to simmer very slowly, so that the water is barely moving, for about four hours. At the end of this time remove the meat and set aside. Take out the bones and strain the stock. Allow the stock to cool and remove the fat.

Return the meat to the stock, test for seasoning and add more salt and pepper and another bouquet garni if necessary. Add the onions and the whole carrots, simmer for another 30 minutes, add the whole leeks and cook until tender.

To serve: start by serving the soup. You can toast some pieces of French bread, spread them with the marrow from the bones, and float one in each bowl.

Serve the meat, surrounded by the vegetables, for the second course. You can serve it with a little of the stock, or make some gravy by thickening some of the stock with a little beurre manié and boiling for five minutes.

Any meat that is left over will taste excellent served cold, with horseradish sauce or mayonnaise, or diced and mixed into a rice or potato salad.

The remainder of the stock may be frozen.

CARBONNADE DE BOEUF FLAMANDE

2 lb (900 g) braising beef	1 tbsp oil
(chuck or skirt) or best-	1 lb (450 g) onions
quality stewing beef, fresh	1/2 pt (300 ml) dark ale or
or frozen	stout
2 tbsp flour	bouquet garni
1 oz (25 g) butter	salt and pepper

Frozen beef should be allowed to thaw until it is soft enough to cut.

Trim the fat off the meat and cut into large cubes. Season the flour liberally with salt and pepper and roll each piece of meat in it. Heat the butter and oil in a heavy pan or flameproof casserole, and quickly brown the meat on all sides. Remove from the pan, add the sliced onions and cook over a low heat until they are soft but not brown. Remove from the pan. Add any remaining flour and stir over the heat for a minute or two. Slowly pour the ale or stout into the casserole, and stir well to dissolve any sediment at the bottom of the pan. Return the meat and onions to the pan, add the bouquet garni, cover, and cook in a slow oven (300°F/150°C/gas 2) or over a very low heat for two hours, by which time the meat should be tender and the sauce quite thick. Remove the bouquet garni.

To serve immediately: test for seasoning and serve.

To freeze: allow to cool, skim off any fat and freeze.

To serve after freezing: allow to thaw for at least three to four hours. Heat very gently on top of the stove, stirring from time to time. Allow about one hour for this quantity.

~

BOEUF STROGANOFF

This is an excellent way of stretching one of the more expensive cuts of beef.

1 1/2 lb (675 g) rump steak,	4 oz (100 g) butter
fresh or frozen	2 onions
8 oz (225 g) mushrooms	squeeze of lemon juice
(or more), fresh or frozen	1 glass white wine
sautéed	1/2 pt (300 ml) sour cream
1 clove garlic	salt and pepper

If you are using frozen meat, it is easiest to slice before it has completely thawed Frozen sautéed mushrooms can be used straight from the freezer.

Slice the beef as thinly as possible. Beat out very thin and rub each slice on both sides with a cut clove of garlic. Season. Cut each slice into strips ½ in (1 cm) wide and 3–4 in (8–10 cm) long. Melt half the butter in a frying pan and fry the beef very quickly on both sides. Set aside and keep warm. Put the rest of the butter in a pan and gently fry the finely chopped onions. When they are soft add the sliced fresh mushrooms and a squeeze of lemon juice and cook for five minutes. If you are using frozen sautéed mushrooms, they should be added at this point. Add the wine and let it bubble over a raised heat, then stir in the sour cream and the strips of beef.

To serve immediately: test for seasoning and heat all well together for not more than a minute or two. Serve with rice.

To freeze: cool and freeze.

To serve after freezing: if possible, allow to thaw for at least two to three hours. Tip into a pan, heat very gently, stirring frequently, and bring to near simmering point, but do not allow to boil. This will take about 20 minutes. You may need to add a little more cream or sour cream.

~

STEAK AND KIDNEY PUDDING

1¼ lb (550 g) chuck steak, fresh or frozen	*¼ pt (150 ml) stock or water*
8 oz (225 g) ox kidney, fresh or frozen	CRUST
1½ tbsp flour	*6 oz (175 g) flour*
1 medium onion	*3 oz (75 g) suet*
	salt and pepper

Allow frozen meat to thaw until it is soft enough to cut.

Butter a 2-pt (1-litre) pudding basin.

For the crust, mix the flour and suet together, season, and add enough water to make a very stiff paste. Roll this out fairly thinly, leaving aside enough for the top, and line the basin.

Trim the fat off the steak and remove the skin and core from the kidney. Cut both into bite-sized pieces and roll in the seasoned flour. Chop the onion finely and mix with the meat.

Put the meat in the basin, add the stock or water, cover with the rest of the suet crust and put a piece of foil over the top, tucking it securely down over the rim. Steam for three hours and turn out on to a warmed dish.

When you serve the pudding you may want to pour in a little hot water to increase the quantity of gravy.

STEAK AND KIDNEY PIE

2 lb (900 g) steak (rump, skirt or chuck), fresh or frozen	bay leaf, marjoram and 2 cloves
8 oz (225 g) ox kidney, fresh or frozen	10 oz (275 g) puff or shortcrust pastry (see p. 218)
2 oz (50 g) flour	1 tbsp sherry
2 oz (50 g) butter	a few drops of Worcestershire or
2 onions	Tabasco sauce
¹/₂ pt (300 ml) stock	salt and pepper

Allow frozen meat to thaw until it is soft enough to cut into bite-sized pieces.

Trim the fat off the steak and remove the skin and core from the kidney. Roll the meat in the well-seasoned flour. Melt the butter in a heavy pan, sauté the chopped onions, and brown the meat quickly. Sprinkle in any remaining flour, allow to cook for one minute, and add the stock, herbs and seasoning. Cover and simmer for about one hour or until the meat is tender. Remove the bay leaf, add the sherry and sauce, and test for seasoning.

Turn the meat into well-greased pie-dishes. The quantities given will make one 2-pt (1-litre) dish or two 1-pt (500-ml) dishes.

To serve immediately: cover the meat with the pastry, make one or two incisions in the top and cook in a hot oven (425°F/220°C/gas 7) for half an hour or until the pastry is golden brown.

To freeze: the pie may be frozen with the pastry cooked or uncooked. If you are freezing it uncooked, allow the meat to cool before covering it with pastry. Wrap and freeze. If you are freezing it cooked, continue as for immediate eating, allow to cool, wrap and freeze.

To serve after freezing: if the pie was frozen uncooked, make one or two incisions in the pastry. Place the frozen pie in a hot oven (425°F/220°C/gas 7). After half an hour turn the oven down to 350°F/175°C/gas 4, and cook for a further 20 minutes if the pie was frozen cooked, or 40 minutes if it was frozen uncooked. If the pastry seems to be getting too brown, cover with a piece of foil towards the end of the cooking time.

Jerusalem Artichokes

To freeze blanched: peel the artichokes and cut into pieces roughly the same size. Blanch for three minutes. Drain, cool and freeze.

To freeze puréed: peel the artichokes and cut into pieces roughly the same size. Cook in a little water or stock until soft. Drain very thoroughly and blend. Cool and freeze.

To serve after freezing blanched: turn the frozen artichokes into a pan with a tablespoon or so of water – just enough to keep them from catching – and a knob of butter. Season, and cook very gently until they are soft.

Tomato purée made from fresh tomatoes (see p. 129) goes well with Jerusalem artichokes. Warm up a little – about 1/4 pt (150 ml) to 1 lb (450 g) artichokes – and pour over just before serving.

To serve after freezing puréed: turn the frozen purée into a pan, add a knob of butter, and warm through over a very gentle heat, stirring from time to time. Add pepper and a little cream, or some fresh tomato purée.

ARTICHOKE SOUP

3 lb (1 1/2 kg) artichokes, fresh, or frozen blanched or puréed	salt and pepper
1 oz (25 g) butter	1/2 pt (300 ml) milk
1 onion	a little cream and chopped
2 pt (1 litre) light stock	parsley (optional)

Frozen artichokes can be used straight from the freezer.

Peel and cut fresh artichokes into roughly equal pieces. Melt the butter in a heavy pan, sweat the chopped onion for a few minutes, add the artichokes and allow to cook for another minute or two. Pour on the stock, season and simmer gently until the artichokes are cooked. Blend.

To serve immediately: return the soup to the pan and add the milk. Test for seasoning. Serve hot, adding if you like a spoonful of cream and a sprinkling of parsley to each helping.

To freeze: cool and freeze.

To serve after freezing: tip the frozen soup into a pan, add the milk, heat gently and serve as above.

BRAISED ARTICHOKES

2 lb (1 kg) artichokes, fresh or
 frozen blanched
1 lb (450 g) button onions,
 fresh or frozen blanched

1 oz (25 g) butter
1 tbsp sugar
salt and pepper

Frozen artichokes and onions can be used straight from the freezer, but do not then freeze the dish.

Peel and cut fresh artichokes into roughly equal pieces. In a heavy pan or flameproof casserole melt the butter, add the sugar and stir. Add the artichokes and onions, cover, and leave to braise over a very low heat for about 40 minutes, or until the artichokes and onions are tender and golden brown (frozen artichokes will not take quite so long). Stir occasionally to ensure even browning. Season with salt and plenty of freshly ground pepper. Serve.

To freeze: cool and freeze.

To serve after freezing: it is important that the artichokes should not turn into a purée in the reheating, so they should be allowed to thaw for about four hours at room temperature, and then heated in a moderate oven (350°F/175°C/gas 4) for half an hour. Do not heat them in a saucepan, as they might become mushy when stirred.

NOTE This dish goes excellently with onion compôte (see p. 72), but in this case omit the onions from this recipe.

Celeriac

Celeriac is an extremely useful vegetable; it freezes excellently blanched or cooked.

To freeze blanched: peel the celeriac and cut into cubes or slices. Blanch for four minutes. Drain, cool and freeze.

To freeze puréed: peel the celeriac and cut up roughly. Put into a pan with some good stock: 1/2–3/4 pt (300–450 ml) stock for 2 lb (1 kg) celeriac. Cover and simmer gently until the stock has been absorbed. If necessary, leave the cover off the pan for the last 10 minutes or so. Blend, cool and freeze.

To serve after freezing blanched: tip the frozen celeriac into a pan with a little water or stock and cook gently until soft. Serve with butter or béchamel sauce, or add to potatoes dauphinois (see p. 190). You can also braise the celeriac (see p. 184).

To serve after freezing puréed: tip the frozen purée into a pan, add plenty of butter and heat through gently. Stir in a little cream, test for seasoning and serve.

The purée can be combined with mashed potatoes beaten up with plenty of butter, hot milk and pepper. The proportion of potato to celeriac is not important.

The celeriac can also be baked with sliced parboiled potatoes. Put the vegetables in a greased baking pan, pour over some olive oil and add plenty of pepper, and perhaps a little grated cheese. Bake in a moderate oven for about 1½ hours.

CELERIAC SOUP

1 lb (450 g) celeriac, fresh or frozen blanched
1 large onion
1 oz (25 g) butter
1 lb (450 g) potatoes

1½ pt (900 ml) stock
salt and pepper

½ pt (300 ml) milk
parsley

Frozen blanched celeriac can be used straight from the freezer.

Peel and dice fresh celeriac. Slice the onion and sauté for a few minutes in the butter. Add the celeriac and cook for a further five minutes. Peel and dice the potatoes and add to the pan, together with the stock. Season. Cook until the vegetables are soft, and blend.

To serve immediately: return to the pan, add the milk and bring to the boil. Test for seasoning, and add more milk if the soup is too thick. Like other root vegetables, celeriac sometimes tastes a little sweet: the remedy is lots of seasoning and above all parsley, which adds a delicious flavour.

To freeze: cool and freeze.

To serve after freezing: tip the frozen soup into a pan and heat gently. Serve as above.

BRAISED CELERIAC

2 lb (1 kg) celeriac, fresh or   ¹/₄ pt (150 ml) stock
    frozen blanched   ¹/₈ pt (75 ml) white wine
1 large onion   (or all stock can be used)
1 oz (25 g) butter   salt and pepper

Frozen blanched celeriac can be used straight from the freezer.

Peel fresh celeriac and cut into dice or ¹/₂-in (1-cm) slices. Blanch for five minutes and drain.

Slice the onion and cook gently in the butter in a flameproof casserole until soft. Add the celeriac and pour on the stock, or the stock and wine. Any stock will do, but the tastier it is the better (pheasant stock is delicious). Season. Bring to the boil, cover, and put in a medium oven (350°F/175°C/gas 4) for about half an hour.

To serve immediately: cook for a further 15 minutes or so and serve.

To freeze: cool and freeze with the cooking liquid.

To serve after freezing: put the frozen celeriac into a flameproof casserole and gently heat through on top of the stove, or put into a fairly warm oven (300°F/150°C/gas 2) for about one hour.

Leeks

Leeks are a splendid and versatile vegetable, useful for incorporating in any number of recipes.

To freeze blanched: trim off the coarse outer leaves and tops and wash thoroughly. Blanch for three or four minutes, according to size. Drain, cool and freeze.

Also freeze some cut into 1-in (2-cm) slices and blanched for two minutes.

To serve after freezing: put the frozen leeks in a little boiling water. As they start to soften, break up the mass gently. As soon as they are soft, drain well and serve with a knob of butter, a spoonful of cream or a béchamel or cheese sauce.

LEEK, TOMATO AND POTATO SOUP

1 lb (450 g) fresh leeks or
³/4 lb (350 g) frozen sliced
2 oz (50 g) butter
1 lb (450 g) tomatoes, fresh or
* frozen raw*
1¹/2 lb (675 g) potatoes

1 tbsp sugar
2 pt (1 litre) stock or water
salt and pepper

3 tbsp cream
parsley

Frozen vegetables can be used straight from the freezer.

Cook the sliced leeks gently in the butter in a heavy pan. Add the peeled tomatoes and cook for a few more minutes before putting in the peeled and diced potatoes. Season, add the sugar, and stir well. Add the stock or water, and cook until the potatoes are soft. Blend and test for seasoning. You may want to add a little more sugar.

To serve immediately: bring to the boil again, stir in the cream and sprinkle a little finely chopped parsley over each portion.

To freeze: cool and freeze.

To serve after freezing: turn the frozen soup into a pan and heat through. Add the cream and parsley and serve.

VICHYSSOISE

This is well worth making in large quantities: not only can it be eaten hot in the winter, but it also makes a delicious cold soup in summer, sprinkled with chives.

2 lb (1 kg) fresh leeks or	2 pt (1 litre) stock
1¹/₂ lb (675 g) frozen sliced	salt and pepper
1 medium onion	
1 oz (25 g) butter	¹/₂ pt (300 ml) single cream
2 medium potatoes	chives

Frozen leeks can be used straight from the freezer.

Chop the onion and sweat in the butter for five minutes. Add the sliced leeks and the peeled potatoes cut into cubes. Cook gently in the butter for a further five minutes. Add the stock (veal stock is best), bring to boiling point, season, cover, and simmer for 20 minutes or until the vegetables are soft. Blend.

To serve immediately:

To serve hot – reheat gently, add the cream and test for seasoning. Serve with a sprinkling of chopped chives.

To serve cold – chill, stir in the cream, and serve as above.

To freeze: cool and freeze.

To serve after freezing:

To serve hot – turn into a pan, reheat gently and proceed as above.

To serve cold – allow to thaw at room temperature or in a refrigerator. Stir in the cream when the soup has thawed. If necessary, chill again in the refrigerator and serve as above.

~

CREAMED LEEKS

1¹/₂ lb (675 g) leeks, frozen	2 egg yolks
sliced	2 tbsp milk
2 oz (50 g) butter	salt, pepper and a grate of
1 tsp flour	nutmeg
¹/₄ pt (150 ml) double cream	
or crème fraîche	

Cook the frozen leeks over a very gentle heat until they are tender, and drain very thoroughly. Put the butter in the pan and, when it has melted, add the leeks, the seasoning and the nutmeg. Sprinkle on the flour and stir well over gentle heat until the leeks are very hot. Add the cream, and continue to stir over the heat for two to three minutes. Mix the yolks with the milk and stir in briefly. Test for seasoning, turn out on to a hot dish, and surround with a border of mashed potatoes.

If you make this dish with fresh leeks, you will need 2 lb (1 kg).

~

LEEK QUICHE

2 lb (1 kg) fresh leeks or	*¹/₂ pt (300 ml) stock*
1¹/₂ lb (675 g) frozen sliced	*4 eggs*
10 oz (275 g) shortcrust pastry	*4 oz (100 g) cheese (optional)*
(see p. 218)	*¹/₄ pt (150 ml) cream*
4 oz (100g) bacon or ham	*salt and pepper*
(optional)	

Frozen leeks can be used straight from the freezer.

Butter one 10-in (25-cm) flan tin or two 7-in (18-cm) flan tins. Line with the pastry.

Put the sliced leeks into a pan and add the diced bacon or ham. Add the stock and simmer for about 20 minutes. When the leeks are tender but not mushy drain and reserve the liquid. Spread the leeks and bacon over the pastry cases.

Beat the eggs lightly in a basin, add the grated cheese and the cream and season. Beat in not more than ¹/₄ pt (150 ml) of the reserved stock and pour over the leeks. Cook in a medium oven (375°F/190°C/gas 5) for 40 minutes.

To serve immediately: cook for a further five minutes, until the top is golden brown.

To freeze: cool and freeze.

To serve after freezing: place the frozen quiche in a hot oven (425°F/220°C/gas 7). After 20 minutes lower the temperature to 350°F/175°C/gas 4, and leave for a further 30 to 40 minutes, according to the size of the quiche, until it has heated right through. Place a piece of foil over the top if necessary, to prevent excessive browning.

LEEKS À LA PROVENÇALE

Serve cold as a salad or hors d'oeuvre.

1½ lb (675 g) leeks frozen	*2 oz (50 g) pitted black*
sliced	*olives*
2 tsp olive oil	*1 lemon (juice and rind)*
8 oz (225 g) tomatoes	*salt and pepper*

Heat the oil in a shallow flameproof dish and cook the frozen leeks gently for about 10 minutes, breaking them up until they have quite separated. Add the peeled and chopped tomatoes, the olives, and the juice and finely grated peel of the lemon, and cook for a further 10 minutes, or until the leeks are soft but not mushy. Season to taste, cool and serve.

If you make this dish with fresh leeks you will need 2 lb (1 kg).

~

LEEK PIE

1 lb (450 g) fresh leeks or	*2 oz (50 g) butter*
12 oz (350 g) frozen sliced	*2 egg yolks*
10 oz (275 g) shortcrust pastry	*2 tbsp cream*
(see p. 218)	*salt and pepper*

Frozen leeks can be used straight from the freezer.

Butter an 8-in (20-cm) flan tin and line with the pastry, keeping aside enough for the top.

Cook the sliced leeks gently in the butter until they are soft. Stir in the beaten yolks and the cream. Season.

To serve immediately: pour the mixture into the flan case and cover with the rest of the pastry. Cook in a fairly hot oven (400°F/200°C/gas 6) until the pastry is done – about 45 minutes. Serve very hot.

To freeze: allow the mixture to cool and, when it is quite cold, pour into the flan case and cover with the rest of the pastry. Freeze.

To serve after freezing: place the frozen pie in a hot oven (450°F/230°C/gas 8) After 30 minutes turn the oven down to 350°F/175°C/gas 4, cover the pie with foil, and cook for a further 30 minutes, or until the pie is heated all the way through. Serve very hot.

Potatoes

There is little point in freezing potatoes, as they are a year-round vegetable, and it is good to enjoy the different varieties in their seasons. However, mashed potatoes, should you have cooked too many, freeze well (they are particularly good if you mash them with olive oil instead of butter). There are, too, a few winter potato dishes which freeze excellently. So when you wish to cook any of the following dishes it is worth making double quantities and freezing half for another occasion.

POTATO SOUP

2 lb (1 kg) potatoes
1 lb (450 g) onions or 4
    medium leeks or a mixture
    of the two
2 oz (50 g) butter
2 sticks of celery
3 pt (1½ litres) light stock

salt and pepper

5–6 tbsp cream
milk (optional)
chopped parsley
croûtons (optional)

Slice the onions or the white part of the leeks, and cook lightly in the butter. Add the chopped celery sticks, the peeled and roughly chopped potatoes and the stock. Season, cover and simmer gently for about 15 minutes until all the vegetables are soft. Blend until smooth.

To serve immediately: return to the pan and stir in the cream. If the soup is too thick, thin with a little milk. Test for seasoning. Sprinkle each serving with a little parsley and serve very hot, with croûtons if you like.

To freeze: cool and freeze.

To serve after freezing: tip the frozen soup into a pan and heat through very gently. Proceed as above.

POTATOES DAUPHINOIS

You need floury baking potatoes for this recipe.

3 lb (1¹/₂ kg) potatoes	*2 oz (50 g) butter*
1 pt (600 ml) milk	*salt and pepper*
bay leaf	
nutmeg (optional)	*2 tbsp cream*

Peel the potatoes and cut into very thin slices. Leave in cold water for at least half an hour to extract some of the starch. Put the sliced potatoes into a large pan of boiling water, bring back to the boil and cook for two minutes. Drain and spread the slices out on a clean tea towel to dry.

Heat the milk with the bay leaf and a grating of nutmeg.

Butter a gratin dish generously. Put in a layer of potato slices, sprinkle lightly with salt and pepper, dot with a little butter, and repeat until all the potatoes are used. Pour on the strained milk (it should come just to the top of the potatoes but not cover them), and bake in a hot oven (400°F/200°C/gas 6) for at least two hours. You can use a cooler oven if you are cooking something else at the same time, but the potatoes will take longer. It is almost impossible to overcook this dish. Push the potatoes down from time to time so that they remain in the milk and the top layer does not dry out. However, it should be allowed to brown towards the end of the cooking time.

To serve immediately: pour the cream over the top of the potatoes about 10 minutes before serving.

To freeze: cool and freeze.

To serve after freezing: put the frozen dish into a hot oven (400°F/200°C/ gas 6) and cook until heated through (at least half an hour, or more, depending on the quantity). Finish as above.

NOTE This dish is also excellent made with a mixture of potatoes and celeriac.

ALIGOT

A warming, rib-sticking dish from the mountain plateau of central France. You need floury baking potatoes. If you cannot obtain Tomme d'Aligot or Cantal cheese, use Caerphilly or a mild Cheddar. Served with a green salad, this makes a simple but excellent supper dish.

3 lb (1½ kg) potatoes	*1 lb (450 g) Tomme d'Aligot*
8 oz (225 g) butter	*or Cantal cheese, cubed*
½ pt (300 ml) crème fraîche	*1 clove garlic (optional)*
or double cream	*salt and pepper*

Cook the potatoes in their skins. Drain, peel and purée as soon as they are cool enough to handle. Return to the pan and beat in the butter and cream or crème fraîche. Add the cheese and the crushed clove of garlic, and stir over a gentle heat until the cheese makes strings when you lift the spoon.

To serve immediately: season and serve very hot.

To freeze: cool and freeze.

To serve after freezing: reheat gently from frozen, season, and add a little butter or cream as necessary.

Chestnuts

Chestnuts are not suitable for long-term freezing (except as part of cooked dishes), as they become slightly musty. However, they are quite all right for three or four weeks, so if you like chestnut stuffing for turkey you can make it before the Christmas rush starts (see p. 205).

Fresh chestnuts are at their best at this time of year, but their preparation involves a lot of time and trouble. Dried chestnuts, though not as good, are a useful alternative.

To prepare fresh chestnuts: cut a cross in the shells and cook in plenty of boiling water for about 10 minutes. Take out three or so at a time and peel off the shell and the brown skin.

To prepare dried chestnuts: soak in a large basin of cold water for 24 hours and drain. Dried chestnuts generally have shreds of the brown inner skin sticking to them which must be removed before they are cooked. They need about twice the cooking time that you would give fresh chestnuts.

CHESTNUT SOUP

1 lb (450 g) chestnuts	*salt and pepper*
1 oz (25 g) butter	
1 onion	*parsley*
1 carrot	*cream*
1 small potato	*dry sherry (optional)*
2 pt (1.2 litres) stock	

Prepare the chestnuts (see p. 191). Melt the butter in a large pan, sauté the diced onion, carrot and potato for two to three minutes, add the chestnuts and the stock, and season. Simmer for about half an hour, or until the chestnuts are tender. Blend.

To serve immediately: reheat the soup, test for seasoning, and serve with a sprinkling of chopped parsley and a swirl of cream in each bowl. A dash of sherry adds a pleasant kick, but be careful not to put in too much as it can easily dominate the delicate chestnut taste.

To freeze: cool and freeze.

To serve after freezing: tip the frozen soup into a pan and heat gently. Serve as above.

~

BRAISED CHESTNUTS

These are particularly good served with venison or game.

1 lb (450 g) chestnuts	*1 oz (25 g) butter*
1/2 pt (300 ml) stock	*salt and pepper*

Prepare the chestnuts (see p. 191). Put in a heavy pan with the rest of the ingredients and simmer, covered, for 40 to 50 minutes, until they are tender but have not disintegrated, and the liquid has all been absorbed. Leave the lid off the pan for the last 15 minutes if necessary. Test for seasoning and serve hot.

To freeze: cool and freeze.

To serve after freezing: tip the frozen chestnuts into a pan and heat through gently. You may need to add a knob of butter or a tablespoon of stock or water.

Citrus Fruits

CHICKEN WITH LEMON

4-lb (2-kg) roasting chicken	SAUCE
2 carrots	4 oz (100 g) mushrooms
4 shallots or 2 small onions	1/2 lemon (juice and rind)
2 tbsp olive oil	2 egg yolks
1 oz (25 g) butter	1/4 pt (150 ml) double cream
1/2 lemon	or crème fraîche
1 clove garlic	1 1/2 oz (40 g) butter
small bunch of parsley	2 tbsp flour
1/4 tsp saffron	salt and pepper
salt and pepper	

Frozen chicken must be allowed to thaw thoroughly before cooking.

Coarsely chop the onions and carrots, and gently cook in the olive oil and butter in a flameproof casserole. When the onions are soft, place the chicken on top, with the half-lemon stuffed inside. Add the crushed garlic, the parsley and the saffron. Season, and add about 1 pt (600 ml) of water (it should half-cover the chicken). Bring to the boil, cover, and simmer gently until the chicken is tender (1–1 1/2 hours).

While the chicken is cooking, start to make the sauce. Cut the mushrooms into quarters. Peel the remaining half-lemon thinly, and cut the peel into matchsticks. Mix together in a bowl the mushrooms, lemon peel and juice, beaten yolks and cream or crème fraîche.

When the chicken is ready, take it out of the casserole and cut into serving pieces. For immediate eating put on a serving dish and keep warm.

Melt the butter in a pan, add the flour and stir until smooth. Gradually add the strained cooking liquid and stir over a gentle heat until the sauce is quite smooth. Add the contents of the bowl, season, and continue to stir until the sauce thickens, but do not allow to boil. The sauce can be made in a double pan if you prefer.

To serve immediately: pour the sauce over the chicken and serve with rice.

To freeze: cool the chicken in the sauce and freeze.

To serve after freezing: thaw overnight in the refrigerator. Warm through gently on top of the stove, stirring frequently to prevent the sauce from separating. Do not leave over the heat for longer than you need, or the sauce may lose its creamy texture and become runny.

LEMON MERINGUE PIE

2 lemons
6 oz (175 g) shortcrust pastry
  (see p. 218)
2 oz (50 g) cornflour
7 oz (200 g) sugar

$^1/_2$ pt (300 ml) water
2 egg yolks

2 egg whites
2 oz (50 g) castor sugar

Frozen egg whites should be allowed to thaw to room temperature.

Butter an 8-in (20-cm) flan tin and line with the pastry. Bake blind in a hot oven (425°F/220°C/gas 7) for about 15 minutes.

Blend the cornflour, the sugar and the water, and stir over a gentle heat for two or three minutes while it thickens. Add the juice and grated rind of the lemons and cook for another minute or two. Beat the egg yolks and gradually add the hot mixture to them, stirring all the time to ensure a smooth consistency. Return to the pan and bring almost to the boil, continuing to stir. Do not allow to boil. Remove from the heat and allow to cool before pouring into the flan case.

For immediate eating: beat the egg whites until they stand in peaks. Add the castor sugar very gradually, beating all the time. Spread over the top of the lemon mixture, taking care to see that the meringue adheres to the sides of the tin, to prevent shrinkage in cooking. Put in a fairly slow oven (325°F/160°C/gas 3) for about 20 minutes, until the top is nicely browned.

To serve immediately: serve warm or cold.

To freeze: cool and freeze.

To serve after freezing: allow the pie to thaw for a couple of hours, add the meringue topping and bake as described above.

RICH LEMON TART

2 lemons (the juice of 2 and
  the rind of 1)
10 oz (275 g) sweetened
  shortcrust pastry (see p. 219)
4 egg yolks
4 oz (100 g) sugar

2 oz (50 g) ground almonds
4 oz (100 g) butter, preferably
  unsalted
¼ pt (150 ml) double cream
  or crème fraîche

Line one buttered 10-in (25-cm) flan case or two 7-in (18-cm) cases with the pastry. Bake blind in a hot oven (425°F/220°C/gas 7) for about 15 minutes.

Beat together the egg yolks and sugar, add the ground almonds, the softened butter, the cream, and the juice of both lemons and grated rind of one. Continue to beat until the mixture is smooth and creamy. Pour into the pastry cases and bake in a fairly low oven (325°F/160°C/gas 3) for 40 minutes, or until the top is golden brown. Serve warm or cold.

To freeze: cool and freeze.

To serve after freezing: place the frozen tart in a hot oven (425°F/220°C/gas 7) for half an hour. Serve warm or cold.

~

LEMON MOUSSE (1)

This sweet is very refreshing at the end of a rich meal.

2 lemons
4 eggs
4–6 oz (100–175 g) castor
  sugar

slightly under ½ oz (12 g)
  gelatine

Separate the eggs, and whisk the yolks with the sugar until they are light and fluffy. Grate in the lemon rind. Sprinkle the gelatine on to the lemon juice and heat until it has completely dissolved. Pour very slowly into the egg mixture, continuing to whisk. Taste for sweetness, and if necessary add a little more castor sugar. Fold in the whites, beaten until they are stiff but not dry. Once you have started to add the gelatine it is important to work fast, otherwise the mousse will begin to set. Pour into a serving dish.

To serve immediately: leave in the refrigerator for one or two hours to set.

To freeze: wrap and freeze.

To serve after freezing: thaw at room temperature for two to four hours.

LEMON MOUSSE (2)

This is a richer version of the previous recipe.

2 lemons   1/2 oz (12 g) gelatine
4 eggs   1/2 pt (300 ml) double or
4–6 oz (100–175 g) castor   whipping cream
    sugar

Make as for the previous recipe until you have beaten the gelatine into the yolks. Lightly whip the cream and fold into the mixture. Complete as for the previous recipe.

~

LEMON HONEYCOMB MOULD

2 lemons   3 oz (75 g) sugar
3 eggs   1/2 oz (12 g) gelatine
1 pt (600 ml) milk or 1/2 pt
    (300 ml) milk and 1/2 pt
    (300 ml) single cream

Make a custard with the egg yolks, the milk, the cream if you are using it and the sugar. Stir over a low heat or in the top of a double boiler until it thickens to a creamy consistency. Melt the gelatine in the lemon juice and heat until the gelatine has completely dissolved. Take the custard off the heat, and stir in the gelatine and the grated peel. Cool. Whip the egg whites until they are stiff and fold into the custard.

To serve immediately: rinse out a 2-pt (1-litre) mould or soufflé dish with cold water, pour in the custard and chill. Turn out when set. It should be in three layers – the top a clear lemon jelly, the middle a creamy milk jelly and the bottom a fluffy lemon mousse.

To freeze: pour the mixture into the mould or soufflé dish, cool and freeze.

To serve after freezing: allow to thaw at room temperature for three to four hours or overnight in the refrigerator. Turn out before serving.

LEMON DRIZZLE CAKE

3 eggs
the weight of the eggs in:
  butter
  sugar
  flour

2 lemons
approx. 8 oz (225 g) castor
  sugar (for the icing)

Cream the butter and sugar until they are light and fluffy. Add the grated rind of the lemons. Whip the eggs and add alternately with the sieved flour, beating well. Line with baking paper a shallow baking tin about 8 in (20 cm) in diameter or 10 in (25 cm) square, and spread in the mixture. Put in the middle of a medium oven (350°F/175°C/gas 4). After 20 minutes turn the heat down to about 300°F/150°C/gas 2. The cake should be done in about 40 minutes.

Meanwhile, make the icing from about 8 oz (225 g) castor sugar dissolved in the juice of the lemons. This is spread on the cake when it cools, and the process is easier if the icing is allowed to stand for an hour or two to set a little. Stir from time to time.

When the cake has cooled, stand on a large board or dish and spoon the icing over it in small quantities. If it runs over the side (as it probably will), scoop it up and put back. This will take time, but eventually it should be possible to spread all the icing on. Leave for two or three hours to harden.

To freeze: freeze uncovered for 24 hours. Wrap and replace in the freezer.

To serve after freezing: allow to thaw for four or five hours.

LEMON CURD

Although lemon curd keeps well in the store cupboard for some time, the advantage of freezing it is that it may be kept indefinitely, and tastes and looks as good as ever when it comes out of the freezer.

3 lemons   *approx. 12 oz (350 g) castor*
2 oz (50 g) butter   *sugar*
                                         3 eggs

Put the butter, the grated rind and juice of the lemons and the sugar in a heavy pan and melt slowly. There should be about $1/4$ pt (150 ml) lemon juice. Do not allow to boil. Beat the eggs just enough to amalgamate the yolks and whites. When the sugar has completely dissolved add the mixture to the eggs very slowly, beating all the time. Test for sweetness. Return to the pan and cook over a low heat, stirring constantly. The mixture will at first become more runny, and then will start to thicken. When it does so (and being careful not to let it boil), take off the stove and pour into jars or pots. These quantities will make about $1^{1}/_{2}$ lb (675 g). Cover.

To freeze: if you are using glass jars with metal tops, it is important to leave $1/2$ in (1 cm) at the top to allow for expansion.

To serve after freezing: thaw at room temperature for three or four hours and keep in the refrigerator.

~

LEMON ICE-CREAM

2 lemons   *$1/2$ pt (300 ml) double or*
6 egg yolks   *whipping cream*
8 oz (225 g) castor sugar

Whisk the egg yolks with the sugar until thick and white. Gradually beat in the grated rind and juice of the lemons. Beat the cream until it is thick but not stiff, and fold into the mixture. Freeze.

To serve: remove from the freezer 10 to 15 minutes before serving.

LEMON WATER-ICE

1/4 pt (150 ml) lemon juice   *1/4 pt (150 ml) water*
(juice of between 3 to 6   *8 oz (225 g) sugar*
lemons depending on size)

Boil the sugar and water for five minutes with the finely grated peel of two lemons. Strain and cool. Add the lemon juice, pour into ice-trays and freeze until the mixture has reached a mushy state. Blend and return to the freezer.

~

LEMON SORBET

Make as for the water-ice, but fold in two stiffly beaten egg whites before returning the ice to the freezer for the second time. If you are using frozen egg whites, allow them to thaw before beating.

~

GRAPEFRUIT WATER-ICE

2 grapefruit   *8 oz (225 g) sugar*
3/4 pt (450 ml) water

Make a syrup by boiling the water and sugar hard for 8 to 10 minutes. Cool in the refrigerator. Finely grate the rind of both grapefruits and add to the syrup, together with the juice. Freeze until the mixture has reached a mushy state. Blend and return to the freezer.

Made with pink grapefruit, this water-ice is particularly pretty.

~

GRAPEFRUIT SORBET

Make as for the water-ice, but fold in two stiffly beaten egg whites before returning to the freezer for the second time. If you are using frozen egg whites, allow them to thaw to room temperature before beating.

ORANGE ICE-CREAM

6 oranges
2 lemons
8 oz (225 g) icing sugar

2 eggs and 2 extra yolks
²/₃ pt (350 ml) double or
whipping cream

Mix the sieved icing sugar with the juice of the oranges and lemons. Beat the whole eggs and the yolks and add. Pour into the top of a double pan and heat gently, stirring all the time, until the mixture starts to thicken. Cool, and fold in the whipped cream. Freeze.

To serve after freezing: remove from the freezer 15 minutes before serving.

~

ORANGE WATER-ICE

7 juicy oranges (smooth-skinned
   navel oranges are better than
   large Jaffas)
1 lemon

³/₄ pt (450 ml) water
8 oz (225 g) sugar
2 tbsp Grand Marnier or
   Orange Curaçao (optional)

Make a syrup by boiling the water and sugar hard for 10 minutes with the finely pared peel of the lemon and of one orange. Strain and cool.

Meanwhile cut the tops off the remaining six oranges and scoop out the flesh from both tops and bottoms, being very careful not to break or injure the shells, but leaving the insides as clean as possible. This is best done with a grapefruit knife or spoon. Reserve the tops. Extract as much juice from the pulp as you can by pushing it through a nylon sieve. If, however, you do not want to serve the ices in the orange shells – and, though this is the prettiest way, it takes much longer to do – you can simply squeeze the oranges in the usual way. Mix all the orange and lemon juice with the liqueur and the cooled syrup. Pour into ice-trays and freeze for one or two hours, until the mixture has reached a mushy state.

Remove from the freezer and blend. Spoon into the orange cups, allowing the ice to come a little over the tops of the cups. Press on the lids and freeze again, keeping the oranges in an upright position in a tin or tray. Or pour into a serving dish.

To serve: remove from the freezer 10 to 15 minutes before serving.

SEVILLE ORANGES

These are available in the shops for only a very short period, so if you do not have time to make marmalade immediately, or if you particularly like the taste of freshly made marmalade, freeze them and make the marmalade at your convenience.

To freeze: freeze whole in polythene bags.

To use after freezing: most people have their favourite method for making marmalade, and frozen citrus fruit can be used in any recipe. If you normally cut up the fruit before cooking, allow it to half-thaw for two to three hours, by which time it will be ready to slice or shred but will not be too squashy.

We give one recipe that is particularly easy to make from frozen fruit, as the fruit does not need to be thawed at all but can be used straight from the freezer and sliced after it has simmered for some time. We give it as a three-fruit marmalade, but it can be made from any combination of citrus fruits or with Seville oranges alone.

~

THREE FRUITS MARMALADE

2 lb (1 kg) Seville oranges
3 sweet oranges } 3 lb (1½ kg) fruit in all
2 lemons
6 pt (3½ litres) water   6 lb (2 ¾ kg) sugar

Put the frozen fruit, whole, into a preserving pan with the water and simmer, uncovered, for 2–2½ hours, or until the fruit is soft. Take the fruit out one by one, starting with the lemons which will probably be soft first, then the sweet oranges and lastly the Seville oranges, and slice or shred each one, putting the fruit in a large bowl. Return the pips to the pan so that they can continue to simmer with the remaining fruit. When all the fruit has been cut up, leave the pips to simmer for a further 10 minutes and then either remove with a slotted spoon or strain the liquid.

Return the fruit and liquid to the pan, and bring to boiling point. Add the sugar, stir well until it has dissolved, and boil fast until the marmalade begins to set. This may take anything between 10 minutes and half an hour.

Yield: about 10 lb (4½ kg).

SEVILLE ORANGE TART

6 oz (175 g) shortcrust pastry	3 eggs
(see p. 218)	6 oz (175 g) castor sugar
2 Seville oranges	¼ pt (150 ml) double cream

Line an 8-in (20-cm) flan tin with the pastry and cook blind for 15 minutes in a hot oven (425°F/220°C/gas 7).

Whisk the eggs with the sugar, cream, orange juice and finely grated orange rind. Pour into the pastry case and cook in a low oven (300°F/150°C/gas 2) for about 45 minutes, until the filling has set. Serve warm or cold.

To freeze: cool and freeze.

To serve after freezing: allow the tart to thaw at room temperature, and warm in a moderate oven (350°F/175°C/gas 4) for about 20 minutes before serving.

Christmas

TRADITIONAL FAVOURITES

Turkey on Christmas Day, straight from the oven, is a pleasure; cold on Boxing Day it can still be enjoyed, but as the days after Christmas wear on, it is generally greeted by groans. So while it is still fresh, and long before the family have reached saturation point, strip the meat off the bones and freeze. Make a stock from the carcass, with plenty of tarragon and lemon peel to counteract the slight sweetness of turkey, and freeze this also. Both the meat and the stock can be used for the following dishes.

Stuffings for the turkey can be prepared weeks in advance and stored in the freezer. On pages 204–6 we give three recipes which are all quite different and complement one another very well.

CHAUD-FROID OF TURKEY

This makes an excellent cold dish for a party. Use the white meat only, and keep the smaller pieces and the scraps for the turkey in cream sauce (see below).

> *3–4 lb (1½–2 kg) sliced*
>   *turkey breast (cooked)*
> *½ pt (300 ml) whipping cream*
> *¾ pt (450 ml) turkey stock*
> *2 good sprigs of tarragon*
>
> *¼ oz (6 g) gelatine*
> *2 tbsp dry white wine or dry*
>   *white vermouth*
> *juice of ½ lemon*
> *salt and pepper*

If you are using turkey from the freezer, this dish should not be frozen. The meat should be allowed to thaw before using.

Simmer the cream, the stock, and one sprig of tarragon for 15 minutes. Remove from the heat and take out the tarragon. Melt the gelatine in the wine or vermouth and the lemon juice and heat until it has quite dissolved. Stir into the sauce. Season and add the remaining tarragon leaves, finely chopped. Leave to cool and thicken a little, and spoon carefully over the meat. It is best to do this several times, so that the sauce does not run to the bottom of the dish but forms a thick coating over the meat.

To serve immediately: chill until set and serve.

TURKEY IN CREAM SAUCE

This is a useful stand-by to have in the freezer. It can be used as a filling for vol-au-vents, omelettes and pancakes, or served with rice as a supper dish.

1 lb (450 g) turkey meat	*¹/₂ pt (300 ml) turkey stock*
(cooked)	*1 tsp chopped tarragon*
2 oz (50 g) butter	*a dash of dry white vermouth*
1 onion	*(optional)*
2 oz (50 g) flour	*salt and pepper*
¹/₂ pt (300 ml) milk	

Frozen turkey meat must be allowed to part-thaw, but if you are using frozen meat do not freeze the dish.

Dice the meat. Melt the butter and sauté the finely chopped onion. Add the flour, stir for a few minutes without allowing to brown, and slowly add the milk and stock. Flavour with tarragon and vermouth, and season well. Stir the meat into the sauce. Serve as suggested above.

To freeze: cool and freeze.

To serve after freezing: tip into a pan, warm gently and serve as suggested above.

~

RICH STUFFING

Cook this stuffing separately in an ovenproof dish; any that is left over will be excellent served cold as a pâté.

8 oz (225 g) mushrooms, fresh,	*4 anchovy fillets*
or frozen sautéed	*1 clove garlic*
2 oz (50 g) butter	*small tin pâté de foie (optional)*
6 oz (175 g) streaky bacon	*finely grated rind of 1 lemon*
6 oz (175 g) loin of pork liver	*1 tbsp chopped parsley*
from the turkey or 4 oz	*pinch each of thyme and*
(100 g) chicken livers	*marjoram*
1 large Spanish onion	*salt and pepper*

Frozen sautéed mushrooms can be used straight from the freezer.

Sauté chopped fresh mushrooms in 1 oz of the butter, or gently warm frozen mushrooms. Roughly chop the meat and the onion and either blend with the rest of the ingredients, or chop all together finely. Melt the remaining ounce of butter and add. Fry a small pat of the mixture in a little butter, taste, and adjust the seasoning as necessary.

To freeze: freeze in an ovenproof dish.

To serve after freezing: thaw in the refrigerator overnight. Dot with butter, and put in the oven for the last 1½ hours while the turkey is cooking. Baste liberally with turkey juice at the end.

~

CHESTNUT STUFFING

These quantities are sufficient for a bird of about 15 lb (7 kg) dressed weight.

2 lb (1 kg) fresh chestnuts or	*2 oz (50 g) butter*
1 lb (450 g) dried	*1 tsp sugar*
½ pt (300 ml) milk	*salt and pepper*
½ pt (300 ml) water	

Prepare the chestnuts (see p. 191) and simmer in the milk and water until they are soft. The time required varies a great deal according to the chestnuts. They may be done in about 20 minutes or may take double that time. Dried chestnuts will probably need at least an hour. Add a little more liquid if necessary.

Blend the chestnuts and any cooking liquid that is left. Add the melted butter and the sugar, season to taste and squeeze into a ball.

To freeze: cool and freeze.

To thaw: thaw at room temperature for three to four hours or in the refrigerator overnight before using to stuff the breast of the turkey.

NOTE If you have cooked more chestnuts than you need for the stuffing, you can use the surplus for one of the simplest and most delectable sweets in the world. Put them through a fine mouli and serve with masses of whipped cream and castor sugar – but you will need literally spoonfuls and spoonfuls of both. If you haven't a mouli you can use a food processor. The chestnuts will not be quite as light, but they will still taste delicious.

FORCEMEAT STUFFING

These quantities are sufficient for a 15-lb (7-kg) bird (dressed weight).

8 oz (225 g) fresh	*2 tsp mixed herbs*
breadcrumbs	*rind of 2 lemons, finely grated*
4 oz (100 g) suet	*3 eggs*
3 tbsp chopped parsley	*salt and pepper*

Mix together all the dry ingredients. Beat the eggs and stir into the mixture, season and press into a ball.

To freeze: freeze.

To thaw: leave at room temperature for two to three hours, or in the refrigerator overnight, before using to stuff the tail-end of the turkey.

~

CHRISTMAS PUDDING

Most families have their favourite recipe for Christmas pudding, but this is a very useful one because it is rich without being too dark and heavy. The quantities given below will fill two 2-pt (1-litre) pudding basins (each enough for about eight people). Save time by making two at once, and freeze one, since Christmas puddings keep for years in the freezer.

1 lb (450 g) cooking apples	*¹/₈ nutmeg finely grated or a*
1 large carrot	*couple of shakes of powdered*
8 oz (225 g) seedless raisins	*nutmeg*
6 oz (175 g) currants	*3 eggs*
6 oz (175 g) sultanas	*approx. ¹/₈ pt (75 ml) brandy*
4 oz (100 g) mixed peel	
12 oz (350 g) fresh	*approx. ¹/₈ pt (75 ml) brandy*
breadcrumbs	*brandy butter*
8 oz (225 g) suet	*whipped cream*

Peel, core and grate the apples and grate the carrot finely. Chop the raisins currants and sultanas. Mix with the other dry ingredients, and add the beaten egg and the brandy. Stir very thoroughly and put into well-buttered pudding basins Put a piece of buttered baking paper over the top and then a piece of cloth an tie securely, making sure that the pudding has room to expand. Steam for five t six hours, take out of the pan and remove the baking paper and the cloth.

To serve immediately: turn on to a warmed dish and, as you bring the puddin to the table, pour over it the warmed brandy and set alight. Serve with brandy butter and whipped cream.

To freeze: cool and freeze.

To serve after freezing: thaw at room temperature for about eight hours. Put a piece of foil on top of the pudding, tucking it securely over the sides of the basin, and steam for three hours. Serve as above.

~

MINCE-PIES

Mince-pies frozen uncooked and put into the oven straight out of the freezer are particularly light and delicious. Mincemeat can be frozen separately, also, and will keep better in this way than in the store cupboard. If you freeze it in glass jars, leave 1 in (2 cm) at the top to allow for expansion.

MINCEMEAT	8 oz (225 g) suet
3 oz (75 g) blanched almonds	6 oz (175 g) currants
12 oz (350 g) raisins	1¼ lb (550 g) demerara sugar
4 oz (100 g) sultanas	1 lemon
1¼ lb (550 g) apples	1 orange
6 oz (175 g) mixed peel	⅛ pt (75 ml) brandy

Chop the almonds, raisins and sultanas. Peel, core and grate the apples. Chop the peel. Mix together the dry ingredients, add the grated rind and juice of the lemon and orange and the brandy, and stir thoroughly. Freeze.

This quantity will yield about 6 lb (2 ¾ kg) of mincemeat.

PIES	1 lb (450 g) mincemeat
approx 14 oz (400 g)	
shortcrust pastry (see p. 218)	castor sugar

Roll out the pastry and line about 24 patty-pans. Fill with mincemeat and cover with the rest of the pastry.

To serve immediately: cook in a hot oven (400°F/200°C/gas 6) for 10 to 15 minutes. Sprinkle generously with castor sugar and serve warm.

To freeze: freeze for at least 24 hours. The mince-pies will then slip easily out of the patty-pans and can be replaced in the freezer, in a plastic box or tin so that there is no risk of their getting damaged.

To serve after freezing: replace the frozen mince-pies in the patty-pans and pop into a hot oven (400°F/200°C/gas 6) for 10 to 15 minutes. Serve as above.

ALTERNATIVES TO CHRISTMAS PUDDINGS

Here are recipes for several puddings that look festive and will be welcomed by those who find the traditional Christmas pudding too heavy.

CHRISTMAS ICE-PUDDING

6 oz (175 g) of a combination	*4 oz (100 g) bitter chocolate*
of any of the following:	*2 good tbsp unsweetened*
raisins, currants,	*chestnut purée (tinned)*
glacé fruits	*¹/₂ pt (300 ml) double or*
4 tbsp rum or brandy	*whipping cream*
¹/₂ pt (300 ml) single cream	
5 egg yolks	**1 tbsp sugar**
5 oz (150 g) castor sugar	**about ¹/₄ pt (150 ml) brandy**

Chop the dried and glacé fruits roughly and leave to soak in the rum or brandy.

Heat the single cream to near boiling point, stir into the egg yolks beaten with the sugar and return to the pan. Stir over a gentle heat until the custard thickens, but do not allow to boil. You may find it easier to do this in a double pan. When the custard has thickened add the chocolate and the chestnut purée and stir well until they have melted and the custard is quite smooth. Test for sweetness and leave to cool. Mix in the rum-soaked fruits and finally fold in the whipped cream.

Line a pudding basin with foil. Pour in the mixture and freeze. When the pudding has frozen, remove from the basin, wrap and freeze.

To serve: remove from the freezer, unwrap, and leave in the refrigerator for about one hour. Just before serving, sprinkle with sugar and bring to the table Heat the brandy, set it alight in the pan and pour over the pudding immediately.

BAKED ALASKA

This is an easy-to-make spectacular which can be prepared two or three days before Christmas, stored in the freezer and put straight in the oven only 15 minutes before it is served. Any flavour of ice-cream or liqueur can be used, but we have found the combination of vanilla ice-cream and Marsala particularly good, as the tart edge of the Marsala counteracts the sweetness of the meringue. The following quantities will serve six, but the Alaska can be made in almost any size.

4 oz (100 g) trifle sponges	*3 oz (75 g) castor sugar*
4–6 tbsp Marsala	
1 pt (600 ml) vanilla ice-cream	*1 tbsp sugar*
3 egg whites	*1–2 tbsp brandy*

Frozen egg whites must be allowed to thaw to room temperature before whipping.

Halve the sponge cakes and line the bottom of a shallow ovenproof dish, making sure it is completely covered. Dribble on about half the Marsala. Mix the remainder of the Marsala into the slightly softened ice-cream and pile this on to the sponge cakes, leaving a 1-in (2-cm) margin of sponge cake uncovered all the way round. Smooth off on top. Place the dish in the freezer while you prepare the meringue mixture.

Beat the egg whites until stiff and add the castor sugar gradually, while continuing to beat. Spread this over the top of the ice-cream and right down the sides, so that it is completely covered and insulated by a thick layer of meringue. Return to the freezer immediately, and wrap or cover lightly when it has frozen. (The meringue mixture never becomes completely hard.)

To serve: take the Alaska out of the freezer 15 minutes before you are ready to serve it. Sprinkle with sugar, and place in a hot oven (425°F/220°C/gas 7) for 15 minutes. Pour on the warmed brandy, set alight and serve.

ICE-CREAM YULE LOG

This can be a children's alternative to Christmas pudding, or with the addition of a liqueur will be enjoyed by adults too. The quantities given will make 8 to 10 good servings.

1 pt (600 ml) vanilla ice-cream	*¹/₂ pt (300 ml) single cream*
1 pt (600 ml) chocolate ice-cream	*4 oz (100 g) plain chocolate*
	liqueur (optional)

Fill a long narrow loaf or cake tin with the slightly softened vanilla ice-cream, which can first be laced with liqueur. Return it to the freezer for a few hours to harden. Invert the tin on a foil-covered tray or dish, wrap a tea towel wrung out in hot water round it and lift off the tin. Cover the vanilla ice with the slightly softened chocolate ice, round off the edges to make a log shape and smooth well. Spread a little chocolate ice-cream over the ends of the log and mix with the vanilla ice to make a pale brown. Make a swirl in the ends with a fork and return the log once more to the freezer for about one hour.

Make the glaze by gently heating the cream with the chocolate, stirring until the chocolate has melted, and boil for one minute, continuing to stir. Remove from the heat and leave to cool till tepid but before it begins to set.

Spread the glaze gently over the log with a palette knife and draw a fork along it lengthwise, to give a rough surface. Return the log to the freezer and take out 15 minutes before serving. Finish off with a sprig of holly or any other Christmassy decorations.

CINNAMON STARS

These traditional German Christmas biscuits not only taste delicious but are also very pretty, and can be used as Christmas-tree decorations. Their flavour is best if you use whole, unblanched almonds.

2 egg whites	ICING
5 oz (150 g) castor sugar	*2 egg whites*
5 oz (150 g) almonds	*6 oz (175 g) icing sugar*
½ oz (12 g) ground cinnamon	*juice of ½ lemon*
pinch of ground cloves	*some nonpareils*
finely grated rind of ½ lemon	

Frozen egg whites must be allowed to thaw to room temperature.

Blanch and grind the almonds. Whisk the egg whites with the castor sugar until very thick and bulky. Blend the cinnamon and cloves into the almonds, add the lemon rind and fold into the meringue mixture. Gather into a ball and chill in the refrigerator for at least 30 minutes.

Sprinkle a pastry board or work surface with a little extra castor sugar and very lightly roll out the mixture ¼ in (½ cm) thick. If the mixture is very soft, roll out half at a time. Cut into stars with a pastry cutter and place on buttered baking sheets. Bake in a moderate oven (375°F/190°C/gas 5) for 10 to 15 minutes, until the top of each star has risen a little and is light and quite dry.

Remove from the oven, allow to cool for a few minutes, then carefully transfer the biscuits to wire racks (they are still quite fragile at this stage). Leave to cool.

Meanwhile make the icing by beating the egg whites with the icing sugar and lemon juice until thick and white.

Using a pointed knife, spread a litle icing on each star, making sure there is icing on each point but leaving a narrow margin round the edges.

When the icing has nearly set, sprinkle a few nonpareils on to the centre of each star and leave to set completely.

When quite dry freeze in biscuit tins. You can thread the stars, using a skewer and some thin cord or ribbon, for hanging on the Christmas tree.

STILTON CHEESE

Any Stilton left over from Christmas can be stored in the freezer, though it may become a little crumbly.

STILTON SOUP

This is a deliciously creamy soup.

6 oz (175 g) Stilton	*salt and pepper*
2 oz (50 g) butter	
1 oz (25 g) flour	*1 tbsp cream*
³/₄ pt (450 ml) milk	*1 tbsp finely chopped*
³/₄ pt (450 ml) light stock	*parsley*

Melt the butter in a pan, add the flour, stir well to blend and cook, without allowing to brown, for three minutes.

Slowly add the milk and stock, stirring to keep the mixture smooth, and bring to the boil.

Remove from the heat and crumble in the Stilton. Add seasoning to taste, return to a moderate heat and stir well. Allow to simmer for at least five minutes.

To serve immediately: just before serving, stir in the cream and sprinkle with parsley. Serve very hot.

To freeze: cool and freeze.

To serve after freezing: tip the frozen soup into a pan, heat slowly, stirring from time to time, and serve as above.

Pasta

MAKING PASTA

Making your own pasta is time-consuming but eminently worthwhile, provided you have a pasta machine, for made at home it is far better, and more nutritious, than even the 'fresh' commercially packaged pasta.

When you make a batch of pasta, always cook the whole lot and freeze the surplus after cooking, as it does not freeze well uncooked. When you want to use it, plunge into boiling water straight from the freezer for one to two minutes.

1 lb (425 g) strong flour   *4 egg yolks*
2 whole eggs   *salt*

Sift the flour into a mound on the work surface and make a well in the centre. Whisk the eggs and yolks together briefly with the salt, using a fork, and pour into the centre. Gradually work the flour into the egg mixture, using the fork to begin with, and finally knead into a ball.

Work through a pasta machine to the required shape and thickness. Leave to dry for an hour or two.

Cook in plenty of boiling water. The pasta will take only one to two minutes after the water comes back to the boil.

CANNELLONI WITH LAMB FILLING

6 oz (175 g) lasagne sheets	SAUCE
	2 oz (50 g) butter
FILLING	*2 oz (50 g) flour*
10 oz (275 g) cooked lamb	*1 pt (600 ml) milk*
4 oz (100 g) mushrooms,	*¼ pt (150 ml) stock*
fresh or frozen sautéed	*2 oz (50 g) grated cheese*
3 oz (75 g) butter	*salt and pepper*
1 oz (25 g) grated cheese	
4–5 tbsp stock	*2 oz (50 g) grated Parmesan*
salt, pepper and freshly grated	*1 oz (25 g) melted butter*
nutmeg	

Frozen sautéed mushrooms can be used straight from the freezer.

Cook the lasagne sheets in small batches in plenty of boiling water, drain, and spread out to dry on clean tea towels.

Chop fresh mushrooms finely and fry in the butter for a few minutes. Mince or blend the lamb and add to the pan, together with frozen sautéed mushrooms (if you are using them), grated cheese, salt, pepper and a generous amount of nutmeg. Stir in enough stock to make the mixture fairly moist and allow to cool slightly.

Cut the lasagne sheets into 3-in (8-cm) squares and lay some of the filling across the middle of each. Butter a shallow ovenproof dish, roll up the cannelloni and arrange in the dish in a single layer.

Make the sauce with the butter, flour, milk and stock, season, and add the grated cheese, stirring until it has melted. The sauce should be thin enough to pour easily, so add a little more milk or stock if necessary. Pour the sauce over the cannelloni.

To serve immediately: sprinkle the Parmesan on top, dribble on the melted butter and bake in a medium oven (375°F/190°C/gas 5) for about 45 minutes, until the cannelloni are very hot and the sauce is bubbling and golden brown.

To freeze: cool and freeze.

To serve after freezing: if possible, leave to thaw for at least two to three hours. Cook in a hot oven (425°F/220°C/gas 7) for 30 minutes, then turn the oven down to 375°F/190°C/gas 5, and leave for another 30 minutes to one hour, according to the size of the dish.

NOTE You can also make the cannelloni with raw minced lamb.

LASAGNE WITH FOUR CHEESES

6 oz (175 g) lasagne sheets

SAUCE
3 oz (75 g) Parmesan
3 oz (75 g) Gruyère
3 oz (75 g) Mozzarella or
Bel Paese

3 oz (75 g) Pecorino or mature
Cheddar
2 oz (50 g) butter
2 oz (50 g) flour
1¼ pt (750 ml) milk
salt, pepper and freshly grated
nutmeg

Cook the lasagne sheets in small batches in plenty of boiling water, drain, and spread out to dry on clean tea towels.

Grate the Parmesan and cut the other cheeses into small dice. Put about one-third of the Parmesan on one side and mix together all the rest of the cheese.

Make the sauce with the butter, flour and milk. Add the cheeses (except the reserved Parmesan). Season with salt and pepper and generously with nutmeg, and leave over a low heat, stirring occasionally, until the cheeses have melted.

Butter a shallow ovenproof dish and put in alternate layers of lasagne and sauce. There should be at least four layers of each. Finish with a layer of sauce, and sprinkle the reserved Parmesan on top.

To serve immediately: cook in a hot oven (425°F/220°C/gas 7) for 20 to 30 minutes, until bubbling hot.

To freeze: cool and freeze.

To serve after freezing: if possible, leave to thaw for at least two to three hours. Cook in a hot oven (425°F/220°C/gas 7) for 30 minutes, turn the oven down to 375°F/190°C/gas 5, and leave for another 30 minutes to one hour, according to the size of the dish.

MUSHROOM LASAGNE

These quantities will make two large or three medium lasagnes, enough for 8 to 10 servings altogether.

8 oz (225 g) lasagne sheets

SAUCE
2 oz (50 g) butter
2 oz (50 g) flour
2 pt (1 litre) milk
¹/₂ pt (300 ml) cream

FILLING
1¹/₂ lb (675 g) mushrooms,
  preferably a mixture of
  different varieties
1–2 oz (25–50 g) dried
  porcini (optional)
3 oz (75 g) butter
large bunch parsley
6 oz (175 g) Parmesan, finely
  grated
salt and pepper

Cook the lasagne sheets in small batches in plenty of boiling water, drain, and spread out to dry on clean tea towels.

If you are using dried porcini, soak in boiling water for half an hour.

Make a sauce with the butter, flour and milk, bring briefly to the boil, remove from the heat and add the cream. Set aside.

Wipe or wash the mushrooms, slice very thinly and cook in 2 oz (50 g) butter. Add the drained and finely chopped dried porcini and their strained liquid, and stir the mixture into the béchamel sauce, together with the finely chopped parsley. Season to taste.

Butter two or three gratin dishes liberally, cover the bottom of each with a layer of pasta, spread with a layer of the mushroom mixture, sprinkle with a little grated Parmesan and dot with a little butter. Repeat until all the sauce has been used, ending with the sauce. Sprinkle with the remaining cheese and dot with the rest of the butter.

To serve immediately: cook in a hot oven (425°F/220°C/gas 7) for 20 to 30 minutes, until bubbling hot.

To freeze: cool and freeze.

To serve after freezing: if possible leave to thaw for at least two to three hours. Cook in a hot oven (425°F/220°C/gas 7) for 30 minutes, turn the oven down to 375°F/190°C/gas 5, and leave for another 30 minutes to one hour, according to size.

VEGETABLE LASAGNE

6 oz lasagne sheets
2–2¹/₄ lb (1 kg) vegetables –
  some or all of the following:
  onions, carrots, celery, leeks,
  pimentos, courgettes
6 oz (175 g) mushrooms
2 tbsp olive oil

1–2 tbsp lemon juice
1¹/₂ oz (40 g) butter
1¹/₂ oz (40 g) flour
1¹/₄ pt (750 ml) milk
6 oz (175 g) cheese
salt and pepper

Cook the pasta sheets in small batches in plenty of boiling water, drain, and spread out to dry on clean tea towels.

Chop the onions and carrots finely and slice the other vegetables. Heat the oil in a frying pan or wok and tip in all the vegetables except the mushrooms. Cover the pan and cook for 20 to 25 minutes, stirring from time to time. Add the sliced or chopped mushrooms for the last 10 minutes. Add lemon juice to taste, and season.

Meanwhile make the sauce with the butter, flour and milk. Add about half the cheese and season.

Butter a shallow ovenproof dish. Put a layer of lasagne in the dish, then a layer of vegetables, and cover with some of the sauce. Repeat until all the ingredients have been used up, ending with a layer of lasagne. Sprinkle with the rest of the cheese.

To serve immediately: put in a hot oven (400°F/200°C/gas 6) and bake for about 45 minutes, until the lasagne is golden and bubbling.

To freeze: cool and freeze.

To serve after freezing: if possible leave to thaw for at least two to three hours. Cook in a hot oven (425°F/220°C/gas 7) for 30 minutes, turn the oven down to 375°F/190°C/gas 5, and leave for another 30 minutes to one hour, according to size.

Pastry

Pastry freezes excellently, both cooked and uncooked, and is one of the most useful items to keep in the freezer.

Even pastry dishes which are to be eaten cold, such as fruit flans, benefit from 15 to 20 minutes in a hot oven when they are taken out of the freezer. After this they can be left to cool and, if necessary, thaw right through. They should then be eaten as soon as possible while the pastry is crisp.

SHORTCRUST PASTRY

1 lb (450 g) flour
4–5 oz (100–125 g) butter
4 oz (100 g) shortening

4–5 tbsp cold water
pinch of salt

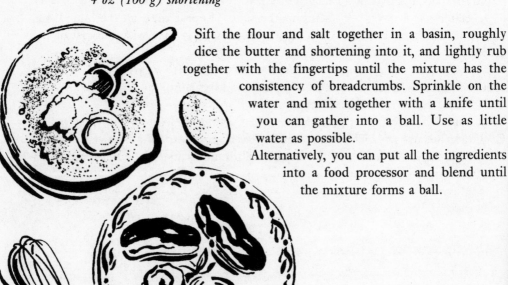

Sift the flour and salt together in a basin, roughly dice the butter and shortening into it, and lightly rub together with the fingertips until the mixture has the consistency of breadcrumbs. Sprinkle on the water and mix together with a knife until you can gather into a ball. Use as little water as possible.

Alternatively, you can put all the ingredients into a food processor and blend until the mixture forms a ball.

SWEETENED SHORTCRUST PASTRY

1 lb (450 g) flour	*1 egg*
2 oz (50 g) castor or icing	*1 tbsp milk*
sugar	*1 tbsp vinegar*
8 oz (225 g) butter	*pinch of salt*

Sift the flour and salt into a bowl or on to a pastry board and add the sugar and the diced butter. Make a well in the centre, break the egg into it and add the milk and vinegar. Chop all well together with a palate knife until it is very fine, and finally knead briefly. When quite smooth, leave to rest in the refrigerator for one hour before using.

Alternatively, you can put all the ingredients into a food processor and blend until the mixture forms a ball.

~

RICH SWEETENED SHORTCRUST PASTRY

1 lb (450 g) flour	*10 oz (275 g) butter*
4 oz (100 g) icing sugar	*pinch of salt*

Sift the flour, icing sugar and salt into a bowl or on to a pastry board. Dice the butter and rub in with the tips of the fingers until the mixture has the consistency of very fine breadcrumbs. Mould lightly into a ball and leave to rest in the refrigerator for half an hour before using, or freeze.

Alternatively, you can put all the ingredients into a food processor and blend until the mixture forms a ball.

This pastry is rather crumbly, and can be either rolled out in small quantities or kneaded or patted into flan tins.

Amounts of shortcrust pastry needed to line flan tins

For uncovered tarts:

To line a 6-in (15-cm) flan tin allow 4 oz (100 g) pastry
To line a 7-in (18-cm) flan tin allow 5 oz (150 g) pastry
To line an 8-in (20-cm) flan tin allow 6 oz (175 g) pastry
To line a 10-in (25-cm) flan tin allow 10 oz (275 g) pastry
To line a 12-in (30-cm) flan tin allow 1 lb (450 g) pastry

For covered tarts allow about half as much again.

CHOUX PASTRY

Choux pastry is extremely simple to make and has an infinite variety of uses, savoury as well as sweet.

BASIC MIXTURE

1/2 pt (300 ml) water   *4 eggs*
bare 4 oz (100 g) butter   *pinch of salt*
41/2 oz (125 g) flour

Put the water and salt into a large, heavy pan, add the butter cut into small pieces and bring slowly to the boil. Stir until the butter has melted.

Sift the flour, then tip the whole lot, all at once, into the pan. Lower the heat and stir with a wooden spoon until the mixture forms one thick, smooth mass and leaves the side of the pan.

Remove the pan from the heat and beat in the eggs one by one, using a wooden spoon. Do not add the next egg until the previous one has been completely absorbed. You will end up with a smooth glossy paste, buttercup yellow, lukewarm, and stiff enough to hold its shape. You can freeze the mixture at this point.

~

CHOUX PUFFS

Allow frozen pastry to thaw.

Using a piping bag with a 1-in (2-cm) nozzle, or two teaspoons, drop small mounds of the mixture on to dampened baking sheets. They should be approximately 1 in (2 cm) in diameter for small puffs, or 2½ in (6 cm) in diameter for larger ones (use two dessert spoons for shaping large puffs).

Bake in a hot oven (425°F/220°C/gas 7) for 20 to 25 minutes, until the puffs have risen and are pale brown.

Remove from the oven and turn the oven off.

Using a sharp, pointed knife, make an incision along one side of each puff, to allow the steam to escape. Put the puffs back on the baking sheets, cut-side up, and return to the oven to dry for about 10 minutes, leaving the oven door open. Remove from the oven and leave to cool on a wire rack.

To serve immediately: finish in any of the ways suggested below.

To freeze: freeze in boxes or tins.

To serve after freezing: place the frozen puffs in a hot oven (425°F/220°C/gas 7) and bake for five minutes to crisp them, then remove from the oven and leave to cool on a wire rack before filling.

NOTE For savoury puffs you can add 4 oz (100 g) grated Gruyère, Parmesan or Cheddar cheese to the mixture. For sweet puffs or éclairs add 1 tbsp sugar to the water at the same time as you add the salt.

~

FILLINGS FOR SAVOURY PUFFS

Savoury puffs can be filled with a white sauce to which you can add chopped ham, sautéed mushrooms, chopped prawns, shrimps, smoked salmon, grated hard cheese or mashed goat cheese.

SAUCE
1 oz (25 g) butter *¹/₄ pt (150 ml) milk*
1 oz (25 g) flour *salt and pepper*
¹/₄ pt (150 ml) white wine

Make the sauce with the butter, flour and wine. Cook for two minutes, add the milk and stir until smooth. Season. Bring briefly to the boil, remove from the heat and add the other chosen ingredients.

Allow the sauce to cool and thicken slightly, then fill the puffs, using a teaspoon. Heat through before serving.

GOUGÈRE

A gougère, or large cheese ring, makes an excellent light lunch or supper dish. It can be served plain, with a salad, or you can fill the centre with a hot vegetable – asparagus, broad beans, or broccoli, for example – topped with cheese or hollandaise sauce.

Make the basic mixture, as on p. 220, but use ½ pt (300 ml) milk instead of ½ pt (300 ml) water. You will also need 4 oz (100 g) Gruyère or sharp Cheddar cheese, cut into small cubes.

When the basic mixture is still warm stir in all but 1 tbsp of the cheese.

Spoon the mixture into a wetted ring mould or spring-form tin with a central funnel. Scatter the remaining cheese on top and bake for 35 to 40 minutes in a moderate oven (375°F/190°C/gas 5), until the top has risen and is golden brown and firm to the touch. Turn out.

To serve immediately: serve as suggested above, very hot.

To freeze: cool and freeze.

To serve after freezing: place the frozen gougère in a hot oven (425°F/220°C/gas 7) for 20 to 30 minutes and serve as above.

~

CREAM PUFFS

Make the basic choux-pastry mixture, adding 1 tsp sugar at the same time as the salt (see p. 220). When the puffs are cold fill with whipped cream and sprinkle with sifted icing sugar.

Allow ½ pt (300 ml) double or whipping cream for the quantity given on page 220, and whip fairly lightly, so that it is not too stiff.

When baking large puffs to be served in this way, it is nice to mark a light criss-cross on each puff before baking. As they rise, this expands to give the traditional cream-puff look.

ÉCLAIRS

Make the sweetened choux-pastry mixture (see p. 220) and either use éclair tins or pipe into the characteristic long thin shape, slightly stubby at each end, by using a piping bag with a plain ½-in (1-cm) nozzle.

FILLING
½ pt (300 ml) double or
   whipping cream
1 tsp icing sugar

ICING
4 tbsp water
1 tbsp sugar
2 oz (50 g) plain or bitter
   chocolate
1 tsp instant coffee powder
3 oz (75 g) icing sugar
½ tsp vegetable oil

Fill the éclairs when baked and cooled (as for choux puffs, see p. 220) with the sweetened whipped cream.

To make the icing, put the water and sugar in a small pan and bring slowly to the boil. Stir until the sugar has dissolved, then boil briskly for one minute. Remove from the heat and add the chocolate, broken into pieces. Stir until melted. Beat in the coffee powder and icing sugar until smooth. Add the oil.

Using a knife, coat the top of each éclair thickly with the icing, and leave to set before serving.

To freeze: open-freeze, and store in rigid containers in a single layer.

To serve after freezing: leave the éclairs at room temperature for at least one hour before serving.

NOTE The éclairs can be frozen before or after filling and icing, but as the icing is soft you may find it easier to store them in the freezer before icing.

Cakes and Biscuits

CHOCOLATE CAKE

This is a rich cake which will please adults and children alike, and is equally welcome for teatime or as a dessert, especially if served with whipped cream or ice-cream.

8 oz (225 g) butter
8 oz (225 g) granulated sugar,
  or half granulated and half
  soft light brown
3 oz (75 g) cocoa powder
2 oz (50 g) drinking-chocolate
  powder
8 oz (225 g) self-raising flour
4 oz (100 g) ground almonds
4 eggs
1 tbsp strong coffee
1 tbsp sweet sherry

FILLING
3 oz (75 g) plain or bitter
  chocolate
1 tbsp strong coffee
1 tbsp sweet sherry (optional)
3 oz (75 g) butter
5 oz (150 g) icing sugar

ICING
4 oz (100 g) plain or bitter
  chocolate
$1/8$ pt (75 ml) water
2 oz (50 g) icing sugar
$1/2$ oz (12g) butter
split blanched almonds
  (optional)

Butter a 10-in (25-cm) round cake tin and line with baking paper.

Cream the butter with the sugar until very light and fluffy. Sift together the cocoa, drinking chocolate, flour and ground almonds. Beat the eggs lightly. Gradually add the eggs to the creamed mixture alternately with the dry ingredients, and finally add the coffee and sherry. Do not overbeat.

Pour into the prepared tin and bake in the centre of a medium oven (350°F/175°C/gas 4) for about one hour, until a skewer inserted into the centre comes out clean.

Remove from the oven and leave to cool in the tin for 10 to 15 minutes, then turn out on to a wire rack and leave to cool completely.

To make the filling, break the chocolate into a small bowl, add the coffee and the sherry, if you are using it, and set over a pan of simmering water until the chocolate has melted. Stir until smooth and leave to cool slightly. Beat the butter with the icing sugar until light and fluffy, then beat in the cooled chocolate mixture.

Cut the cake in half horizontally and sandwich together with the filling.

To make the icing, break the chocolate into a pan, add the water and icing sugar and bring slowly to the boil, stirring all the time. As soon as the mixture begins to thicken and large bubbles appear, remove from the heat, stir in the butter and pour quickly over the cake, smoothing the icing if necessary with a wet palette knife. (If the icing sets too quickly, heat again with a little more water.)

Decorate with split almonds, if you are using them, before the icing sets.

To freeze: allow the icing to set and become completely dry, then either freeze in a box or tin or open-freeze and wrap in foil.

To serve after freezing: unwrap and thaw at room temperature for six to eight hours.

STOLLE

Halfway betwen a fruit loaf and a fruit cake, a Stolle is traditionally eaten at Christmas and Easter. It is much lighter than Christmas cake, and can be eaten plain or buttered.

1 lb (450 g) currants	14 oz (400 g) butter
10 oz (275 g) sultanas	6 oz (175 g) chopped mixed peel
4 tbsp rum	4 oz (100 g) chopped blanched
2¼ lb (1 kg) flour	almonds
2 oz (50 g) yeast	
½ pt (300ml) milk	**melted butter**
4 oz (100 g) sugar	**icing sugar**

Soak the currants and sultanas in the rum.

Sift the flour into a warmed mixing bowl, make a well in the centre and crumble in the yeast.

Warm the milk to blood heat, add a spoonful of the sugar and stir the milk into the yeast. Work a little of the flour into the yeast mixture, sprinkle with a little more flour, cover with a tea towel and leave in a warm place to rise (about 15 minutes).

When the yeast mixture has trebled in volume (it will rise up like a little ball in the middle of the flour) melt the butter gently and work the flour and all the remaining ingredients into a dough, leaving the fruit and nuts to the last.

Knead the dough well, put back into the bowl and leave to rise for about an hour, or until it has doubled in volume. Knock down and leave to rise again.

When it has once more doubled in volume (about 30 to 45 minutes), divide into two or three and roll out each one into an oblong about 1½ in (4 cm) thick. Fold one side towards the centre lengthwise, to form a split loaf shape.

Place on buttered baking trays, or use baking parchment, and leave to rise again for about 15 minutes. Bake in a moderate oven (350°F/175°C/gas 4) for about one hour, until the loaves have risen and are firm, and have a light-brown crust. Remove from the oven and leave to cool slightly, then turn out on to wire racks.

To serve immediately: when the loaves are cool, brush with a little melted butter and dust thickly with sifted icing sugar.

To freeze: cool, wrap and freeze.

To serve after freezing: unwrap and leave to thaw at room temperature for six to eight hours, or preferably overnight. Finish as above.

ORANGE SNOW CAKE

This cake keeps beautifully moist, and has an unusual flavour and texture.

6 oz (175 g) butter
finely grated rind of 1 orange
6 oz (175 g) castor sugar
2 eggs
1/8 pt (75 ml) water
10 oz (275 g) self-raising
  flour

3 tbsp thick-cut marmalade
2 oz (50 g) candied peel
3 oz (75 g) walnuts or pecans

ICING
2 tbsp orange juice
icing sugar

Butter and line with baking parchment a 7-in (18-cm) cake tin.

Cream the butter with the grated orange rind and the sugar until light and fluffy. Separate the eggs and beat the yolks with the water. Add the flour and the yolks alternately to the creamed mixture, beating in each addition well before you add the next. Stir in the marmalade, the finely chopped candied peel and the chopped walnuts. Fold in the stiffly beaten egg whites.

Pour the mixture into the prepared tin and bake in the centre of a medium oven (350°F/175°C/gas 4) for 1¼–1½ hours, until a skewer inserted into the centre comes out clean.

Turn on to a wire rack and leave to cool.

For the icing, mix the fresh orange juice with enough sifted icing sugar to make a mixture sufficiently stiff to spread over the top of the cake. Leave for two to three hours to harden.

To freeze: open-freeze and, when the icing has set, wrap and return to the freezer.

To serve after freezing: unwrap and thaw at room temperature for four to six hours.

HONEY CAKE

6 oz (175 g) honey
4 oz (100 g) soft light-brown
  sugar
5 oz (150 g) butter
1 tbsp water

2 eggs
7 oz (200 g) self-raising flour
1–2 oz (25–50 g) flaked
  almonds

Butter an 8- x 12-in (20- x 30-cm) tin about 1¼ in (3 cm) deep and line with baking paper.

Weigh the honey. There are two ways of doing this: you can either weigh the sugar, spread it over the weighing bowl and weigh the honey on this bed, so that you have 10 oz (275 g) of sugar and honey combined; or you can place the honey jar on the scales and remove 6 oz (175 g).

Put the honey, sugar, butter and water into a pan and heat gently until the sugar has melted. Transfer to a mixing bowl and add the well-beaten eggs. Stir in the sifted flour.

Pour into the prepared tin and scatter generously with flaked almonds. Bake in the centre of a medium oven (350°F/175°C/gas 4) for 30 to 35 minutes, until a skewer inserted into the centre comes out clean.

Turn out on to a wire rack and leave to cool completely.

To freeze: wrap and freeze.

To serve after freezing: unwrap and thaw at room temperature for four to five hours.

~

OATMEAL BISCUITS

6 oz (175 g) porridge oats
4½ oz (125 g) butter

2½ oz (65 g) sugar
½ tsp baking powder

Mix all the ingredients firmly together and knead until the mixture is pliable. Generously flour your hands, the rolling pin and the pastry board and roll out the mixture fairly thinly – ⅛–¼ in (¼–½ cm), according to how thick you like the biscuits – and cut into rounds. Place on floured trays and bake in a medium oven (350°F/175°C/gas 4) for about 20 minutes, until the biscuits are light brown. Remove carefully to a wire rack as soon as they are firm enough to handle.

To freeze: freeze in boxes or tins.

To serve after freezing: the biscuits can be served straight from the freezer.

CRISPY BISCUITS

The quantities given below make dozens of crisp, delicious little biscuits.

4 oz (100 g) butter   *1 egg*
4 oz (100 g) sugar   *2¹/₂ oz (65 g) currants*
4 oz (100 g) self-raising flour

Cream the butter and sugar until fluffy. Add the flour and the beaten egg alternately, beating each in well. Stir in the currants.

Flour baking trays and drop on little bits of the mixture, about the size of a 20-pence piece. They should be about 2 in (5 cm) apart, as the mixture spreads. Bake in a hot oven (400°F/200°C/gas 6) until light brown. Take out each tray the moment the biscuits are cooked and transfer them to a rack. This must be done very quickly, as they harden immediately and are then very difficult to remove without breaking. The easiest way is to run a palette knife under each biscuit as soon as the tray comes out of the oven.

To freeze: cool and freeze in boxes or tins.

To serve after freezing: the biscuits can be eaten straight from the freezer.

Using Up Egg Whites

Egg whites need no preparation before freezing. Simply put into small containers and label with the number of whites.

Once thawed, they can be whipped very successfully, but they must reach room temperature first. It is also important to keep them absolutely dry, so if ice crystals have formed on top, scrape off thoroughly before leaving the whites to thaw.

MERINGUES

4 egg whites   8 oz (225 g) castor or icing sugar

Frozen egg whites must be allowed to thaw to room temperature. Whip the whites until they reach the soft-peak stage. If you are using castor sugar, gradually beat in half. Fold in the remaining castor sugar with a metal spoon.

If you are using icing sugar add it all to the egg whites before you begin to beat. It will take longer to beat the mixture to the required thickness, but some people find this method more reliable.

Line baking sheets with baking parchment and either pipe on the mixture or shape the meringues with two spoons. Bake in a very low oven, starting at 200°F/90°C/gas ½. After half an hour turn the oven down to 100°F/45°C/gas ¼ and bake for at least a further two hours. If necessary turn the meringues over for the last half an hour to dry off the bottoms.

Meringues can be unpredictable. If they refuse to set, leave them in a very low oven overnight.

MERINGUES WITH CHESTNUT

4 egg whites
8 oz (225 g) castor or icing
  sugar
8-oz (225-g) tin sweetened
  chestnut purée

½ pt (300 ml) double or
  whipping cream

Frozen egg whites must be allowed to thaw to room temperature.

Make the meringues as described on p. 230, spreading the mixture in three circles on the baking parchment.

When they are cooked, lay one of the circles on a round serving dish and spread with half the chestnut purée. Lay a second circle on top and spread with the remaining purée. Lay the third circle on top of this and cover with the cream, whisked until it stands in soft peaks.

As an alternative to the meringue rings, make small meringues and sandwich them together with the purée and whipped cream.

~

MACAROONS

These little macaroons are quickly made and go well with ice-cream or water-ice and many other cold desserts.

1 large egg white
4 oz (100 g) ground almonds
8 oz (225 g) castor sugar

6–7 drops almond essence
rice paper

Frozen egg white must be allowed to thaw to room temperature.

Mix together the ground almonds, sugar and almond essence. Stir in the lightly beaten egg white until the mixture is a smooth paste. With floured hands, shape the paste into about 24 small balls, flattening them slightly.

Lay the rice paper on baking sheets and place the macaroons on top, leaving a little space between them as they will spread during baking. Bake in a moderate oven (350°F/175°C/gas 4) for 10 to 15 minutes. They should be no darker than the lightest golden, for if they cook too long they will become hard.

Remove from the oven and leave on the baking sheets until cold, then trim away excess rice paper. Freeze in boxes or tins. The macaroons can be eaten straight from the freezer.

CAROLINA COOKIES

These delicately spiced biscuits are the perfect accompaniment to ices, sorbets or fruit compôtes. Keep a supply in the freezer, as they take virtually no time to thaw.

2 egg whites	*4 tsp ground cinnamon*
1 lb (450 g) butter	*2 tsp ground ginger*
12 oz (350 g) soft light-brown	*pinch of salt*
sugar	*1¼ lb (550 g) plain flour*

Frozen egg whites must be allowed to thaw to room temperature.

Cream the butter with the sugar until very light and fluffy. Beat in the egg whites until the mixture is smooth and very light. Sift the spices and salt with the flour and fold into the mixture. Beat briefly until smooth.

Butter baking sheets and spoon on the mixture. Pat out quite thinly. Bake in a medium oven (375°F/190°C/gas 5) for 15 to 20 minutes, until light golden brown.

Leave to cool for a few minutes, then cut into diamond shapes and cool on wire trays. Freeze in boxes or tins. The cookies can be eaten straight from the freezer.

~

APRICOT SHORTCAKE

1 egg white	*4 oz (100 g) castor sugar*
6 oz (175 g) flour	*1 whole egg*
4 oz (100 g) butter	*about 8 oz (225 g) apricot jam*

Frozen egg white must be allowed to thaw to room temperature.

Sift the flour into a mixing bowl. Add the butter and rub in. Stir in half the sugar and the egg yolk. Knead until the mixture comes away from the side of the bowl. Press into a floured 8-in (20-cm) flan tin and bake in the centre of a hot oven (400°F/200°C/gas 6) for 15 to 20 minutes, until the shortcake is light brown and just firm to the touch. Remove from the oven and leave to cool in the tin for about 20 minutes.

Spread the shortcake generously with apricot jam. Whisk the two egg white until they stand in stiff peaks and fold in the remaining castor sugar. Spread over the jam. Cook in a moderate oven (350°F/175°C/gas 4) for 20 to 30 minutes.

Serve warm or cold.

LEMON FLUFF

3 egg whites   *4 oz (100 g) castor sugar*
1/2 oz (12 g) gelatine   *2 lemons*
1/2 pt (300 ml) water

Frozen egg whites must be allowed to thaw to room temperature.

Sprinkle the gelatine over the water in a small pan and leave to soak for a few minutes. Add the sugar and stir all together over a gentle heat, until the sugar has dissolved and the liquid is clear. Remove from the heat, add the grated rind and juice of the lemons, and leave to cool.

When the mixture is completely cold, but before it begins to set, add the egg whites and beat in an electric mixer at top speed for about 10 minutes, or until the mixture is thick and white.

Pour into a serving dish, chill until set, and sprinkle with flaked almonds, or (for children) hundreds and thousands or chocolate vermicelli. Serve with a little cream and some light biscuits, such as the Carolina cookies on p. 232.

~

ROSY MOUSSE

You can make this mousse with freshly puréed fruit or with frozen fruit purée. Any red fruit can be used. Do not make more than two or three hours before serving.

4 egg whites   *finely grated rind of 1/2 lemon*
2 tbsp kirsch or orange liqueur   *2 oz (50 g) flaked almonds*
4 tbsp fruit purée

Frozen egg whites and frozen fruit purée must be allowed to thaw to room temperature.

Stir the kirsch or liqueur into the fruit purée.

Whisk the whites until they stand in very stiff peaks, then slowly but thoroughly fold in the fruit purée and the lemon rind. Pile into individual serving glasses.

Roast or toast the almonds and scatter over each glass.

Refrigerate until ready to serve.

Index